Lives of the Poem

*Community and Connection
in a Writing Life*

Richard Hague

WIND PUBLICATIONS

International Standard Book Number: 1893239268
Library of Congress Control Number: 2004109576

First edition

Front cover art is by Terri Kern, a Cincinnati ceramist. Of her work for *Lives of the Poem*, she writes, "The illustrations are clay tiles that have been hand-painted with multiple layers of underglaze. Once the color has been painted on the surface, all the detail work is done by a combination of brushwork over the colors and sgraffito work etched back into the colors. The pieces are then finished with a clear glaze."

Acknowledgments

I thank the editors of the following, in which these poems first appeared, sometimes in slightly different form:

Appalachian Heritage (Berea, Kentucky) — "Breaking Its Own Rule, The Poem Attempts An Answer To The Question, 'What's A Poem?'," "What Can You Use A Poem For?"

Appalachian Journal (Boone, North Carolina) — "Talking Together," *Appalachian Journal* 24.4 (Summer 1997):438-439. Used with permission.

Athenaeum: (Cincinnati, Ohio) — "Writing During January Rain," "Poem Entering The House After A Winter Walk"

Birmingham Poetry Review: (Birmingham, Alabama) — "The Poem Taken Home And Left Unread In The Gym Bag," "The Poem Wakes And Receives Visitors," "The Stupidity Poem," "Swayed By Popular Opinion, The Poem Gets Its Posthumous Credentials," "Questions They Kept Asking Him," "Bone Yard"

Beyond Doggerel (Auburn, Alabama) — "Turning To A New Notebook Page"

ByLine (Edmond, Oklahoma) — "Where Does The Poem Live?," "The Poem Acknowledges It's Out Of Practice," "What Should A Poem Do?" "The Poem, Disguised As His Coy Mistress, Goes A-Maying," "Naming A Few Bones Of The Poem"

Catching Tigers In Red Weather: Poems from A Workshop (Hamilton, Ohio, Redbud Hill Press, 2000) — "Catching Tigers In Red Weather"

Confluence (Marietta, Ohio/Parkersburg, West Virginia) — "The Poem Turns Back Toward Familiar Territory And Fails"

Coffeehouse Poetry Anthology (Bottom Dog Press, Huron, Ohio) — "Mixed Blend: Coffeehouse Poetry"

Hackberry, Purcell Marian's Literary Magazine (Cincinnati, Ohio) — "Chaos Poem," "Big Poetry Mama Gives The Beginning Poets Some Groveling Lessons," "The Little Students Get Their First Glimpse Of The Big Poetry Mama, " "What Big Poetry Mama Thinks About Grammar And Punctuation And Usage And Such," "Big Poetry Mama Warns About Backseat Drivers," "Where Does Big Poetry Mama Live?" "'I Don't Do Titles,' She Said"

The Heartlands Today: Ohio Turnings And Crossings (Bottom Dog Press, Huron, Ohio) — "What Good Does A Woodchuck Do?"

The Journal of Kentucky Studies: (Highland Heights, Kentucky) — "The Poem Lures Her Along, Shows Her The Promised Land," "From The Porch To The Page: Memory, History, And A Poem," "How The Poem Listens,"

"The Poem Finds Its Poet," "The Poet At Fifty Walks Away From Writing"

Mediphors (Bloomsburg, Pennsylvania) — "The Poem's Brother-In-Law, A Doctor Working On A Chapter For A Book, Calls Asking For Lines About Blood"

Ohio Council Teachers Of English Language Arts Newsletter — "The Poem In The Back Of The Classroom"

Ohio Writer (Cleveland, Ohio) "Writing About Writing Contest" — "The Company Poetry Keeps" (Second Prize), "Poems When Nobody's Looking" (Honorable Mention)

Pine Mountain Sand & Gravel (Whitesburg, Kentucky/ Cincinnati, OH) — "Not Long After Jim Wayne's Death, I Remember That Frost Once Called Poetry 'A Momentary Stay Against Confusion'"

Poetry (Chicago, Illinois) — "The Poem Starts To Start Over," Vol. CLXIX, No. 5 (March 1997) Copyright, *Poetry*, 1997, Reprinted with permission of the Editor.

Poetry In The Park (Columbus, Ohio) 1989 Chapbook — "Spiel For Opening Day Of The Workshop"

Red Crow Review (Hamilton, Ohio) — "The Poem Teaches Him His Name," "The Poem Turns Mean"

Soaptown: (Cincinnati, Ohio) — "On Reading That The Little Man Inside The Poet Isn't Very Happy With His Life"

Word, newsletter of the Northern Kentucky University Dept. Of Literature and Language (Highland Heights, Kentucky) — "The Company Poetry Keeps"

Writing On The Edge (Davis, California) — "Finding The Poem," "The Advocate Speaks In Defense Of The Poem's Rights"

In addition, "The Advocate Speaks In Defense Of The Poet's Rights" appears in my chapter "Joining Up: How To Become An Effective Department Member" in *Adolescents And Inclusion: Transforming Secondary Schools*, ed. Annie Bauer and Myree Brown (Brookes Publishing Co. 2001)

I thank Rick Stansberger, editor of *Soaptown: A Magazine Of Cincinnati Writing*, and my colleague for many years in the Writing Program at Purcell Marian, and F. Keith Wahle, author of "Autobiography of a Poet" for kind permission to reprint. I thank Joe Enzweiler and Graywolf Press for allowing me to include "Porch In Winter" here. I thank Pauletta Hansel, Kathy Rich, Katie Schlosser, Mike Herring, Laisha Dumas, Mary O'Connell, Jeannie Sanders, Colleen Glenn, Steve Stricker, Tony Ruter, Dan Striley, Joanna Bach, Nickie Barnes, Joe Patt, Katie DuMont Merz, Robert J. Collins, Jason Haap, Charles C.M. Kellom, F. Keith Wahle, Dave Cross, Sarah Humble, Joe Dumont, and Patrick Hague for granting me the privilege of including their poems. I am grateful to Mary Pierce Brosmer, whose thoughts on names and name-calling which first appeared in *Hackberry* are excerpted here. I thank Jerry Williamson, Peter Davison, and Robert J. Collins for permission to include their letters. I also acknowledge George Ella Lyon's "The Mean Poems" and Jim Wayne Miller's *Vein Of Words*, which appeared during the time of this collection's inception, and so are ancestors of this work. Thanks also to the editors of *Nimrod* and to judge Olga Broumas; a selection of these poems was named a Finalist in the 1989 Pablo Neruda Poetry Prize competition. Thanks to Larry Smith and Bottom Dog Press, publisher of *Coffeehouse Poetry*, in which my little essay "Mixed Blend" first appeared.

Thanks to Mary Ellen Miller for permission to reprint "Cheerleader."

Thanks to Steve Scott of major help in the cover design.

Thanks to the Ohio Arts Council and the 1994 and 1999 Individual Artists Fellowships which helped me to complete the first draft of this book and later the near-last. Thanks to the English-Speaking Union, which awarded the Purcell Marian High School Writing Program First Place in the United States in its 1994 "Excellence In English" Award.

Special thanks to Claude (Bud) Smith of Ohio Northern University's English Department. He was the Ohio High School Poetry Contest's administrator for many years, and served the lives of the poem admirably and memorably.

The passage from Peter Elbow's *Writing Without Teachers* is used with permission of Oxford University Press.

Excerpt from "Intricacy," page 143-144 of *Pilgrim at Tinker Creek* by Annie Dillard. Copyright (c) 1974 by Annie Dillard. Reprinted by permission of HarperCollins Publishers.

And finally and especially thanks to all the workshoppers and classers and contributors, whether one-timers or long-termers, spanning the late Sixties, Seventies, Eighties, and Nineties of the 20th Cenuty, and into the Oughts of the 21st: *Muchas gracias*.

for my students, my teachers,

in memory of Jim Wayne Miller,

and in thanks to Pam and Patrick and Brendan,

who put up with my long abductions by these lives

Contents

. . . a spur to the young,
a delight to the old;
an ornament in prosperity,
a consoling refuge in adversity;
they are pleasure for us at home,
and no burden abroad;
they stay up with us at night,
they accompany us when we travel,
they are with us in our country visits . . .

— *Cicero*

Take what you have, and make what you want

— *James Baldwin*

And your very flesh shall be a great poem

— *Walt Whitman*

Preface

"Only connect." —E. M. Forster

One of my purposes in this gathering of poems, notes, chronicles, coincidences, and commentaries is to examine some of the patterns of my life, and to celebrate and commemorate all those who have journeyed along the way of poetry with me. Perhaps more importantly, my purpose is to celebrate with teachers, students, readers, and writers of poetry the proposition that poems are living things. Like bees, they are gregarious; they die in isolation from another. And because they are living things, the same degree of attentiveness and the same diligence and tolerance and creativity necessary to establishing and maintaining human friendships are necessary to developing a friendship with poetry.

To illustrate the complexities of the lives of poems, I record in this book much of what in others goes unrecorded. This is a collection of poems, but it is also a running commentary on the conception, gestation, birth, and socializing, so to speak, of the poems and of the ever-widening circle of friends and associates and supporters—and occasional enemies—of the poem and the poet. Under other circumstances, critics and reviewers and interviewers and biographers do much of this work; in this case, the poems and the poet do it. The model in the back of my mind is Frost's "Education By Poetry," a concept with much to recommend it. But such a brief book as this cannot hope to develop as complex a curriculum as Frost had in mind; it can only make a start. A start, a beginning, is what this is intended to be.

Looked at from a slightly different perspective, the book might provide some ways of thinking about these questions:

What is poetry?
What is the nature of the relationship between poetry and the culture and community it arises from and dwells in?
What is the nature of the relationship between the poet and the poem, and vice versa?
What does "doing poetry" or "being a poet" look like?
How much "real life" can get into a person's poems?
To what extent are our poems shaped by our relationships and connections with others, especially others who are writers?
What makes poems good?

1

Of course, everything here is offered as *an example*, not as *the model*. Poetry is so abundantly vital and evolving that it is always larger than our ideas about it and more extensive than our varied practices of it. It will not be contained by definition or prescription.

The epigraphs to the book are my way of suggesting some ideas about poetry which I have come through experience to believe are the truth. Poems are among the best companions we can have, trustworthy over an amazing breadth of circumstances. Cicero speaks across the centuries to us, suggesting the varied uses and consolations of poetry, and of the loyalty of the poem, especially when we memorize it and can call upon it in times of jubilation, rage, sorrow, or desolation. The day after the September 11 attacks, my classes and I remembered and reread (and wept with) Whitman's lines from "Song Of Myself:"

> I am the mashed fireman with breast-bone broken,
> Tumbling walls buried me in their debris,
> Heat and smoke I inspired, I heard the yelling shouts of my comrades,
> I heard the distant click of their picks and shovels,
> They have cleared the beams away, they tenderly lift me forth . . .

Also, I have heeded James Baldwin's advice: "Take what you have, and make what you want." What I have are thirty-five years of teaching practice, forty years of writing and submitting poems and having them accepted or rejected, even sometimes commented upon. I claim also, and no less importantly, the accumulated peeves, hassles, failures, uglinesses, successes, triumphs, and excitements of those years, and the students, colleagues, readers, and editors who populate them. What I choose to make of them all is this book. I hope it might be of interest to general readers interested in creativity, to other teachers and writers and to those who want to catch an inside glimpse of the lives of the poem. But mostly, I do it because it's what I have and it's what I want to do. This is the special freedom of the writer.

The second epigraph is part of a longer passage—one of the great secular hymns to democracy—a kind of Romantic Ten Commandments and Beatitudes all rolled into one. Here is the complete injunction, from Whitman's Preface to the first edition (1855) of *Leaves of Grass*:

> This is what you shall do: love the earth & sun & the animals, despise riches, give alms to every one that asks, stand up for the stupid and crazy, devote your income and labor to others, hate tyrants, argue not concerning God, have patience and indulgence toward the people, take off your hat to nothing known or unknown or to any man or number of men, go freely with powerful uneducated

persons & with the young & with the mothers of families, reexamine all you have been told at school or church or in any book, dismiss whatever insults your own soul, & your very flesh shall be a great poem and have the richest fluency not only in its words but in in the silent lines of its lips and face and between the lashes of your eyes and in every motion and joint of your body.

I don't know anywhere else in American writing where I have found so completely and thoroughly spelled out a philosophy of life—and an approach to writing—that inspires me more. I hope that something of its spirit infuses these poems, even when they're ornery—even when they're wrong.

Speaking of when they're wrong: this is not primarily a handbook about how to write poetry, though frequently I make some suggestions I hope might prove useful. Nor is it primarily a guide to studying poems, although, once again, it may offer some sidelong suggestions. It is foremost one writer's testimony about the lives of the poem. It is an attempt to show the complexity of what happens in an individual poem and to plumb the wonderful cross-fertilization and complex inter-relatednesses that constitute the lives of the poem. And so it must also be about mistakes, just as the work of any poet must contain many mistakes; just as the work of younger writers must also. Truly bad poems must happen to us all; we need at once to recognize them and to thank them for what they teach us. Somewhere I was reading about successful management styles. The author at hand, an accomplished businessman, said something to the effect that he'd rather hire a person who made five hundred mistakes and a couple of utterly great right moves than one who rarely made mistakes and no great moves—because the one who makes no mistakes isn't trying hard enough, isn't risking anything, and is unlikely to make anything truly wonderful happen. So this book is not a handbook about having success in writing poetry, but is more a gathering together of notions and ideas—and examples, in the poems themselves—of how to live in a way that is open to poetry, that finds the poem everywhere, that may expose us to some significant successes now and then. It also tries to be a book that is tolerant of confusion, uncertainty, false moves.

One final point. The widespread bias (and I use an editor's word, here, not mine) against poems about poems and poetry-writing, a bias which I have encountered for years, is another reason I indulge myself in this book. In a time when the process approach to writing is taking hold everywhere, when metacognitive studies suggest that learners profit by paying attention to the ways in which they learn, it seems to me that poems about poems and poetry-writing might be one way of gaining such knowledge.

I am willing to concede that editors may get many terrible poems about poetry and writing poetry. Those bad ones should not blind them to the good and perhaps even instructive ones that come along now and then. *ByLine* magazine welcomes openly and regularly poems about the craft and the prestigious *Poetry* magazine publishes the occasional fine and provocative poem about poetry. All power to them.

*   *   *

Some may prefer to read this book from beginning to end, but let me suggest an alternative. It might be interesting to explore it at first, haphazardly, ignoring the commentary and just sampling the poems, expecting the serendipitous, the chance connection, the unpredictable linkage of one poem or idea to another—or the fruitful contradiction. Later, after wandering around in it, maybe a sequential reading would be worthwhile. But not at first. Informally, get the lay of the land, the drift of its ideas, the patterns of its images. Ask some questions. Begin to argue with it.

I hope that the book is actually larger than it seems to be. I hope that it opens up, like some hypertext stack in a computer, in ways the Notes and Divagations don't even hint at. I know that many of its readers will be smarter than it is, and read it in ways I didn't expect.

So I hope readers will respond to it, dropping me a line (or a poem) when they discover something interesting or inspiring or contradictory or impossible or stupid or mediocre in it. I hope that the conversation that it is already a part of continues.

Cincinnati, Ohio, 1987-2003

4

The Poem Wakes And Receives Visitors

It rises early from the mute tide of sleep.
Across Ohio, night's seethe withdraws,
pebbles, bones, fossils rattling.
Fumbling in the kitchen,
the poem litters the floor with starfish
still moving in the dampness off its feet.
Sea oats rustle in the kettle's wheeze.

Outside, the blue jay on the feeder
shouts in Nepalese. Clouds gather
at the summit of the ash tree.

Three, something says to the poem,
and it sits at the table
and opens the newspaper to that page.

Nothing: everything. A man in California
reports sighting Bigfoot
in a redwood grove north of Arcata.
Quintuplets are born in Bowling Green, Kentucky.
A young councilman from Tulsa marries
a grandmother whose son
is older than he is.
A local store advertises a new perfume
called "Seduction."

The poem smiles.
This is how it is,
the poem begins,
and keeps trying,
all the crowded morning,
to catch up.

Notes & Divagations

I learned the word "divagations" from a former student of mine, Bruce Rich. He was an early member of the writing workshop I held in my home from 1971 to 1991. I recall that at one point, while I was vigorously challenging him to confront and explore difficult personal and social issues in his journal, he demanded I show him my own. I did, and he took the liberty of making notes (with a pencil, thank goodness) in the margins, pointing out where my theories about life and my practice of it diverged. He pulled no punches. I was at once appalled and amused by his snoopy commentary, and we have been friends ever since.

A few years after the writing workshop, in his mid-twenties, Bruce decided he'd learn the piano. Not only did he learn it, but he began to compose his own music. I attended his first concert, and he called it "Divagations." Of course, the music did not "wander aimlessly," as my *Funk & Wagnall's* offers as its first definition. But it did start in one place, and interestingly go to another; it did "digress." I hope something of the same for these notes and comments.

Acknowledgments

Even the acknowledgments tell an important part of the lives of the poem. The poem gets around. It gets to know people. It's sociable, at least part of the time, otherwise it is condemned to live in a small town of one citizen with no address and no telephone or Internet connection, alone as a lost sock. On the other hand, poetry does not party to the point where it spends all its energy on crowds and wild-eyed blowouts. It knows the costs, often hidden, of technology, and has read Wendell Berry's essay "Why I am Not Going To Buy A Computer." It knows it owes almost everything to solitude, that friend, teacher, confidante, that source of power. As in so much, balance is a key. (Though not the only one; Excess can also be a key, as can Asceticism. See the epigraph to "She, Imperturbé, Cosmologique, Composes Her Body of Work." You ought to know which way—or which several ways— are your own.)

In the meantime, you need to research where to send your poems out, or you will waste a great deal of time, money, gasoline, and patience. Most of these journals were familiar to me before I sent any poems; if I had not seen and read a copy or two, I had met the editor, or at the very least had looked the magazine up in *Poet's Market*, an annual list and description of thousands of poetry reviews and journals and little magazines which is updated each year. Available in the Reference section of your library, it will help you make an educated guess as to whether or not a particular magazine is likely to take your poems. If *Poet's Market* or the *Dustbooks International Directory of Little*

Magazines is not available, ask your librarian to order one or both of them. (And make sure you patronize your local library. To hope to get any better at writing poetry without reading lots of poetry, past and present, is utterly futile. All poets are knowers and users of poetry, just as surgeons are knowers and users of the lore and history of their practice, of the latest and most time-tested-techniques, and of the current developments in their field.)

The Poem Wakes And Receives Visitors

How do things get into poems? Why pebbles, bones and fossils? Why Nepalese (if there even is such a language)? Why Bigfoot and quintuplets and a brand of perfume?

I can only answer this: Richard Cortez Day, author of the short story collection *When In Florence* and a colleague of mine at the Appalachian Writers Workshop in Hindman, Kentucky, lives in Arcata, California. Another Hindman staffer was Jim Wayne Miller, one of whose collections of poems, *Vein of Words,* is mentioned in the *Acknowledgments.* Jim Wayne, who died in 1996, a few months before my own father, was a poet, short story writer, playwright and essayist as well as one of the great teachers in America. He lived in Bowling Green, Kentucky. There are hundreds, probably thousands of us, who miss him, and always will.

You'll have to ask the poem about the rest.

As far as I can determine, I didn't know anyone from Tulsa until I began to send poems to *Nimrod: International Journal.* Then I began to at least exchange letters with a few people there. Eventually, a selection of poems from this book was published there.

Where Does The Poem Live?

Your first impression
is that it lives in school,
flattened like a pressed violet
between the pages
of a book.
But no one lives in school,
not even the maintenance man.
Even he goes home
in the evening to drink his beer,
turn a few fancy chair legs
on his lathe in the basement.

The truth is,
poetry comes from wherever
you live,
has an address
that is like the formula for blood;
it lives inside you
like your bones
or eardrums;
like your lungs,
expanding
with air,
ready to
help you sing.

Where Does The Poem Live?

Many of us seem to have a kind of identity crisis. We think that success does not live in our province, that there is nothing poetic in our hometowns or native counties, that only people somewhere else are writing good poems, and that there must be some sort of secret to writing well that only other people have. Some of us think that we have to live in New York City or London or Beirut to have anything interesting to write about, or to have a local writing community.

Wrong. Or so the poem says.

Here's what G.K Chesterton says, about Chaucer, but it is good advice to many of us who think we're cut off from poetry.

> Chaucer was wide enough to be narrow; that is, he could bring a broad experience of life to the enjoyment of local or even accidental things. Now, it is the chief defect of the literature of today that it always talks as if local things could only be limiting, not to say strangling.

"A broad experience of life" brought to the "enjoyment of local or even accidental things." Yes. Perhaps the dangerous distrust of the local, or unwillingness or inability to find life and poetry in the native, the common, the close-at-hand, is no better evidenced, unwittingly perhaps, than in this, from the Preface to *The Morrow Anthology Of Younger American Poets*, edited by Dave Smith and David Bottoms. They write, "Who is the younger poet here? [He] is thirty-seven years old, married with children, has been or is an editor of a literary magazine, has published widely . . . has been awarded a grant . . . *and rarely lives where he grew up* (my italics).

But if what Smith and Bottoms observe is true, then American poetry has a problem. Thoreau claimed:

> A man is worth most to himself and to others, whether as an observer, or poet, or neighbor, or friend, where he is most himself, most contented and at home. There his life is the most intense and he loses the fewest moments . . . The poet has made the best roots in his native soil of any man, and is the hardest to transplant. The man who is often thinking that it is better to be somewhere else than where he is excommunicates himself.

Here's one of my poems (it's really a kind of prayer, or even a vow) about this important sense of place:

9

Placed

Placed here,
gifted with senses,
I live to see tanager
and bunting
sing air into an artifact,
a thought,
of which I am a part.

I live to hear
the hornet charge
the hillside
with its yellow hum,
the chord of my spine,
music for my walking.

I live here to feel
the full moon's hymning
fill my skull,
to hear stars' codas
richen my throat,
the musky press
of shadows
whisper my name.

The voiceless world of plants and animals and weather and light requires of its poets that they speak for its many manifestations, that they attend to its detail and secrets, that they stay put long enough to know it. This is equally true for those poets who live in cities and towns. Each homeplace in America ought to have its own poet, and that poet ought to be known to everyone in town, and ought to be as valued a member of the community as the mayor, the police chief, the justice of the peace, the family doctor, the priest, the rabbi, and every teacher in the school. Whitman again says it best, in his poem which describes his ideal citizen-poets:

Mediums

They shall arise in the States,
They shall report Nature, laws, physiology, and happiness,
They shall illustrate Democracy and the kosmos,
They shall be alimentive, amative, perceptive,
They shall be complete women and men, their pose brawny and supple, their
    drink water, their blood clean and clear,
They shall fully enjoy materialism and the sight of products, they shall enjoy the
    sight of the beef, lumber, bread-stuffs, of Chicago the great city,
They shall train themselves to go in public to become orators and oratresses,
Strong and sweet shall their tongues be, poems and materials of poems shall
    come from their lives, they shall be makers and finders,
Of them and of their works shall emerge divine conveyors, to convey gospels,
Characters, events, retrospections, shall be convey'd in gospels, trees, animals,
    waters, shall be convey'd,
Death, the future, the invisible faith, shall all be convey'd.

See also "Talking Together" below, under *Things To Learn In Preparing For The Poem.*

By the way, I would be less than candid if I did not add that except for my age (I am older than their thirty-seven somethings) and except for the fact that I do not appear there, I fit every detail of Smith's and Bottoms' description of who they published in their book. This is in no way meant as a boast; I regret most deeply that I no longer live where I grew up.

The Poem As Audio-Visual Aid

Its on switch
is in your head.

You have one,
don't you?

The Poem As Audio-Visual Aid

Because teaching poetry is one of the great joys and one of the most earnest occupations of my life, I am sometimes frustrated that my attempts to help others enjoy it often fall short. I'll be worked into a lather in class, exploring, say, Emily Dickinson's little jewel "A Route of Evanescence," and I'll stop suddenly and ask some questions. A few brave souls will raise their hands, but I can tell by the look on the other faces that I might as well be speaking, well, Nepalese.

I frequently tell my students that poetry is one of the great mind-altering substances, certainly the healthiest one, the least dangerous to your well-being; for visions it is unsurpassed, for dreams the main thing, for wackiness hardly excelled.

So this little poem, in mock anger and frustration.

By the way, is the "on switch" of poetry really in the head? Or is it in the heart? Or the glands? Your choice as to which one or ones. Is poetry a matter of ideas, primarily, or of physical sensations and feelings, primarily? If you've not thought about these questions before, spend a little time thinking and writing about them now. And read with an eye to seeing what other poems imply about the physical "place" or source of poetry, and to what other poets have written about the matter.

* * *

Write a few short, pithy poems in which you play the smart aleck. Aim them at phonies, extremists, people suffering from too much pride or self-importance. Try for one-liners, or at most two- or three-liners. Afterwards, find a good dictionary of literary terms and look up "epigram." See if any of the things you've written might qualify.

The Poem Taken Home And Left Unread In The Gym Bag

It is like a cat
in C-clamps,
a snake pinned
underfoot,
music locked
in a piano.
Whatever, it wants out,
onto the warm lap
of a reader,
into the ferny woods
of a mind,
into the flesh
like a dancing clock.

But all evening,
zipped in its smothering nylon,
it is pummeled by
Twisted Sister.
The telephone
shreds its
finely-tuned nerves.
Drowning in
Pepsi, it
wants wine
and attention
and quiet,
but all
it gets
are socks
and mascara
and jockstraps.

The Poem Taken Home And Left Unread In The Gym Bag

At a reading during the Appalachian Writers Workshop in Hindman, Kentucky, the poet, essayist, novelist and teacher Barbara Smith snickered after I had finished, "Mascara *and* jockstraps? That's a pretty strange gym bag."

Well.

I once received as a subscribing bonus a very nice pencil from the Teachers & Writers Collaborative. Printed on it was a quote from Whitman: "I contain multitudes."

It's what the poem says always.

The Poem In The Back Of The Classroom

To a few of you, rightly,
it's a kind of riddle:
ice in a bonfire,
an empty glove,
something weird made of rubber.

But too soon
you take hammers
to it,
shouting, "Tell me! Tell me!"

You push splinters
of No. 2 pencils
under its fingernails.
You stomp on its delicate feet.

You turn it around and
around till it's dizzy
and lost.
Suspecting something's there,
but half afraid of it,
you lift its skirts
and snicker.

The Poem In The Back Of The Classroom

You know who you are and you should be ashamed of yourselves: a mottled pox on ye.

"Neither great works of art or science speak for themselves. Their capacity to function as mind-altering devices demands more than a quick fix. Learning to see these complex and subtle images is as intellectually demanding a task as we know." That's Elliot W. Eisner, in an essay called "On Reading The Images of Culture."

It's a quote that I've carried through many notebooks. Finally it has come out into my writing. Of the hundreds, perhaps thousands of quotes I've gathered, how could I know this one would come forward, discover its own destination? And all the rest of the things I've gathered: will they all come forward, too? Or are most of them destined to stay in the dark between closed notebook pages? But they are all necessary; they are all potential food for poems; and the poet must take whatever seems savory, or interesting, or strange: *omnes, omnes, omnes.*

See also "Hidden Meaning" and the Notes and Divagations on it.

* * *

For me, there are two kinds of notebooks, both essential to the job of writing. The first might more accurately be called a Commonplace Book or Day Book, and it is where I jot down passages that interest me, or titles of things I want to read, paste in photocopies of charts or columns, and jot brief speculations on things, sometimes noted by subject. This type of notebook is a joy; it is a private museum which I visit time and time again, happy to return to favorite exhibits and to muse about them anew. I become so familiar with this notebook through review and rethinking, in fact, that I know almost exactly where a specific item is in it. (Actually there are about forty of these notebooks now, dating back more than a quarter of a century, aligned on a shelf in my study, where I can refer to them whenever I need to.)

The other kind might more accurately be called a Workbook, and it is where I draft poems and essays and stories. Of the two, the Workbook is by far the most dangerous and frightening, because at first it contains so much white space: a kind of blizzard waiting for me on a bad day when I seem to have been wiped dead blank.

Turning To A New Notebook Page

Goodbye to that world I lived in,
all tracks obscured.
Winter is renewed,
that white-out I have to find my heat in.

I strike a small spark
on the edge of my thumb,
fire among crystals.

Big wind coming.
Snow like the ghosts of smoke.
Sometimes I think
I hear voices.

The Poem Clears Its Head

A kid's toybox crammed with Ninja Action Figures,
    Silly Putty, plastic grenades, matches, rocket launchers,
    football cards, bullets made of old chewing gum, squads
    of GI Joes, inflatable Death Stars, a stolen pack of
    cigarettes, die-cast HO-scale land mines, Green Lantern
    Comics, model Polaris submarines:
Ah, throw it out.

A young woman's desk full of failed dates, Barbie clothes,
    misspelled love letters, paste rings, false eyelashes,
    seventeen lipsticks, fake fingernails like crimson scoops,
    small change, pulp romances set in Boston and Argentina,
    foam rubber bra inserts, prom bids, soccer trophies,
    ticket stubs from the Motley Crue concert, mascara,
    copies of *Bride* magazine:
Ah, throw it out.

An old man's war chest full of checkbooks and shares,
    the dried eye of an enemy like a shriveled pea, pills,
    credit cards, surgeons' bills, the title to the third BMW,
    plug nickels, bad seeds, dreams of blood, the deed to the
    Florida condo, merger memos, insurance policies:
Ah throw it out.

There. Now you're ready, the poem says.

Fill it up again. This time, be more careful.

The Poem Clears Its Head

So the poem says. I don't agree. Bad advice. The poem is thinking like the wrapped-tight, somewhat puritanical (though eminently admirable and sincere) Henry David Thoreau. He admonishes the writer to take care with what he or she fills the attic.

Though I think that Thoreau has a point, and though I explain to my students when I ask them to memorize poems that they already have filled their heads with the words of McDonald's advertising ditties and that I want them to balance that hollow commercial language with powerful poetry, I still prefer the advice I have already quoted from Walt Whitman. In "Song Of Myself," he writes, "I am large, I contain multitudes." Poetry is not, as Thoreau was, a rather picky eater. It is omnivorous. It eats, again as Whitman says, "omnes, omnes, omnes."

See also "What You Should Eat Before Reading The Poem."

Do I contradict myself?

* * *

Perhaps it is in part from my love of Whitman that I have become a fan of the catalogue—the list, the enumeration—as a poetic device. I do not particularly enjoy the long parades of generals and admirals and ships that you find in epic catalogues, but in such catalogues as I've built in "The Poem Clears Its Head" I find a useful and, what I hope in this case, is a damning accumulation of detail. In his essay "Some Remarks On Rhythm," Theodore Roethke explains the catalogue in poetry best: "There are areas of experience in modern life that simply cannot be rendered by either the formal lyric or straight prose. We need the catalogue in our time. We need the eye close on the object . . ."

* * *

Think about some area of your life or experience which might be best revealed through the use of a catalogue. Write a small handful of poems employing this device. Make sure you really push it. It is often instructive to see how far you can take such things before they break down. It is equally instructive to explain to yourself *why* your catalogues have broken down.

20

Entering The Poem

As all houses have doors,
so poems: some up front,
well-lit, the steps
polished and inviting.
Names over the brass
mailbox, letters
in the slot. Pull them out
and read them,
get to know
these neighbors,
where they're from,
what they eat,
what catalogues they collect.
Learn the languages they speak.
In the homeland
of the poem there's no law
against it: snoop.

But others have entrances
underground, cellar
doors obscured
with dust and cobwebs.
The keys to them
are hidden under
stones in the garden,
below the rusting Ford
abandoned in the field,
lodged far down
in the watch-pockets
of your dreams.
And some of them
are woven tightly
into the bindings
of old books.

To find such keys,
such doors they will open,
you have to be
studying all the time,
feeling the world

21

with your fingertips
as you turn its pages,
reading its plot
with your skin
like you read
the wind
on the side of
your face,
finding the way
like you follow
the map in your legs
that leads you
home in the dark.

Entering The Poem

There could have been other metaphors, of course: reading (and writing) poetry is the exploration of an undiscovered country; it is a slow fall into language as if one is falling into love; and so on and so on. But a thought has been hanging around in my notebooks for almost two decades, and seems to need to come out here. It's from George Santayana, the American philosopher: "There are books in which the footnotes, or the comments scrawled by some reader's hand in the margin, are more interesting than the text. The world is one of those books."

I have to admit that when I first read that and copied it down, I thought it marvelous. But I have come slowly to disagree with it because it makes the world inferior or secondary to human consciousness, whereas they are probably, in some mysterious and as yet incompletely understood way, a partnership of the closest kind. No mind, no Nature; no Nature, no mind.

Still, the idea of human participation in the writing of the book of Nature is exactly up my alley, and the place of instinct (the "natural" as distinguished from the "learned") in the process is of great interest. The poem agrees, too.

The Poem Approaches Physics

Told light is like waves
one moment, then particles
the next, the poem,
interested in science,
climbs into its pickup
and drives to the creek.
There it finds
light at home, its neighborhood
of flashes and dazzles.
They talk a while.

"Off that bluegill's back,"
the poem says,
"what are you—waves?
Or dots of something,
mica flakes,
mirror's silver,
what?"

           "Yes,"
light says, speaking
from a dew bead.

"And off that spicebush
blossom—
are you like a tide
or like an avalanche
of mountain?"

           "Yes,"
light says, nodding
like wet jewelweed.

"And off those gravels
there, and off the
riffles here—are
you moving all at once,
or bit by bit?"

           "Yes,"

light says,
inside out and
grinning.

That's all the poem
needs.

Tonight,
sitting by its unlit lamp,
it writes light's name
in the dark,
sits still.
Soon, sun rises
there,
flame on paper,
a bursting
standing fast.

The Poem Approaches Physics

Poetry can be one of the great interdisciplinary endeavors of the arts. Likewise physics nowadays is perhaps one of the most fruitful scientific realms for poetic exploration. What you know about chemistry may seem to have little to do with architecture (though it does with cooking, and gardening, and reproduction, right?) but it might just turn out to have a lot to do with poetry.

After taking a close look at these poems, how many branches of science can you see which have at least a reference, if not a larger place, in any of them? In what ways is poetry "science-friendly?" In what ways is science "poetry-friendly?" What's to be done with the connections such friendships engender?

Chaos Poem

at the boundary, life blossoms
—James Gleick, *Chaos*

Out at the edges
                    of words, seeking
turbulence and speed
                    the poem shapes
up a paisley
                    of curves and spurts, masses
merging, strange
                    attractors packing in
patterns,
                    sounds, lines, and arcs like
letters
                    or pictures, or picture-
thoughts:
                    then suddenly: image
jeweled and
                    honed, its peened intricate
edges goldglint
                    or flashing
brass or cut
                    diamond, infinitely moonshined
and reflecting:
                    reflecting, image
out at the edges
                    of words, seeking
turbulence and speed:
                    image
teased out of random
                    ness like smoke
through teasel
                    webbed, spiked, cat's cradled, for
a moment each trend
                    of breeze a sleave
of braids: image
                    suddenly there, placed, particular,
though spacious as
                    sponge or bird's airy
bone: image plain as
                    grass in windwarped hummocks,
or saddles, gravels,

                    the ovals of eggs: image
clear as smoke in a
                        still room rising (the first
inkling) then
                        suddenly crazy, aswirl (the
rush, the pouring, the
                        embedding blessed random-
ness) spills
                    over into pattern, and out
again, and over—
                        impossible! but there,
the unfolding beauty
                    textures of surprise, the
shape out of
                    shattering, out of
scintilla, blot
                        spot: image
as clear as
                    clumped wet grapes or
penguins, ten
                thousand on a beach,
or bison,
                    unraveling skeins lumbering
into the bunch
                        and gather of time,
or haystacks, in a
                    bright days' ending,
settling, every
                    needle in the wonder
of them pointing
                for a moment
                        the same way.

Chaos Poem

I suspect that more poems will come out of this subject. Remember what Emerson says about books in "the American Scholar": "Books are the best of things, well used; abused, among the worst. What is the right use? . . . They are for nothing but to inspire." James Gleick's *Chaos: The Making Of A New Science*, is one of the books to inspire me. Reading it, I was reminded of a theme that an earlier favorite of mine, Annie Dillard's *Pilgrim at Tinker Creek*, elaborated and explored: intricacy in Nature, the fluted, saw-toothed, fractal edges of things, from sea-coasts to elm leaves to the unpredictable yet orderly flow of currents and eddies in rivers. Just listen to this:

> The rolling of eddies, the unfurling of ferns, the creasing of mountain ranges, the hollowing of animal organs all followed one path . . . It had nothing to do with any particular medium, or any particular kind of difference. The inequalities could all be slow and fast, warm and cold, dense and tenuous, salt and fresh, viscous and fluid, acid and alkaline. At the boundary, life blossoms.

That's Gleick. And this:

> Our life is a faint tracing on the surface of mystery. The surface of mystery is not smooth, any more than the planet is smooth; not even a single hydrogen atom is smooth, let alone a pine. Nor does it fit together; not even the chlorophyll and hemoglobin molecules are a perfect match, for, even after the atom of iron replaces the magnesium, long streamers of disparate atoms trail disjointedly from the rims of the molecules' loops. Freedom cuts both ways. Mystery itself is as fringed and intricate as the shape of the air in time. Forays into mystery cut bays and fine fiords, but the forested mainland itself is implacable both in its bulk and in its most filigreed fringe of detail. "Every religion that does not affirm that God is hidden," said Pascal flatly, "is not true."

That's Annie Dillard.

Sometimes you read books that speak so clearly and so excitingly to you— and it seems, to you so personally and privately—that they change your life, they change the way you see the world; they shift your paradigms. Such books are a central part of the lives of the poem. They lurk in libraries, used book stores, Heart Marts and Goodwills and St. Vincent DePaul storefront second-hand emporia. One of the great accomplishments in life is to find these books and be changed by them. I would go so far as to say that if you've never been knocked to the floor by a book, your education is not complete. I remember the afternoon in college when I first read Sylvia Plath's book *Ariel*, which includes, among others, "Lady Lazarus," a poem of white heat, dangerous as nuclear radiation. At one point, I simply threw the book across the room, shouting "No!" at how hysterically beautiful and fatal the passions and language in the poems were.

The lives of the poem require that you expect such books, and that you keep a sharp lookout for them, and that you acknowledge your debt to them when you finally discover their importance in your life.

See "The Poem Braids Its Lover's Hair" for another take on intricacy and pattern. See Andy Hull's "Creation Day One" for another poem related to science.

The Poem Three-Railing Into The Mind

Three weeks' steady rain:
dampness makes
the shape of fish
along the cellar wall
as gradually as
years leach gray
his beard.
Shooting pool
down there,
the victim
suddenly sees
the poem,
vivid as the
three-ball
before him,
casting
a solid shadow.

Of course.
He knows:
poetry, that shapeshifter,
leaps from rail-shot
and talcum
as well as from
nightingales
and death.
His fingers blue
with chalk,
the poem helps him
play successfully
the green lit world,
his hands uncommonly steady,
his shots occasionally true,
his english nearly perfect.

The Poem Three-Railing Into The Mind

The things I like the most about shooting pool are that it requires you sometimes to go out late at night to places which aren't too clean, it sometimes involves you with persons you might not otherwise encounter in a white-collar life, and it always tolerates smoking, drinking, spitting, and cussing. These last four things include two of the basic tools of the trade of the writer, according to William Faulkner (his exact list: paper, tobacco, food, and whiskey.)

Another thing I like about pool is that it is applied geometry, and physics in action. It requires not only skill but careful foresight, diligence, and patience, and in the course of one game all of this can be canceled at any time by blind luck. Pool is therefore, like poetry, one of the great human adventures, especially when we remember the roots of the word "adventure," which mean "what is to come." There is no certainty in adventure, except that something will, indeed come. Exactly what, is anybody's guess.

Anyone who has written poems for any time knows something about adventure. How many times we start writing, thinking we might know something about where the poem is going, what it wants to say—and suddenly, it takes a strange or unpredictable turn on us, and we career after it, laughing or grimacing, trying to catch the tiger by the tail.

Anyone who has shot pool knows about adventure, too. My friend Joe Enzweiler taught me about "riding" the nine-ball in the game of Point Nine-Ball. The object in Nine-Ball is to pocket the nine after making the first eight in sequence; in Point Nine-Ball, if you hit and pocket the one, the five, or the nine in combination during the regular sequence, they count, and get placed back on the table. So "riding" the nine-ball means that even if you're shooting the four, if the nine is within range, you try to hit it, too, employing the spin on the ball that is known as "english" and that provides me with a pun near the end of the poem. If the ball goes in after a few rails, wonderful. Though for experts like Joe, this is not so much an adventure as an elegant geometry exercise, for lesser mortals like me, there is a lot of luck involved. Sometimes the nine goes in, unexpectedly, "a gift."

Poetry ought to take us places we haven't been before, and with new ears and eyes and hearts. Writing and reading it ought to "disorient" us, so to speak, as a preliminary to the larger, newer orientation to the world and its ways which is poetry's gift to us.

*   *   *

Write some poems that seem to be about sports, but that are about something else, too, maybe even about poetry and its relationships to other forms of play.

Things To Learn In Preparing For The Poem

In the morning,
on the honeysuckled porch
that draws bright hummingbirds
to flash and hover,
how to put your pencil,
for an hour,
to the paper
so its point
will find
a true direction,
like the golden plover
over tundra.
In the afternoon,
how to fly across the garden,
and flying,
sing when dead drunk
like the crazed birds
sucking too-ripe pawpaws
in the woods.
Then later,
on toward evening,
before Arcturus brightens
over dusty Master's Knob,
how to read the lines
in stones
hard frosts have heaved
wide open—
scrawled passages
in light and dark
almost impossible in words.

Things To Learn In Preparing For The Poem

Joe lives in a cabin he built himself outside Fairbanks, Alaska. He's not only a poet but also a physicist, billiardist of course, and a knowledgeable astronomer. I remember, one summer evening many years ago, his pointing out Arcturus through the branches of a wild cherry tree in Monroe County, Ohio, where I was living in the woods for a season. Along with Sirius and Canopus, Arcturus is one of the three brightest stars in the sky. Master's Knob, mentioned in the poem, is just down the road from that wild cherry tree, and a Geodesic Survey benchmark identifies it as one of the highest points in the county.

Arcturus, on the other hand, is 36 light-years away from the earth. Getting that star and Master's Knob together in the neighborhood of the poem, closing the incredible distance between them, creating some meaning in their relationship—that's what poetry does. That's what makes it worth getting ready for.

By way of learning a little more about the lives of the poem: how many passages throughout these poems and poems later in the book might be attributable to my friendship with Joe, to our mutual pursuits and interests, given what I've told you about him so far and what you will learn later? Are friendships important in general not only to our personal lives but also to the lives of the poem?

And finally, here's a poem that uses that same image of the tree and Arcturus (what does it mean that the image reappears? is it okay to repeat an image in different poems?) and that is about the connections of friends and place I've mentioned.

Talking Together

Annual meeting of the Southern Appalachian Writers Cooperative,
Highlander Center, Tennessee, 1982

Lord, how our voices often mingle,
creeks rounding down from a thousand miles
to wed the same bright river

And how we mouth our favorite names:
say *poplar, sycamore, broom sedge*
like prayers

And how we have seen the same birds

34

flock among the white pine groves
of the oldground we've helped heal,

And how we seem to have heard the same stories,
seen the same men on street corners
of small towns so barren
they have no football team

And how we have loved women who look and speak like sisters
And how we have hunted the same deer
on stands decades apart,
And how we have found the same stones in creeks

And how we have seen the same wonders at night
in places hundreds of miles distant
(wild cherry branches shuttling in the breeze,
Arcturus living like an eye above the oak)

And how we have failed the same jobs,
workers slumped over Chevys and Fords,
machinists hurt in our hearts by slivers of steel,
hunters limping upridge with bloodied feet

And how, when we find ourselves together,
standing around gas pumps or stoves in old stores,
waiting for tires to be changed,
for children to be drilled by the clinic dentist in town,
for fathers to die in the hospitals of county seats

We find something to say that means us,
that names us neighbors and kin,
that finds within us words to connect:
coon hounds loved in common,
a relative with the same name,
a character true to type in all our places:

Lord, how our lives often mingle,
how we mouth our favorite names,
how we sing in voices old, flat, or sweet:

How we know one we know another,
how we love even what we hate
for how it brings us together.

*　*　*

On this score, here is a letter I wrote to the editor who at first turned down "Talking Together." I had submitted to him, just a few weeks later, a number of poems, three of which appeared in 1988 in a collection of mine called *Possible Debris*. He wrote back, taking me to task in several areas, and my letter, beginning with my parenthetical wincings to passages from his, was the result.

I did not send the letter to him; why not, I don't know exactly. Maybe I wasn't sure that I explained myself clearly. Maybe I wasn't sure that I'd learned all I could from writing the letter, that I needed to keep it and study it, and see if I really believed it all. At any rate, here are both letters:

October 30, 1987
Dear Dick:

This I love:
> Alive above the freeway,
> it is knot, storm, pounder:
> a fist of sight
> clenched to hammer movement
> into food.

That's a hard little hammering knot of words—just beautiful! But I wish I liked the rest of the poem as much. You swash some buckles, you out-Dickey Dickey. The *art* that composed those opening five lines and made them air-tight like a well-woven basket to catch the metaphysical weight of *food* —that art gets too artful for me, and that's what I don't like about the rest of the poem. I shouldn't be lecturing you, but since I'm sending these back to a friend, I feel like trying to explain. It's so much a matter of dey goostibus, anyway. I like poetry that *is* experience itself, but I feel you *composing* so much, it becomes *reporting* for me. It seems more consumed emotionally by its artfulness (that extended metaphor at the end of "Agnes" is just the end!) so that I don't any longer feel the immediacy and the electricity of an active mind *thinking*. It's more like posing. (Have you been reading a lot of John Donne lately? The classroom is going to despoil us all!) Maybe it's me. But I think I see you selecting ripe plums—"splashed blood," "boomed confusions," "the whole everlasting crazy"—not that I don't admire their grandness, but it's too much display, too little immediacy. It's the

36

feeling now I have of someone trying to explain the ineffable grandeur of the way he feels about existence & nature. And being perverse, I try to dodge the lecture. I don't want you to go academic on me—no way!—and I think that's what's happening, that show-off syntax, for example ("rising unsuccessfully adult to office, work,/ and traffic").

As I say, maybe it's me, and dey goostibus ain't what dey used to be. And maybe you won't get mad at me, and maybe on the other hand you'll tell me to take a flying f . . . at the moon . . .

All best wishes,

Jerry Wayne Bushman

Dear Jerry Wayne:

I

" I don't want you to go academic on me—no way!" (Yikes!)
"Showoff syntax." (Ouch!)
"Art." (Oooo.)
"Posing." (Well! I say old sport!)
"Ripe plums." (The pits!)
"Too much display." (Zap!)
"Too little immediacy." (Like, hit me with that there hammer, Bubba.)

II

Thanks for the note, really: I know you wouldn't bother if you didn't care. And I know you're coming from a sincere position, and I know you're talking a matter of taste, and all. But let me try to make some sense, if I can, of where I stand now as a poet.

First, I don't like to be pigeon-holed; if some of my work can appeal to those interested in the more natural immediacy your comments suggest is important to you, fine and dandy. But that's not the only voice I have. There's a real feeling for the ceremonial quality of language in me; I like the extra charge that syntax and sound can create, the density of packed metaphors and the artfulness, artifice, if you wish, of carrying metaphors for more than a line or two.

Ornament is attractive to me, in the same way it is to a jazz musician doing riffs, or a Victorian carpenter gingerbreading with his band saw. Excess is always lurking at the end of the street, I know, but I ain't afraid of him, in whatever business I'm engaged in when he shows up, be it swarping in the mountains or teaching Seamus Heaney in a sweat, or trying to make some sense of Hurricane Agnes in a poem. Me and Excess have lived together for a long time; we keep in touch.

Or to strike another analogy: there's something in me that likes to garden. To *make* a garden. You can't let one happen. You have to make it, order it, pattern it. No pattern, no garden. No artifice, no garden. Same with poems as I see it. No texture, no tension—or no healthy self-consciousness, no deliberate, willed collaboration of the resources of language and syntax—no poem. I'm a putter-inner, along the lines of Melville, not a taker-outer, like Williams. And I like Baroque music, better than ballads, almost. I like a poem that draws me to it as a performance as well as to its subject; I like the reward not only of saying something, but of singing it too, charging the language a pitch or two higher than usual.

I think you're right that it's a matter of taste, and it ought to be, and it ought to stay that way. And what also ought to stay is the freedom for a fella to mess around, fooling with language to see what it will do, goofing off and then riding the high horse, loafing then burning hot. There are a lot of poems you and I would agree strike some magical, wonderful balance between the artfulness and the immediacy explicit in your comments, but my bet is that right now, I'd like a bunch of the ones that you wouldn't. There'd be a line you wouldn't cross and I would, the hell with it, let's look at the language here and the sounds and textures of words *en soi, por soi*, separate from the political or social or conventional realm. What can hyphenated constructions do? What is it about the kenning that is so attractive? What about a conceit that distances and engages all at once? What's going on here in this place called language, and what lives in it that I'd never find if I didn't give it its head now and then and let it run? And what lives in it that I'd never find if I didn't tie myself down to some form or pattern and so slow down and take a closer look?

Hell, what I've got in mind is a book of poems that are as different from one another as could be. That goes full against the grain of the academic point of view that insists on a poet finding and cultivating " a distinctive voice," and of there being such a unity in a collection, or even in an entire body of work. Hell, why not be a mimic, a strange crow with a split tongue, a mockingbird, or even a polyglot starling, full of chitters, whistles, and wheezes—all in the same collection?

One other thing. Remember that "what you look hard at looks hard at you." If I were to try to infer your notions about poetry from your comments, I would first be struck by your sensitivity to artifice—perhaps, even, a hypersensitivity. When someone who once smoked like a forest fire but has now quit begins to sermonize about the smoking, I'm with you—I "dodge the lecture." But could it be that you've had some crisis that has carried you away from a realm you once moved in, vividly, and powerfully, but were finally made ill by? And now, as a result of this crisis, you work out of an anti-intellectual, anti-artifice stance, making lectures for the other side? I remember you telling me once that you were growing sick of your own voice in the classroom, by which I took you to mean that you were disgusted by the merely academic approach to poetry. In your letter, you write, "The classroom's going to despoil us all." Really?

Bushman, the world—and poetry—is bigger than that. There's room for more than the speaking voice in poetry; there's room for more than the looseness of colloquial syntax; there's room for self-consciousness as long as it's not poisonous; there's room for *movement* in poetry, movement from one mode to another, from one tone or subject or style to another, from one register of language to another, and there's room in life for more than one change of mind or direction or attention. And there's room for more than one taste.

You've set me to thinking, Bushman—I thank you; editors and friends are supposed to do that. But thinking about what, exactly, I'm not sure. Maybe about life. Maybe about the right uses of language. Maybe about the fit of my underwear. But one thing your letter has confirmed in me is that all talk, finally, of individual styles is talk about individual styles, not talk about poetry. Poetry itself is large enough to contain and comprehend all this talk, and not be shaken by it, as the ocean remains serene just a few feet below the hurricane. It will take care of itself, poetry will, for all our weather. That's where my faith lies—in that calm deep that at its upper edges is still sunlit and familiar, that is still mixed with the common, but which at its depths, shades off into the dark that is full of the unknown and the unspoken. I like Melville's whale, that plunges from sunlight into the depths, and rises scarred with the marks of what no one's seen yet. I can't get there on a raft; I've got to push off, dive in, explore. Even if I meet the Dean at a thousand fathoms, his eyes aglow with accusation, in his hands sheaves of my own poems, their metaphors all smeared, their syntax skewed. . . .

(Here, as the metaphors heat up intolerably, the letter ends, thank goodness.)

But obviously, back there in in 1987-88, I was in some sort of tizzy. At almost exactly the same time, I had submitted a batch of different poems to another editor-friend of mine, this time in Alabama. He accepted one of the poems, but of one that he rejected, he wrote a comment that got my dander up. So I wrote him a letter, too. It also remained in my papers, unmailed. (I must write such unsent letters because they afford me a familiar and specific audience against which to bounce my ideas; once I have written them, and clarified the subject for myself, I avoid any argument or conflict by putting them away. Not good. Now that I see this avoidance, I promise to avoid it.)

Here's the Alabama letter:

Dear Bob,

Thanks for the letter accepting "Toward Fall" for B[irmingham] P[oetry] R[eview]. Glad you liked it. As for "Weeding" sounding to you like Wendell Berry, certainly you should know. [Bob did his dissertation on Wendell Berry; stupidly and unfeelingly, upon reading its first page, I dismissed it as "pedantry" in an attempt at humor that backfired. Don't mess with a guy's dissertation.] As for me, though, I've long ago stopped worrying about whether my poems sound like someone else's: my primary loyalty is to the individual poem, whether it has taught me something, revealed something to me I hadn't known or articulated to myself before. If it does so in a voice different from my other poems, or in a voice similar to someone else's—so be it. Poetry's larger than whatever notion of my own voice I might have—a notion which is fragmentary and inconclusive at best anyway, and likely to change from poem to poem and year to year as the world and my connections to it change and develop. Would we expect a bachelor's poems to see the world in the same way as a husband and father's? A few years ago I got back a manuscript I'd submitted to the Ohio Arts Council, and it had a note jotted on it that I think is indicative of what's wrong with part of the world of poetry these days. It said, "Well-crafted but nothing new."

"Hmph," I said to myself. "The same could be said of the Appalachian Mountains. The Grand Canyon. An iris blossom."

My *last* thought when I write is whether or not I'm being original; it's whether or not I'm being true—to my own perceptions (perhaps profoundly influenced—and so what? What are we reading poems for, if not, among other important things like pleasure, to change and heighten our understanding of the world?) and to the event that the poem becomes, and to the resources of language that present themselves to me during the time of writing. That's the craft; poetry isn't primarily new ideas, is it? Rather it's the contemporary expression of what Pound called "the news that stays news"—a comment that implies the perennial nature of poetry's interests and of the interests of its readers. Themes like death and love and isolation and communion. The sea. The land. Gardens and rivers and dreams. The effect of not worrying about whether I sound like someone else or not is liberation: I can damn well write about what I please, in the way that seems right. I do not look over my shoulder: that's death to any freedom. And the challenges to the writer's freedom are many, and by far the worst are from the interior: insecurity, the disease of self-consciousness, knowing too much about poetry, reading too much poetry, and so on.

In a review of my first full-length book *Ripening in Athenaeum*, Norman Finkelstein made the remark that one or two of the poems seemed derivative; he mentioned especially W.S. Merwin. Now the fact is, I hadn't read much Merwin since college, and didn't care too deeply for his work at the time. It's a pretty interesting trick to derive from a writer you've hardly read and don't much like in the first place. This hunting for sources and such is interesting, I suppose, but most writers are even more of a compost pile than that: no one, for example, has ever said anything about Shakespeare"s influence on my work, but if you ask me, the Bard's more of an inspiration to me than almost everyone else. And Dylan Thomas. And James Wright, and so on and so on—and each for a different reason.

I didn't mean to go on like this. I apologize. It's just that as I've been writing and publishing over these years, I've seen the inevitable attempts at categorizing: here's an Ohio River poet, here's a regional poet, blah, blah, blah. Fine. I acknowledge it as long as it's true. But poetry, as I said, is always larger than all that, and it's cutting my freedom and possibilities to buy into any of that stuff too seriously. Each poem is new, and difficult, and may require a change of pitch, or even a kind of ventriloquism, for me to flush—or tease— from its

41

hiding place. The hunter who knows only one way to hunt misses all the game that requires a different set of techniques, a different stalk, a different kind of patience. And if, in varying the attack, so to speak, I find myself in Wendell Berry's shoes, or in Walt Whitman's, or in Roethke's, or in Ogden Nash's, even—well, what goes around comes around. The only risk I run is that I don't do it as well as they did. And if I worry about that at all—in the slightest—then I ruin whatever chance I have of finding what it is I do best, what part of the world of poetry I've been given to stalk or to till. I trust that influences and models will evaporate on their own, leaving the residue of what's "original" in my work, if anything in it is. Of course, as I've said, I can't worry about that.

To put it another way, I try to maintain my amateur status as a poet. Perhaps if I cut off some small portion of the world and said to myself, "This, and no more," and careered that small hunk into some kind of reputation, I would be in the mainstream where the good old boys and girls, like those faked photos of Chairman Mao in the Yangtze River, swim along for the edification of the masses. But what I'd miss! The silly poems, the funny poems, the poems "uncharacteristic of the canon" and so on. To hell with that damned consistency. It's still fun writing poems, and I've not grown sick of myself or them. And it's because I'm resisting these dangerous threats to my freedom, my amateur status. Or I'm trying to, and in letters like these I'm finding out just exactly what I think.

One final thing—you and I both know that a poetic reputation rests largely in the hands of the academics who create it. And you know that much—not all, I know, I know—of the writing is an attempt to classify and categorize, to place the work in a tradition, to sniff out patterns, and to base the criticism on the consistency of those patterns. It is reductive, in a word. But the writing of criticism and the writing of poetry are two hugely different things, as far apart as gynecology and making love.

O I do go on. But I realize now it's because of the basic schizophrenia involved in being both a teacher and a writer, both a critic and a creator. I wonder what poetry would be like today if the 90 per cent of poets who are teachers were freed from those dual and sometimes contradictory loyalties? If instead of studying and teaching poetry all day and writing poetry at night—a hell of a way to run a railroad, analogous to requiring all bridge-builders to also practice sabotage—they were expressly forbidden to do both. Either teach, or write: never both. In saying this, I know that much head work gets done in teaching, head work that sometimes pays off in the writing of poems later—but I suspect that keeping a little more distant from literature and a little closer to the rest of life might help in the long run.

I'm getting hungry. I have to stop and eat lunch.

Best to you,

Dick

Now, to further complicate matters, I resubmitted "Talking Together" to Jerry Wayne in 1996, and he accepted it! I had accompanied it with a letter to the effect that I'd been miffed, but because a mutual friend of ours, Pauletta Hansel, had spoken to me, I was ready to make up, let bygones be bygones. I admit that I was sulking for those years; it was all on my part, as Jerry's reply makes clear:

August 2, 1996

Richard (Wayne) Hague
6203 Erie Ave.
Cincinnati, OH 45227

Dear Dick:

I swear, old bud! but you have taken me aback. I didn't know there was a feud. I didn't know I had pissed you off. (I ain't exactly *surprised*, either, given my innate and wholly unconscious talents in that direction.) And as you say, I *never asked*, which is—you're right—the bigger fault.

Generally, I don't write letters like that—only to people I care about, and well, you see where that lands me. But I swear I never turned "Talking Together" down. How could I be so stupid! I swear I've never seen that poem before. But if I have seen it, and if I did that awful thing to it, then verily I am a ass and a idiot (to quote some Dickens character I used to know the name of). And I guess it's long since published somewhere else, so any hope of redeeming my mortal soul is precluded. Maybe God *is* a Catholic after all.

And now I have to fall to worrying about how many other oddly silent people there are out there boiling a grudge in a covered pot, all because I articulated too precisely a hesitation that had no particular shape to it until I started trying to explain it, an inchoate hesitation

43

that just had to stand up corporeally and pretend a logical shape and be *analyzed*. In other words, explanations suck along with editors. But I guess I had (and still have) the need to explain myself, which is skidding on black ice with detrimental results. Nobody wants explanations. Just results. And preferably positive ones.

Well, that's Jerry Wayne's letter. His prose style lets you know right off that he's a peach, a smart fellow, and a friend. And he certainly is. The poem appeared in the Summer 1997 issue of *Appalachian Journal*, and we have lived happily ever after.

*   *   *

Write a letter to an editor, explaining why you disagree with his or her decision not to print your poem. What exactly were you up to in your poem? What might the editor have missed? What makes your poem good? What makes it new? Should "new" be a criteria for judging the goodness of a poem? Just what makes a poem "good" anyway?

It pays to think about these things; know, however, that the answers are long and hard, and may not be fully attainable in your lifetime. But that does not exempt you from exploring the questions as well as you are able to do.

*   *   *

Reading, of course, may help you to find some answers. Though I am tempted to append a list of poems that everyone simply *must* read, I distrust such reading lists for several reasons. For one thing, any list will be less than the perfect one for each individual who reads it. The perfect one is the strange, haphazard mix of good and bad that a person experiences on his or her own. There is no map to "Poetry" except the one built into each of our adventures. (See again "Entering The Poem.")

Having said this, I still admit that there are a few essays and a number of books (as well as the thousands and thousands of poems I have read, which constitute a kind of topsoil out of which everything else has grown) I have found useful, and that in some ways provide part of the architecture of my ideas in this book. I list a few here, with brief comments, not because I think everybody has to read them, but because, for me and for *The Lives Of The Poem*, they were important.

"A Felt Linkage." Jim Wayne Miller, *Mountain Life & Work*

Quoted in Notes & Divagations to "Spiel For Opening Night Of The Workshop." In his essay Jim Wayne also writes:

> When we get used to walking around in our lives with . . . distorted images of ourselves, distorted because we have forgotten who we are or can't acknowledge who we are and what we came from, then we are profoundly confused. This confusion is the root of sickness, despair, alienation. We are then what Alan Watts calls "genuine fakes." Weird. Grotesque. Spiritual disaster areas.

If you need some thought-provoking guidance on the matter of identity as linked to place and poetry, read this essay.

"Can Poetry Matter?" Dana Gioia, *Atlantic Monthly*

Among many other provocative things Gioia writes, ". . . the country is full of young poets and readers who are confused by seeing mediocre poetry praised, or never attacked, and who end up doubting their own perceptions." Also: "It is time to experiment, time to leave the well-ordered but stuffy classroom, time to restore a vulgar vitality to poetry . . . "

"Knowing The Mediocre And Teaching The Good." David Brendan Hopes, *English Journal, Sept. 1986*

An essay about mediocre poetry being praised. In many ways, this essay helped me sustain the courage to continue criticizing student poems, and calling for fluent writers to press the limits of their experience and voice. I have heard of university writing teachers, poets themselves, who offer few, if any, criticisms of the poems in their workshops. This is right and good—at the beginning stage. I would expect that university students in creative writing programs might be a bit beyond the beginning stage.

The thrust of Hopes's essay is that there *is* such a thing as a mediocre poem, and it is identifiable, and it needs to be pointed out as mediocre. There is nothing more cruel than encouraging, by default, mediocrity; there is nothing more difficult (nor more necessary) than criticizing respectfully, but firmly, that which is less than good.

Practically all the common objections to poetry—that it is sentimental, that it is wafty or effeminate, that it is irrelevant to the concerns of the contemporary world—are really objections to half poetry, to bad poetry, to poetry poorly taught or ignorantly read, to the mediocre. The only objection registered rightfully against the genuine as much as the mediocre is that it is difficult . . .

If you're approaching poetry as a learned parlor entertainment, you'd best start over. Poetry is a way of knowing, a method of organizing perceptions; in the family of the mind, poetry stands between science and theology, possessing the keenness of observation of the one and the will to faith of the other.

"How Do You Know It's Good?" Marya Mannes, in *Edge of Awareness*, ed. Hoopes and Peck, Dell Publishing Company, New York: 1966.

Mannes's essay begins:

Suppose there were no critics to tell us how to react to a picture, a play, or a new composition of music. Suppose we wandered innocent as the dawn into an art exhibition of unsigned paintings. By what standards, by what values would we decide whether they were good or bad, talented or untalented, successes or failures? How can we ever know what we think is right?

Good questions. The essay goes on carefully to answer them, and to take a stand on the responsibility of all of us to make judgments about art, including poetry. A fine essay to read and reread as your education progresses.

"Salt Crystals, Spider Webs, and Words." John Engle, in *Edge of Awareness*, ed. Hoopes and Peck, Dell Publishing Company, New York: 1966.

Engle writes:

[S]ome will argue: writing, like all art, is intuitive, and any intrusion of the reason will destroy the lovely, natural thing. This is dead wrong. It reduces writing to the level of a child babbling without regard to the shape of what he is saying. It is, indeed, so much like the uninhibited confessions from the psychiatrist's couch, sodium amytal cheerfully flowing through the veins and breaking down shyness, that it would seem proper to give inhibition-removing drugs to the writer. He could sit there gaily listening to the rustling of his unconscious. And of course the hallucinatory state would be the most creative of all . . . Yet surely the great and structured works of writing are done with the intelligence playing over against the intuition, each bracing the other, the mind giving form and sense, the intuition giving immediacy of impression, the stored-up memory, the deeply instinctive phrase.

Such stimulating observations about poetry exist all around is in the lives of books. Look for them. Expect to find good advice and counsel. There's much to learn in preparing (and continuing to prepare) for the poem.

The Poem Plants

In its pocket seed packets
like drafts of possible cantos.
The garden, that tradition,
both old and new before it.
On its knees, the poem crafts furrows
with a handy apple branch.
Soil opens, falls to either side,
darker and more rich
the deeper.
In a highday dazzle
of light it plants
half-blind, trusting to touch,
the balance of feel,
inspired by world's
heady smell.

Knowing growth is never sure,
over its seed lines
it tamps the moist earth,
palming the soil
for luck and good contact,
shaping a place,
if the weather is right,
where roots can take hold
and make of its work like a question
their deep and perennial
answers.

The Poem Plants

One night during the poetry workshop I used to hold at my house for whoever wanted to come, Joe, in Ohio for one of his lengthy stays before returning again to Fairbanks, and who always likes to have something to do, some job of work or challenge of one kind or another, said, "Let's write poems about poetry that aren't."

A pretty transparent attempt, this one. But I like "perennial answers" because it suggests the permanence of the lives of the poem. There can be a devastating drought in the poet's life, or an emotional flood that obliterates the familiar banks of his thoughts, or some tornado of spirit that explodes the barns and outbuildings of his mindscape, or a series of actual plagues and deaths that rob the poet of everything, as happened to Job. But if he or she is lucky, and has been faithful to the craft, after a few months poetry will arise again, like fireweed in Yosemite. As a matter of fact, poetry as a tough weed is a rich metaphor, more right than it is wrong, and worth developing.

Someone out there: go ahead.

Naming A Few Bones Of The Poem

1: Metaphor

These are the legs it stands on,
muscular, a leaper's springs,
broad-jumping rivers with verbs.
When the legs go
so does the poem.

2: Simile

Twins, they tell
us, "I am like her,
she is as I am."

Only they don't mean
it, exactly. They make
us see double.
Both of them.
At once.

3: Personification Articulates With Simile

For example, this
poem with hands.
It takes yours
in its own
and helps you
down to the
bottom
of this sentence
like a ladder
to the period
like a stone
underfoot
in the lawn
and says:
Look.

Naming A Few Bones Of The Poem

It has always seemed to me that this poem should be larger, more ambitious, more comprehensive. It should have zeugma in it, and chiasm, and symbol and alliteration and so on, all these wonderful, strange bones of poetry. But that period at the end of its last line just stalls me, stops me in my tracks.

The Poem Lures Her Along,
Shows Her The Promised Land

Over there, beyond the Kentucky Fried Chicken,
out across the freeway to the Video Store
and the mall, left at the Bowling Alley Boutique,
then right again at the Ribs Joint:
the world. Turtles and newts,
bluegrass and geology. Every stone
along every suburban driveway
a monologue spoken
for a million years.
Every wind rustling the kitchen curtains
carrying news in from Africa,
Shanghai. Every face in every yard
the history of evolution,
the current event.
Yet, struck blind and dumb
by TV's glow, success's robot eyes,
her own senses' sleepy daze,
she turns her back on it.
In school, stunned and blinking,
she thinks there is nothing
she can write about,
nothing she can say.
Meanwhile, her body, that community—
mitochondria, wise tenants with their own DNA,
bacteria in her guts signaling every other—
whispers poems to her, urgent and imploring.

At last, she listens:
pioneering the territory of herself,
she builds a lean-to of words
against the trunk of her spine,
camps for a season
near her own heart like a spring,
studies its upwellings and eddies.
Healing, her strength coming back,
she risks the ridges of dreams,
halloing in the dark.
And from a breathing hollow

nearer than she ever knew,
she hears arise her own voice,
rich as birdsong and wind.
Fed on memory's honey and fruit,
it chants its cardinal reply:
"You're here,
you're here.
Begin."

The Poem Lures Her Along, Shows Her The Promised Land

This poem is the source of the imagery of this book's front cover. I sent a number of the poems to Terri Kern, ceramic artist, who then designed several dozen tiles to illustrate the poems. When I went to her studio to see the finished series, I was utterly astonished at their vitality and energy and charm. The lives of the poem had taken form in another medium. Connection and collaboration: yes.

Trying To Write A Bunch of Metaphors,
She Stalls and Can't Go Anywhere,
As If She's Astride An Arabian Stallion
With A Mind Of Its Own And The Amazing Capacity
To Run Very Fast While Getting Nowhere

for Colleen Glenn

Whoa! she cries, thinking
if she stops it, maybe
she can get it pointed in some fruitful
direction, or at least
catch her own breath.

Without warning it
screeches to a halt,
exactly like the roadrunner
at the cliff's edge
in the cartoons.

In fact, the horse has been transformed;
she finds her legs
wrapped around
the stinking body of Coyote,
who, she sees with a start,
is eyeing her over his shoulder
and grinning.

She tries to dismount,
but Coyote revs up his Acme
Powerpack
and they're off,
hurtling across the desert
like Chuck Yeager in a rocket sled.

Breath rips through her mouth,
her tongue numbed by the pealing air,
her lungs force-fed and spinning
like fan-jet engines.

She feels the rpms
increasing inside her,
movement incarnating,
swelling her like a sudden
baby of speed,

Then wham, gives birth,
right there on Coyote's back,
a bloody advent of verbs amuck,
nouns shrieking like V2s
over the London of her former peace,
and explosions—muffled thumps,
a long way off,
begin to move toward her,

Until, after a long ridiculous cry
yiyiyiyiyiyiyiyiyiyiyiyi,
one direct hit,
middle of her head,
breaks open her skull
like a pomegranate
and inside there
are seeds, thousands of them,
each a poem still wet with its revealing,
still mumbling the strange noise
that will coalesce into English
and speak name upon name
to the shouting, shrapnel-filled air,

While Coyote howls like a cruise missile
and she clings to his back
like a bronco rider,
flailing her arm,
punctuating like flak-explosions
some vivid line
that leaps and flares and dives,
as large and full of light
as the whole round sky of day.

Trying To Write A Bunch of Metaphors, She Stalls And Can't Get Anywhere, As If She's Astride An Arabian Stallion With A Mind Of Its Own And The Amazing Capacity To Run Very Fast While Getting Nowhere

At the beginning of the 1994-95 school year, Katie "The Red" DuMont and Colleen Glenn approached me and asked if I might be able to meet them once a week or so for a poetry writing tutorial. My schedule as Coordinator of Writing Across The Curriculum allowed lots of flexibility, their guidance counselor, Pam Dolan, was all for it, and so I jumped at the chance to work with two very promising writers who also happened to be outstanding and beautiful people, too. As it worked out, we were able to meet twice a week for fifty minutes, sitting three abreast at the old cafeteria tables in the tiny Writing Room at school, each of us at a computer. We would talk, write, make assignments for one another, read our work aloud, critique it, and every so often I'd ask Katie and Colleen to switch seats, so that we sat adjacent one another for something approaching an equal length of time. I had noticed that the person sitting closer to me often got more comment and criticism, so we played musical chairs to overcome that odd dynamic.

One day I asked Katie and Colleen simply to write a bunch of metaphors—to heck with trying to make any kind of coherent poem. Just make a bunch of metaphors, and we'll see if they take us anywhere. Colleen, whose poems were almost always relatively short, tightly-crafted, single-minded lyrics, sat there grinning and red-faced, and at last crashed. We laughed, and talked about it, and then I started up on this poem, again just for kicks. It kept growing and going on me, so I rode it to the end. Six months or so later, I had a reading at a local bookstore, and I knew Katie and Colleen would be there, so I read the poem, trying to watch Colleen's reaction over the edge of my manuscript. Characteristically, she grinned and blushed and seemed to like it— she's a great sport, as is Katie.

As for the poem—it seems to me to be trying, almost by magical incantation, to get Colleen over the hump that was blocking her, to help her rise and fly in the face of what must have seemed to her a daunting chaos.

Coyote, the famous trickster figure of Southwest Native American lore, was familiar to us because of some work in fairy tales and folklore we'd done in our World Literature class together. He's in the poem because for me he's one of the personifications of the Wild Mind that Natalie Goldberg celebrates in her writing and teaching, and that she explores in her book of the same title. And I think he is also there because of the Roadrunner cartoons; Coyote is always coming up with some Acme-built contraption to match the Roadrunner's speed, but he never quite catches up. Instead, he fails and fails and fails, each time rising broken, blown up, sieved, smashed, shredded,

57

pancaked, or turned inside out, for the next disaster to happen to him—so that he can arise again. His story is one version of the lives of the poem: a long history of failure after failure, punctuated momentarily by competence and maybe even wild brilliance, only to be followed by catastrophe upon outlandish catastrophe once more. But if we never go along for the ride, never fall out of the saddle, never get bombed in the head, never careen to the top of the mountain and over the top, never plunge to the bottom of the gulch, never get called to account by an editor or friend, never make mistakes, we never get anywhere interesting.

*　*　*

Katie, along with others of my students, struggled with physics, so in our tutorial we wrote and talked together and started to write, for kicks, some physics poems. Here's one of hers.

Mr. M's Physics Pulley Demonstration: Wizard of Awes

The aisle clears:
students bow to remove their clutter
making way
for the Prince of Pulleys,
the King of Clank,
the High Muckamuck of movement.
Escorted to its stately place,
the classroom front,
the grand Vizier of Vectors
applies its force
on the honored shoulders
of the appointed student,
rising above all others
as Governor of Gravity.

Following the procession's progression,
a wave
of watchful pupils,
a common class,
from all realms of Physicsdom,
gathers to see the royal demonstration—
a courtly concatenation.

The Magician of Motion, Mr. M
smiles his loyal way
to the right side
of the Lord of Laws,
readying the moment
for the sorcery
of torqued turns to begin.

He raises his arm
and in an extravagant smoke
preludes the climactic pull
with a haze of commotion,
brooding cumulus clouds of confusion
before the crowd's eyes
with his fancy fog
of centripedal wrist action.
Then, in one brief tug
he casts into the air
a spell of awe
as the deflated purpose
goes flying over the heads
of all those assembled.

The Magician lowers his magic hand-
holstering his wand,
and nods regally,
as the Gathered
wipe the mist from their sights
and find the Emperor of Energies disrobed.

*   *   *

The tide of the masses
ebbed away in time,
searching the skies
for any glimpse
of whatever it was
that just went soaring by.

Though this draft of the poem is a little unclear in its situation at this point
in its development, and is in need of some shaping and editing—all that critic's
business—its high-energy playfulness, and its mixing of a physics demonstrat-

ion with folklore and literature—*The Emperor's New Clothes* and *The Wizard of Oz*, most obviously—is a lot of fun. And Katie's imaginative attempt to make something out of her physics class reminds us of the magnitude of potential poetic material. If only we could go to every class in school primed with the expectation that a poem, or a story, or a song, or a drawing, or a dance, might arise from it—we would see with different eyes, hear with different ears, move with different limbs, and "our very flesh become a poem."

* * *

Together, Colleen and Katie and I played with physics and poetry, among other subjects, so I had a handful of physics poems when, in the later Fall of '94, I came across a notice in *Education Week* magazine about a series of Arts in Education Awards to be made by the Council For Basic Education with the support of the J. Paul Getty Foundation and the National Endowment for the Arts. I proposed a course of study and the writing of a series of poems about physics, came up with a reading list, and applied. Early in 1995, I received word that I had been awarded a $3250.00 grant (the $250.00 dedicated solely to books!) to spend six weeks reading and writing. My friend Joe Enzweiler, who has already appeared here, and is a graduate of the Geophysical Institute at the University of Alaska, Fairbanks, served as my science advisor, and we exchanged letters and audio tapes concerning the science (or lack of accuracy or depth in it) in the poems. A great time was had by all, and the result is a book entitled *The Time It Takes Light*, the poems in which have appeared in a dozen places, and which at last, after nine years of maturing, has found a publisher.

But what a narrative of connection and coincidence this all is. The lives of the poem are multiple, overlapping, unpredictable—literally marvelous.

"I Don't Do Titles," She Said

for Colleen Glenn

Neither did God,
self-invented physicist,
swashbuckling buckaroo
breaking the bronco Chaos,
tied to the pommel as tightly as His tongue
was tied inside His mouth (nothing else around, no need for talk)
then left-handing this into creation, that into being,
upchucking forms and shapes by the tens of thousands
and all wordlessly, obscurely
nimbused and swooping here and there,
lassoing His strings into and out of Creation,
dragging nothingness down into form like a calf in the dust,
but always, (according to old Nicholas of Cusa)
nowhere,
and always (though gospelled as the Word at the Beginning)
saying nothing,
He sowed everything in silence,
grim planter.

But later, coming to,
Adam saw the mess He'd left
and so, mumbling, started in, sorting and arranging:
grampus, weevil, sneezeweed,
dik-dik, bongo, oryx,
earwig, chafer, pillbug,

and then some others
followed, Adam's grandsons,
(O yes he named them, and named them good:
Hamphat and Shadrack and
Spitnshine) and they, to
get revenge, continued, always naming,
always poking words
at things until they stuck:

hellbender, platypus,
ichneumon,
Coleoptera, Coelenterata,

coelocanth and ouzel,
Wiwaxia, Opabinia,
Hallucigenia,

until all had a lettered address,
a handle, sobriquet,
most carefully binomially nomenclatured,
and would, if rightly called,

answer to a name: hadrosaurus,
smilodon, paramecium,
Popilla japonica, Rana pipiens,

spadefoot, hornbill, horntoad,
rufous-sided towhee:
and so to all (and you, my title-less dear,
and your dear name-hungry reader)
to all a title says:
I have a name,
I live in this world:

hello, hello.

"I Don't Do Titles," She Said

Perhaps just a little peeved at me, this is what Colleen said when I went into my speech about how poems without titles are like children without names—worse: babies without heads. Why go to all the labor of bringing a poem into the world, only to abandon it before you do what a poet does best: naming things? As I have mentioned, I had begun, with some of Katie's and Colleen's classmates, to write some poems about physics, and some of that business leaked into this poem. But mostly it's full of the names of things. As John Hollander's poem "Adam's Task" points out playfully, the first namer— the first nominator—was Adam. (Before I go on, I want to point out a wonderful little fiction by Ursula le Guin, called "She Unnames Them," which appeared in *The New Yorker* several years ago. It reinforces the power of naming in obverse; Eve, grown wary of the "capturing" and artificial categorizing that Adam's naming involves, unnames the beasts and so frees them.)

But to return: I like the connotations of the word "nominate," for there is something official, something ceremonial about the word, and certainly the naming of things is a kind of ceremony: think of baptism, confirmation, Bar and Bat Mitzvahs, political conventions, the naming ceremonies of Native Americans, the Second Commandment. Names can be used to include and to exclude—as my friend Mary Brosmer, writer, mentor, educator, and founder of Women Writing For (a)Change, points out in an essay commenting on her poem "What I Seem To Have Forgotten," published in *Hackberry, Purcell Marian's Literary Magazine*—names and name-calling must be paid attention to:

> I go back by remembering, or trying to remember, the 'names of things.' My father taught my brothers and me the names of every tree, wildflower, and mushroom we encountered in our rambles through the woods of our Northern Ohio home and visits to the hills and woods of his boyhood in Southern Ohio. I am 'haunted by all my forgettings' and by the forgettings of us as a people: we have no time to learn the names of things, and even laugh at people who bother to try. (It is common to hear someone say blithely, 'Oh, I'm just terrible with names,' as if no effort were required to remedy it.) What's in a name? What's in naming? I think only—urgently—the willingness to be in relationship, to honor the world we come from and the one we are creating. I mourn, perhaps in the poem, not only the goings of my people from the world, their deaths, but the going away of naming (poetry-writing, botanizing, composing litanies of the honored)

toward an anonymous world where the joyous and loving activity of naming is replaced largely by the hostile and competitive practice of name-calling.

"To honor the world we come from and the one we are creating." What better expression of the responsibility of the poet to name her work than that?

There's more to talk about in the life of this poem, too. A year or so before I wrote this poem, I had read Stephen Jay Gould's *Wonderful Life*, a book about the Burgess Shale fossils. If you haven't heard of them, get this book and read it, for it is not only a book about fossils and the latest notions about evolution, but it is also a detective story of sorts, a book about naming, and an exploration of one of the most fascinating and fundamental questions of all—how do we *know* something? How do we prove that we know?

At any rate, the book's central subject is a set of fossils that, for many years after their discovery and preliminary misclassification, lay stored away in dusty drawers, their stories untold. Then a couple of fellows came along and took a second look and as a result, rewrote the history of the Cambrian Era, and perhaps of life itself on our planet.

One of the tasks they faced was to name this profusion, this explosion of astonishingly diverse and profoundly eerie life forms, and I think they did an excellent job, for the most part. Imagine what an animal named *Hallucigenia* might look like, then go to this book and be even more surprised.

So I had been carrying these wonderful names around in my head—as I had been carrying the Latin name for Japanese beetle and leopard frog and others for nearly all my life—and at last they found a place to come into being in, a poem that provided them, so to speak, with the conditions necessary for life. *Lives of the Poem*, indeed.

* * *

Write a poem about your name. Then, write a poem that name-calls, that assigns labels to things or to weaknesses or to virtues that you perceive in yourself or others. Where does this naming lead to? Is naming not only a poetic act, but a political one, involved, somehow, with the world and how we choose to perceive it? Is naming involved with power?

I include this poem because I think it's a nifty little exercise, suggested by my friend and mentor Jim Wayne Miller. Writing it surprised me a bit (and that's always good); I had to do some research too (that's always good). I found out that my last name is linked to an Irish word that means either "one who argues over fences," or "one who lives within a fenced enclosure." The wonderful thing about this is that I am, indeed, a rather argumentative sort of person, and, amazingly enough, every house I've ever lived in had, at one time or another during my dwelling there, a fence or hedge around it. How did my name know all that, even before I had lived into it?

The Poem Teaches Him His Name

I hear tell you hung over fences
in the old time, got a name
for arguing and haggling
over the hedges that
enclosed your camp:
so it's a fence,
two-posted,
one stringy rail across,
you start with,
right next to a pumpkin
with a little stem.
But in the middle
lives a root,

Hague

curling underground.
I think that's love
for you,
that heading down,
that adventuring.
Then two short pickets,
then your hopeful ending—
how you turn back,
rise up and around;
how you slowly circle,
as if relishing once last time
the lay of the land,
then go on
and disappear.

* * *

Write a series of short poems in which you name your secret fears or nightmares or insecurities, and let them speak as if they have not only a name, but a life, of their own. Below is an example from a series of poems I wrote

65

when I was just out of graduate school, and trying to recover from a suddenly failed marriage. It is one of about forty short poems in which I gave voice to mostly demonic forces which threatened to disintegrate me. Years later, I was invited by Yvonne Foley, a colleague of mine at Purcell Marian, to talk to Katie The Red's religion class. I believe it was when they were preparing their Life Philosophy papers, and I read from these poems as a way of talking about my own life's journey, its ordeals and trials and darknesses. Here's one.

The Beast of Waking Up

Sometimes I'm as sluggish as a gnu,
but sometimes quick to strike,
the boomslang of the harried and
undreaming.
I'm life's essential problem.
You cannot choose me and you cannot lose me.
I'm with you like your skin
You're stuck. Wake up.

Here's a another little footnote to the lives of the poem. I wrote these poems, as I said, many years go, in the the early Seventies. A handful were published by my friend Robert Collins, then editor of *Ohio Journal*. (See "Night Stop At The Crossroads," below). The poems then lay dormant for more than two decades, until I decided to collect them together in a chapbook; they appeared from Pudding House Publications in 1996.

Four years later, Keith Wahle called and asked if I would like to read some poems as a part of a performance series he was involved in producing. He knows my work, and suggested either some of the Lives of The Poem poems, or some of the Beast poems, which he had heard me read at one of York Street International Cafe readings that Terri Ford and Jim Palmarini organized. I said I'd think about it. Originally, he had simply wanted me to read the poems, but I thought of perhaps dramatizing them, since I had just that summer taken part in a workshop with Marc Mocahbee, an actor, teacher, and movement coach, and was thinking about ways of doing poetry beyond the traditional podium-bound reading. I thought immediately of Katie The Red, who had had extensive experience staging poetry during her undergraduate days at Xavier University. I asked her if she would help me in staging some of the poems. (Exactly thirty years after I graduated from Xavier, Katie served as Host, or President, of Mermaid Tavern, the writing fraternity at X.U. I had held the same post that same thirty years before.) "There is more here than meets the eye!" the poem exclaims.

And so, since it seemed to be in the stars, Katie agreed. She made a cutting of the poems, selecting ten (we had fifteen minutes for the production) and we rehearsed for a couple of months. In December of 2000, we performed them two nights running at the College Hill Town Hall, the home base of the Contemporary Dance Theater, host of the Performance Arts Series. Katie was the star of the performance, her voice, her presence, her delivery, her movement, her hair—all stunning. And the opening poem, spoken by her, the projection of the poet's tortured imagination, as she writhed ominously awake on stage, was "Waking Up."

Poems written almost thirty years ago, left alone for twenty, then published as a book, then collaborated upon with a friend and former student who was not yet born when the poems were written, and then, together with that friend, performed. This sort of intergenerational wonder cannot have happened in many human lives, and I am aware of its blessed uniqueness and of its power. It is a gift the lives of the poem have made to me, and to Katie, and to Keith, and to Kosmos and to all of us involved in this chronicle of interconnectedness and language. Lives of the poem? Yes. More than the cat's nine, and more marvelous, and strange.

* * *

"Works of art participate in our lives; we are not just distant observers
of their lives. They are in conversation among themselves and with us.
This is part of the description of human life. We do the way we do
partly because of things that have been said to us by works of art and
because of things we have said in reply."

— Wendell Berry

Think about this. It is one of the most amazing facts about literature, and about the lives of the poem. I have before me right now a poem by my friend Kosmos. (By the way, Kosmos was a fellow member of the same Mermaid Tavern I mentioned just above, at exactly the same time; his nickname was finally nailed down with the initial "K" supplied by—you guessed it, Katie The Red, shortly after meeting him—and not long after that she wrote the play, highly poetic and wildly imaginative, entitled "Kosmos"). The poem at hand was written here in Cincinnati, after a particularly fine January day, mild and sunny, that Kosmos and I shared on my back porch—a gift in the middle of winter. As intensely present to that day we both were, the poem, collected in Joe's *Stonework of The Sky* and published in 1994, nevertheless remembers a long, long time ago, in a far, far country:

67

Porch In Winter

Games of pool, blue twilight
river towns and the orange noise
of strangers through the screen door
that drew us there.
Of our victories and their thin escapes,
driving the high ridge midnight road
where the fog laughed
and fireflies joined the stars.

All talk is, in the end,
the talk of home. Twenty years
we have been friends.

From these chairs
we lean into our words tonight
like sails as the sun shifts,

board by board, behind the winter elm.
Then you lean back, unburdened, laughing
and I laugh too, in an hour forgetting.

It's what porches are for, to sit
awhile, watch before supper the cold
parabola of swifts
and think of nothing more;

to talk, to listen for what is older
than ourselves. The heart. The rhythm
of the sea. Odysseus, who still longed
for home, though he was offered immortality.

From southwestern Ohio to ancient Ithaca—and the places all over that ancient world where Odysseus roamed. It's another of the fine aspects of the lives of the poem—through poetry we can connect present and past; after sweet solitude or finest quiet company we can rejoin the noisier circles of existence, we can participate in, be shaped by other imaginative views of life. Joe's life and my life are made larger by the lives of the poem.

"To listen for what is older/ than ourselves." Now there's a business that's little practiced these days in our culture. I have a favorite little speech I give my students when the occasion arises, involving King's Island, a huge so-called amusement park in this part of the country. I remember when King's Island was not there; where now there are acres and acres of asphalt parking lots, there were formerly fields sown to corn and soybeans, interspersed with little windbreak woods and creek-bank thickets. I ask of my students that, when they go there the next time, they pause in the parking lot to listen. I tell them to hear the vanished birds, and the sound of the gone creek, and the rustle of wind through the extinct corn—I want them to realize that there is the past all around us, above and beneath us. I want them to consider the possibility that the present is not always an improvement. I want them to understand the full and real cost of their "amusement." I want them to consider whether it's "amusing" at all to bulldoze, then pave over a piece of land to make way for roller coasters and cotton-candy booths.

At any rate, it seems important to me that we get an accurate sense of perspective. Where do we stand in time? Where do we stand in relation to other living things and to the land? These are some of the things Joe's poem invites us to reflect seriously upon.

* * *

Write a series of poems that "listen for what is older/ than ourselves." Maybe they will be based on a place or places you are familiar with and that you hold in memory. Maybe they will be about heirlooms that your family possesses. Maybe they will give voice to objects that have lain silent in your life up until now. See again "How The Poem Listens."

* * *

There's another kinship expressed, somewhat secretly, in this poem, too. Remember that poetry is a conversation, ongoing and uninterrupted down through the centuries. In the poem above, Joe has a brief conversation with Homer, nodding in acknowledgment of his great epic poem and his clever, many-faceted character, Odysseus. But he's also having a conversation with me. Here's a poem from my first full-length collection, *Ripening*, published in 1984, and written about a trip Joe and Bob Collins and Jim Quinlivan and I took in 1976.

Night Stop At The Crossroads

Where we started from
that time, city's high summer
bred its thick prose
choked with detail,
so we drank our way
across the state
till dark fell
like a single, simple line.

In the Crossroads Bar
at Malaga, Ohio,
we took the table
closest to the night
that poured fragrant
through the door,
and shot pool
until the bright felt
bleared, until
the gaudy balls
in dawn's light
softened.

Then, down 26 from Rich Fork
clear to Graysville,
laughing, weary,
we recalled our
better shots.
and dreamed of shots
we'd take.
And for a time,
we were satisfied
that our lives, our worlds,
were as certain as our games,
and that the fog,
as it did that time,
would roll
forever cool across
the creek and road,
forever true and steady
toward familiar corners.

Reread "Porch In Winter." The lives of the poem are endless; they reproduce themselves.

Breaking Its Own Rule,
The Poem Tries An Answer To The Question
'What's A Poem?'

Out in the country,
a man from the city
drives his new car
down the middle of the road.
He's lost and doesn't even know it.
He's smoking a cigar,
talking to Chicago on his cellular phone,
making big deals.
But he's no poem.

So he doesn't see the pack of dogs,
feisty beagles and mutts from all over the county,
racing along at wheel-level beside him,
nipping at his tires.
They're poems, all of them.
deep-winded natives,
sharp of tooth, and lean.

And he doesn't see,
a mile down the road near the old wooden bridge,
the county sheriff
(he's a poem too,
half laughter and tobacco,
half jokes and barbed wire)
waiting to catch him breaking the law.

And he doesn't even imagine—he can't—
how back at the Court House,
hunching in the dark,
the judge (a poem too,
formal and strict as a sonnet,
but nowhere near so pretty)
sits waiting and ready
to throw his ass in jail.

Breaking Its Own Rule, The Poem Attempts An Answer To The Question, "What's A Poem?"

It was Shelley who called poets "the unacknowledged legislators of the world." Here, they're the policemen and judges, too.

What crime has the man driving the car committed? I recall that scene from *Death of A Salesman*, as the central character, Willy Loman, is in a severe decline. His wife says, "Attention must be paid." She was speaking of her husband, but perhaps this poem is suggesting that it won't do to cruise through somewhere (or through some subject, or some culture other than your own) with a kind of supercilious self-centered disregard for what's out there. Attention must be paid to places and customs and laws—both the written ones and the unwritten—or else we run the risk of being punished or at least embarrassed by our own ignorance and arrogance. I speak from painful experience in this, having embarrassed myself more than a few times. What Wendell Berry says is true: "A man may be provincial only by being blind to his own province." Where do you live? What are its laws and customs? What are its beauties and excellences? Who are its poets? What are it flaws and shortcomings? Are you blind to them, or are you ready to sing about them?

* * *

On another track: can poems really say things like "Throw his ass in jail"? I guess so. If it's right for the poem. Is it right here? Where wouldn't it be right? Write a poem that rejects such language, then a poem in which such language is clearly out of place, then a poem which absolutely calls for such language, and lots of it.

In The Bedroom of The Poem

There are things familiar
and strange. On the table
by the bed, a set of false
teeth in blue water:
they are waiting till
you are old
and need them
for eating
the tougher truths.
On the window seat
a cat sits
and you touch it:
made of stone.
As you turn
away, it purrs.
Two shoes
by the fireplace,
their laces untied,
an empty brandy snifter
beside them,
and an open book
of poems:
glancing, you
see your own face
on the cover.
And in the bed,
someone is sleeping,
inventing your life
in her dream.

In The Bedroom Of The Poem

I've heard this, in several versions, from several writers belonging to several groups—ethnic, racial, political—outside the mainstream, whatever that is these days. "If we don't tell our own stories (and poems), someone else will, and they'll get them wrong."

Claim your lives and hold on.

Hidden Meaning

Everybody knows that poets
are grave-loaders, packing
the damp earth
of their poems
with elaborate coffins.
And everybody has heard about
what's in them:
history, sex, onomatopoeia,
wyverns, similes,
moles, bridges, spiders,
empty bottles,
favorite nightmares,
pictures of cousins
who were mean:
even, now and then,
our own friends,
victims tattooed like Queequeg
with essay questions
from the College Boards.

But what many don't know
is this: all it takes
is a change of clothes—
a disguise—
a little planning,
a scheme as diabolical as theirs,
a little motherwit and mother tongue
and a night of sweat
and watching
to catch them at it,
red-handed, those ghouls:

Smiling guiltily,
like brothers or sisters
wearing our stolen coats,
they'll confess
to everything.
Often, when pressed,

they'll let drop clues
to other crimes:
"I committed Beauty."

"I kidnapped Chaos
and led her into Order."

"I got back, and even."

Hidden Meaning

Why does a writer write? Speaking of stories, but truly as well about poems, Paul Gallico, in "One Writer's Life," says,

> For many reasons—an urge, a gripe, the need of a buck, the need to get something off his chest, the desire to support his family, the hope of expressing something beautiful he feels inside him, the wish to entertain, to be admired, to be famous, to overcome a frustration, to experience vicariously an unfulfilled wish, or just for the pleasure of taking an idea and sending it flashing through the air, like a juggler with many silver balls, or the dark satisfaction of pinioning that same idea or thought or human experience and dissecting it to its roots.

Some young writers I know, asked recently why they write, answered, it's "blowing off steam," it's "getting something out of you," it's "escaping—going to other worlds," it's "relaxation and a self-clarification," it's "because I have to—if I don't I'll blow up," it's "to talk about things in a different way," it's "to get 'it' down right," it's "to talk to yourself and still stay out of the loony bin," it's "to capture and preserve moments."

That's a good list, too, very fine.

See "The Poem Does Lunch Out East" for exemplification of another motive for writing, one of the sweet pleasures for sinners like me, at least. If you haven't got the time to read "Out East" right now, the motive is named explicitly in the last line of "Hidden Meaning."

The Poem, Disguised As His Coy Mistress, Goes A-Maying

She drives a '55 Chevy
with Hurst lifters
and moon caps,
wears see-through
painter's pants,
reads Henry Miller,
Erica Jong.
This afternoon, she's
cruising Ault Park,
driving through clouds
of dope smoke
and barricades of smashed
beer bottles,
singing,
"I Want To Hold Your Hand."

He's following
on his ten-speed,
checking out her
rhyme scheme
from the rear.
When she pulls over
by the woods,
he knows
he'll have her.

She looks back,
shakes her sweet
couplet,
and smiles.

The Poem, Disguised As His Coy Mistress, Goes A-Maying

Poetry and sex? Yes, and probably from the very beginning: Adam was the first poet, and the first seductee. *O felix culpa.*

* * *

And if you don't recognize that last phrase above, stop whatever you're doing right now (adventures often begin unexpectedly, even irritatingly) and find out. Keep a little log of all you had to do to find out the meaning and significance and origin of this phrase, and then consider this: is there a place in the lives of the poem for research? Do poems always come from what you already know, or do some poems require you to go out and learn something new, and sometimes something very complicated and extensive?

* * *

Get to know Andrew Marvell's "To His Coy Mistress." Memorize it. Know how it works, how it's put together, appreciate its strangenesses. Say it to yourself and your friends whenever you can. If nothing else, you'll get a reputation of some sort. "Grow a beard," one of my college teachers suggested, grinningly. "Or an extra ear."

The Poem Braids Its Lover's Hair

She smells of oranges.
For this also the poem loves her.
It grasps, gently, rounds
of her coppery hair,
weaving them,
fragrant and flashing,
over and under,
under and over,
then drifts into trance,
then likenesses:

How bodies move
like this in love,
legs twined
in the afternoon sun;
how bindweeds climb
a chain-link fence,
their stems overlapping
brilliance and shadow,
plaiting light and form
to design;

How the poem's very self
of words
works this way too,
nouns its warp,
verbs its weft,
all the warm loops and coils
of the world
its dreamy affairs,
its sensuous interweavings.

The Poem Braids Its Lover's Hair

For many of these poems, I have only sketchy remnants of the drafts they went through; to keep all that stuff would make my study a fire hazard. But with this poem—not a very successful effort, I'm afraid—I kept everything, including a running commentary on the writing of it, which I made for my students who were studying revision. Here it is, pretty much unedited, as it happened.

Revising The Poem

We have not really talked much about revising the poems we are writing. In some ways, learning to revise the poem will help us pick up skills useful in revising other kinds of writing. So here are the drafts and revisions of a poem I wrote last year. Maybe in talking about them, we can uncover some of the things that work for me, and that may work for you.

First, a few words about how this poem began. In 1987 I started deliberately working on a series of poems about poetry and about teaching and learning to write poetry. (I had committted a few such poems all along, begining in my college days—but in 1987, I set out to do a series of them.) One evening, I just made a list of possible titles for poems in that series. That, for me, was a brainstorming or clustering session; I let whatever craziness and unlikeliness that wanted to happen come out. A year later, I came back to that list, and was still interested in the idea that one of the titles suggested. So I started a draft.

By the way, the idea of this poem was suggested to me in homeroom one morning. I was watching one girl braid another's hair. There was something about this little scene that caught me; it seemed calm and loving, and, pardon the pun, touching. I don't know why it took hold of me that way, on that particular morning. On some other day, I may well have shouted, "Girls, this is not a hair salon," and asked them to stop. But I didn't on that day. It made an impression. And it gave me a poem.

Draft 1

The Poem Braids Its Friend's Hair

She smells of oranges.
The poem xxxx holds rounds of
her copper hair and
weaves them, fragrant and
flashing, over and under,

81

under and over,
and thinks of likenesses:
how bodies move
like this in loving,
legs twined
in the afternoon light;
how bindweeds xxxx climb
the a chain-link fence,
xxxxxxxxtheir stems overlapping,
twining,
weaving,
how words
work this way, too,
nouns the warp,
verbs the weft,
(and the great whole)
the world the weaver,
xxxxx xxxxxx
xxxx xxx xxxxx
       xxxxxxxx xxxxxxxx

Well, I had gotten hold of something, at least. Where that first line came from, I don't know. Maybe there had been someone eating an orange in homeroom that morning, or maybe the hair spray reminded me of the scent of oranges—I just don't know. But it showed up as a way to start, and though I couldn't account for it, I took it, let it be a place to start.

If nothing else, it gave me the color of the hair—"copper"—orange-red hair, my favorite for some reason, maybe my Irish roots. Anyway, "oranges" goes with that color. Maybe I knew unconsciously that the hair would be red later in the poem, and so "oranges" came first. Again, I don't know. But I went with it.

Then things started to roll pretty well. I got the scene of the braiding going, and then, I got some other similar things going: bodies braided in love, bindweeds climbing a fence (here I could see very clearly the way the bindweeds, which are wild morning glories, by the way, on the chain-link fence around my yard twisted their stems tightly around the fence wire—and I like getting my house and yard into my poems: it feels "at home" to do this). And then I saw how to get the Poem—that is, the main character in this *Lives of the Poem* poem into this a little more—how a poem's words are like the strands of fiber in weaving. I had to go to the dictionary to make sure I was using "warp" and "weft" correctly. These are words I first ran into many years ago when I was first reading *Moby Dick*. So they came into this poem from a long way off. But there they were.

Then the poem died on me; it ran out of gas. I had no idea how to close it off. I struggled with a couple of possible lines, but scratched them completely.

And that was that: the first draft. A mess, a failure—but a failure I learned a lot from. Mostly what I learned was that I did not know what I wanted to say, exactly. I did not know how to end the poem. I did not know, yet, just how the Poem-as-character fit into it. But from experience in writing, I trusted that if I kept on working, I would discover what I needed to know.

And then right after that, to try to get back into the flow of the poem so that I might be carried through it again to an ending, I wrote this:

Draft 2

The Poem Plaits Its Lover's Hair

She smells of oranges.
For this, the poem loves her.
(if for only this, the poem loves her.)
It holds   grasps gently   rounds of her
copper y hair (the poem is partial to such color.
                          xxxit knows secrets, it is wise.)
weaving them, fragrant and flashing,
over and under,
under and over,
and thinks   drifts into xxxxxx warm of likenesses: drifting into trance,
how bodies like this xxxxxxx softness   then
likenesses:
how bodies move
like this in love
legs twined
in the afternoon light;
how bindweeds climb
a chain-link fence,
their stems overlapping,
twinning, xxxxxx and crossing
how its very self of words   the poem's very self of words
works this way too,   works this way too,
nouns the warp,   nouns the warp,
verbs the weft,   verbs the weft,
all the soft warm lengths   reaches and xxxx coils

of the world
its patient
interweaving

    its caresses and interweavings,
    its thoughtful   dreamy caressings,

    its xxxxxx   xxxxxxxxx interweavings.
      attentive
      amorous

Even more of a mess now! But that's exactly what happens to me in revisions: I add, cut, make notes, go off on tangents to explore new possibilities. After all—what I have is right there in front of me; I'm not going to lose it. So I can explore other ideas and not worry that I'll lose anything that I've already found. That's *writing*—not just thinking. Or to put it another way, that's writing-while-thinking, or thinking-while-writing. Or to put in another way, that's writing to think straight; that's writing in order to discover what I mean to say. (Or even more precisely, what the poem means to say.)

This draft is obviously a little longer than the first. And there's a little more of an ending, though still unsatisfactory. Notice that some of the lineations are changing slightly; compare the first five or six lines of Draft 1 with the first ten or so of Draft 2 and you see that I am feeling the line-ends a little more surely. I'm still crossing out words and phrases, not settling for the first thing that comes to mind in some cases. And I've gotten the Poem-As-Character into the second draft a little more directly—that seems to be one of the things the poem is trying to get me to do. After all, the central idea of the whole series of poems is "Lives of the Poem."

"The poem is trying to get me to do." I'm not so much writing the poem at this point, as *listening* to it, trying to understand what it needs to say. I'm very conscious of the fact that a poem is connections—connections between words, images, sounds, actions—so I'm trying to find the words, images, sounds and actions that go together best, and that will thus suggest to me what the poem wants to say, and how it wants to mean.

Finally, notice the changes in the title. From the original starting point—a girl braiding her friend's hair in homeroom—the poem has now become clearly a love poem. There are several reasons for this that I am conscious of, and I am sure several more I am not conscious of. One conscious reason is that I'm feeling the poem as a love poem—it's not just friends here. Another is that the images themselves suggest something deeper than just friendship. A third is that I needed a love poem for *Lives Of The Poem*, and this seemed a likely candidate. Another change is due to the fact that I want to save the word "plaits" (in the original title) for the body of the poem. I don't want to repeat it. Now:

Draft 3

The Poem Braids Its Lover's Hair

She smells of oranges.
For this also the poem loves her.
It grasps, gently, rounds (of her)
of her coppery hair, (then begins
begins,
weaving them, fragrant and flashing,
over and under,
under and over,
then drifts into trance,
(and then likenesses:)

how bodies move
like this in love,
legs twined
in the afternoon light;
how bindweeds climb
a chain-link fence,
their stems overlapping,
twinning and crossing,
plaiting light and form
to design;
how the poem's very self
of words
works this way too,
nouns (the) its warp,
verbs (the) its weft,
all the warm, (reaches) loops and coils
of the world
its (dreamy) thoughtful caressings,
its amorous interweavings.

The mess continues! But there are some things that are now beginning to sort themselves out; there are some passages that have remained relatively unchanged since the first draft. That they have tells me that they might be right; my re-visions, my re-lookings at the poem have confirmed their rightness through three drafts now.

And also there are things that showed up in Draft 2 that are no longer around. "The poem is partial to such ideas,/ it knows secrets, it is wise"—all this goes away now (and good riddance). What was it doing there in Draft 2 and why isn't it there now? Several reasons. First, it is too much of a telling, rather than a showing. I hope that the Poem's knowing things and wisdom and partiality is evident in the actions it performs—it doesn't need to be said. Second, I think that I needed to say that to myself, to keep the character of the Poem straight, to remind myself of something about it that was important. Once I'd done that, I could get on with the poem itself, suggesting things in the action and imagery. Third, it's out because it's a little too arrogant for a tender poem such as this one. It's crass and bragging, and though there is much room for crassness and braggadocio in poetry, not in this one. It just doesn't belong.

And the design of the poem is beginning to emerge, too, in this draft. It's pretty clear that it's more than one part, logically, and I've divided the first stanza from the second, the major reason being to focus attention of the "likenesses."

And finally the end of the poem is beginning to take shape: the Poem-As-Character is right there, at the end now, as it should be. And it is there as a lover, again as it should be, given all that's happening earlier. And those "warm loops and coils of the world"—yes. There's a detail that connects with the weaving and braiding imagery, and it suggests what I want to suggest— that the Poem is the world's lover—it loves all, not just the girl whose hair it braids—and this image of the loops and coils of the world covers a lot of territory—growing things (like bindweed), the way water flows, the serpentine intricacies of the *Book of Kells*, the ways clouds and all curved and soft things flow. (See " Chaos Poem" again) And also, since the images just before are of nouns and verbs—the loops and coils suggest, if I am not stretching this too far, the very letters of the alphabet that are woven together to make those words. [See "The Poem Teaches Him His Name."] Yes, the ending is beginning to come into focus in this draft. I feel good. I do another draft, again writing all the way from the beginning to get back into the flow of the whole poem.

Draft 4

The Poem Braids Its Lover's Hair

She smells of oranges.
For this also the poem loves her.

86

It grasps, gently, rounds
of her coppery hair, begins,
weaving them, fragrant and flashing,
over and under,
under and over,
then drifts into trance,
then likenesses:

how bodies move
like this in love,
legs twined
in the afternoon light;
how bindweeds climb
a chain-link fence,
their stems overlapping,   brilliance and shadow, xxxxxx xxxxx
twinning and crossing,
plaiting light and form
to design;

how the poem's very self
of words
works this way too,
xxxxx sounds
nouns its warp,
xxxxxxx sense
verbs its weft,
all the warm loops and coils
of the world
its (thoughtful) amorous (gorgeous) (involvements)
its (amorous) sensuous interweavings.

Now this is a mess that's beginning to un-mess. I'm "cleaning up the verbal situation" in a more orderly way, now. Most obviously, the structure of the poem has become clear to me: the three parts, each developing one scene or set of ideas that are linked. How do I know it's the right form for this poem? It feels right, is all I can say. When I re-read the poem out loud (and I always do, when I'm working on one), it feels right this way.

I'm still making additions, and still wrestling with the ending—things I've done all the way through the process. But I don't let these things bother me; I know that if I keep trying, and keep thinking, keep re-seeing the poem as I let it cool off between drafts (that cooling off may only be a few moments—I like to do drafts of poems as much at once as I can, while my concentration is high, these things will work out.

But sometimes they don't. That's when I put the poem away for a week, or a month, or even longer. Then I'll come back to it, and often, somehow, the problems will have worked themselves out. Not always, but frequently enough for me to trust this approach. So I'll come back to it, and I'll see what it needs me to do. It's as if my unconscious mind has kept working in secret on the poem during those weeks or months that I've set the poem aside, and when I finally come back to it, I'm ready. Or it's ready. Same difference.

I've also let myself experiment a little here: "nouns its warp,/verbs its weft" has been in the drafts almost from the beginning. Now, later in the life of this poem, I'm fiddling around with those lines, seeing if something else will work better. At this point, I don't think it does, so I'll bet that the original lines show up gain in the next draft. Let's see:

Draft 5

The Poem Braids Its Lover's Hair

She smells of oranges.
For this also the poem loves her.
It grasps, gently, rounds
of her coppery hair,
weaving them, fragrant and flashing,
over and under,
under and over,
then drifts into trance,
then likenesses:

how bodies move
like this in love,
legs twined
in the afternoon light;
how bindweeds climb
a chain-link fence,
their stems overlapping,
brilliant and shadowed,
plaiting light and form
to design:

how the poem's very self
of words

works this way too,
nouns its warp,
verbs its weft,
all the warm loops and coils
of the world
its daily caressings,   involvements,
its sensuous interweavings.

Things are definitely shaping up now, At this point I've worked on the poem for about three hours. Most of the work has been, obviously, revising to clarify for myself what the poem wants to say and be, and how it wants to say and be it. So the entire process has been discovery—remember that all I started with was a title, and a remembered scene from homeroom. I did not know ahead of time what I wanted to say—I only knew I had a picture in my mind of a girl braiding another's hair, and that I had a working title. I can't stress this point too much—I did not know what I wanted to say—nor what the poem wanted to say—until I went though all this.

In this draft, then, the structure of the poem has solidly emerged. Its's the way it wants to be, the way that makes sense and feels right. There is one addition: the "brilliant and shadowed" image of the bindweeds. It showed up in the last draft, and it seemed right after a little tightening, Visually, it's another "weaving."

I'm still having trouble with the final lines. They still don't have enough punch, vividness, surprise. I'm sure that in the next drafts, they'll get worked on. But I'm feeling pretty satisfied now with the poem. It has arrived, and I think what it says is true, and it probably "works."

Post Script, Several Months Later

About those final lines; many months have passed, and I still was not comfortable with them. But I did choose some other words. Here's the last stanza now:

how the poem's very self
of words
works this way too,
nouns its warp,
verbs its weft,
all the warm loops and coils
of the world
its dreamy affairs,
its sensuous interweavings.

"Dreamy affairs" conveys some of the quality I wanted to capture in the poem's relationship to the world: "dreamy" remembers the "trance" of the first stanza, and it suggests something about the poetic process. "Affairs" is not only literal, meaning the business of the poem, its daily work, but also suggests romance (though its connotation of *illicit* romance is not exactly right. I think I need to do better here.)

And also I am not happy with "interweavings." It is a repetition, and not an effective one. Surely I want to close the poem on the image of weaving or braiding, but I do not feel comfortable with this bald repetition of a word appearing earlier in the poem. So I am still looking for a better word. I could go to the thesaurus, but I never do that. I want to write in my own language, my own vocabulary, and though the thesaurus might seem to solve my problem in the short run, it won't feel right. I know I'm a little cranky on this count, but unless I've met and come to know a word in its natural habitat—in an essay, or novel, or poem, or news article, or in a conversation on the street or in the country somewhere—or, as with "divagations," in the program of a friend's piano concert—I don't feel I've earned my use of it.

So, though the poem is "finished" in one sense, it's still living and developing in my head. I'm letting the underground workshop—one writer's name for the subconscious creativity of the mind—continue working on it. I hope that I will find the exact images to close the poem with. I'm pretty sure I will; I just don't know when.

And it is just right here, at this stage in the process (I have learned this over and over through experience) that I confront two of the writer's deadliest enemies: settling, and impatience. Settling is the enemy of excellence; just settling for something, saying to yourself, "Well, this is competent, this is okay; there's nothing embarrassingly bad in it" is the road to ruin. Equally so is impatience. It seduces you to settle for less than excellence; it talks you out of working hard, really hard, to finish something off. And so it is the enemy of good writing, too, because the finishing off is also crucial to excellence.

Here's Paul Engle, in his fine essay, "Salt Crystals, Spider Webs, and Words:"

> . . . what the writer is doing is not so much writing a poem or play or story that he has firmly in mind, but rather is using his writing to discover what it truly is he is trying to say. Often he will not know until the final revision of the last page what he had been trying to do from the start.

Post-Post Script, Several Years Later

It was Auden who said, "A poem is never finished; it is just abandoned."

So it has been with this one. Sometimes excellence is unattainable. What to do with those poems that fall short? As well ask what to do with children who fall short.

No other choice but this, as I see it: love them for what they are, what they try to be. Know that they aren't what you had hoped, but keep quiet about it. Don't nag, don't bitch too much. (A little self-pity is okay, and therapeutic, and a kind of recompense for your time and sweat, but only in private, among friends. There is nothing more boring and ludicrous than an artist whining about how hard, or how unrewarded, art is, especially in some public forum.) Life is larger and at the same time both less and more perfect, less and more fair than your hopes or mine for it. So too the lives of the poem.

Writing

Every moment unfolds like a world of blossoms.
Our waters listen with their salty ears.

Let us pray our words are not
tricksters that betray us.

How The Poem Listens

Fides ex audio.
— St. Paul

The poem has seen pictures
of Indians by the railroad,
ears to the iron
for the bad news coming.
So the poem lays its head
against earth and hears:
the groan of continental plates
subducting, crackling boil
of magma cooked
a long way down.
Hears earthquake, mumbling its faults
to itself, readying
for some great release of grief;
soil's own infinite revisions,
low sizzle of leaves into humus,
fiber into mote,
mote into atoms of carbon,
the mournful passage of snails,
the intricate routines
of polypods and earwigs
over earth,
gas hiss, twig rot,
rock spall.

And so long at this,
lost, entranced in damp,
the poem's face
sprouts roots,
a thick beard white
and clinging, delving,
that binds it
to the ground.

Now the poem cannot stand,
but giving in,
stretches out,
going green with moss

along the fence,
hearing its name called
from the veins of clay,
the hallways of each leaf,
all back doors
where world sneaks in
from starburst
and recycling,
from beginnings whispered
like the Word.

How The Poem Listens

Sometimes the poems just keep leading back, by various and unpredictable routes, to the same destination. Here was another item in my notebooks, the quotation of St. Paul's, ("faith is from hearing") and I wanted to explore it. And what happened was that a painting by Frederick Remington, or some other artist of the American West, got mixed up with plate tectonics (there's science again), the Book of Genesis, and decomposition, among other things.

* * *

Someone said that the ideal poem would approach, if not fully achieve, silence. It seems like a contradiction until you think about it, and remember that music would not be music if it were not for the silences it contains. If it were simply a steady drone of noise, always at the same tempo and pitch, it would kill us. So St. Paul had something right—poetry not only accomplishes what it does through language, but also through pregnant silences built into that language, spaces in which we can listen for the what-is-not-there as well as the what-is.

I had a student in the third year of my creative writing class in school whose work was among the most original I have seen. Laisha Dumas approached the subject of silence head-on, personifying it as the *Lives of the Poem* personifies the poem.

Silence Has Found A Voice

Sitting around observing and absorbing energy,
silence is tired of.
She gets up, moving and expressing her mystery.

The diva of deception on the top floor,
who is finished playing loud lungs
with the python of the week,
is ready for a sweet but sweaty noiseless sleep.

Silence comes stomping softly, bringing noise with her,
disregarding the Do Not Disturb sign
diva of deception has on her face.

94

Noise is into silence the way
every python was into the diva of deception.
Expressing her mystery is light for him.
She's giving eternal internal beauty to the world.
For all the deception divas who live for
pure silence after loud lungs,
and for the rest of the world,
neverending silent noise.

Wandering And Wondering

Sitting impatiently in a rocking chair
Waiting for her smile as she reads my poem,
Her face shines like a brand new Cadillac as she reads
My fourth line.

Said parts tasted
Like peaches
Newly fresh, not out of the refrigerator.
But other parts were hard to slip her fingers through,
Like coarse hair.
Said I keep some of my words in pockets
And underneath the earth
Like a groundhog,
Yet interesting to play with
Like a slinky.
She got lost and liked it,
In my cathedral of mazing words,
Wandering and wondering.

Flatlined

Littles and smalls have limited sight,
becoming only what their eyes allow them;
Having blinded sight, where life is flatlined.

For those used to seeing down heads, life is short.
Where babies breathe black air, this is home.
Adolescent moms go to school with uneducated legs.
Adult moms circumnavigate the buildings
for left-behind pleasure.

Chains from necks are ripped, and many fall.
They don't bother to get an ambulance,
The black hearse is immediately called.
Happy masks in the daytime are what many wear.
Talk of each other is the daily meal,
Eating up one another as they burn the same things.
Music that screams with burning mouths is their teacher.

Those from the loving living land come rarely to help,
Leaving kids thirst for a sip.

Opportunities are few,
keeping sterile brainwaves low.

Clothes hold young women tight,
Busting the pureness out.

Where life dies and death lives,
This is home.

Finally, here's a poem that came as a result of my failing to get her name right early in the year. I like it as a poem; I like it also because it brings poetry to the elegant resolution of a little interpersonal conflict; its existence suggests that the lives of the poem have many "uses" in the actual world. Imagine all the areas where what poetry can do becomes a way of exploring issues and communicating conclusions: ethical issues, justice issues, race and class issues. How much could poetry contribute to these dialogues if it were publicly acknowledged and encouraged as a way of navigating, reporting on, and revising society?

Lay-ish-uh

Her syllable personalities
are often overlooked, but
work well with the tongue
in creating neon names from
a name that stays away
from bright light.
Laeesha. Lakeisha, Leanecia,
Lacrecia, Lyesa, Louisha, Luisha,
Lyeeshe.
Names that are rock concerts.
LACRECIA. Laisha. LEANICIA.
Laisha.
Her calm, simple syllable personalities,
like an abused child, when hit with flash.
Lay-ish-uh. Laisha.

And here is a remarkable document, written by Laisha after I asked her the story of her name. See that names continue to occupy an important place in the lives of the poem.

Laish

My mother's friend, Laish, a Rastafarian man whom I am named after, invited me into the mysterious, playful, and satisfying world of poetry. He is my muse because he speaks in poem. Everything he says sounds as if he is reading a poem from a poet who won a Pulitzer prize. His words, like poems, get me thinking of things in new ways; they enlighten me and sometimes they make me believe that he isn't real. I tell him all the time that I think he can change the world because his words have muscles, they are strong. Like Hitler, he could have many followers, only Laish will lead his followers in a positive, promising direction.

When I talk to people about Laish, they think I am making him up because I talk about him like he is an angel. I'm glad I don't have to make him up because fifty per cent of the genuineness I need would be lacking. A lot of people in my life don't come with any originality or difference, but I get new meals from Laish while a lot of these other people feed me leftovers. A lot of people don't understand my need for originality, but Laish does and he is my originality doctor.

Laish inspires me to write poetry simply because he speaks. Because he speaks, I learn new and different ways of thinking. He doesn't inspire me because of any personal advice he gives me. He inspires me by having simple conversations. These conversations turn into a school that I enjoy. Laish gives me more to write about. Without him, I think writing prompts would keep me limited to typical and non-creative.

I do more than appreciate Laish. I honor his ability to make my mind more righteous, to inspire me to write beautiful and original poems, and his ability to make me dream when I'm not sleeping. Most of all, I am glad that Laish speaks.

*　*　*

And before we go on, here's yet one more poem about silence, and a brief discussion of its origin. Its author, Nickie Barnes, was a person of what would be called the Goth style: dark lipstick, red cropped hair, black fingernails. She was smart, writhy, not easily swayed to anything too distant from her experience. She wrote some small, good poems.

A Story Of Almost Silence

In my fourth bell class on B day I sat listening to the instructions for our fifteen-minute writing assignment. Mr. Hague said that some philosophers believe that "the best poetry is that which most closely approaches silence." My first thought was to jump and say, "If it's silent, then why should we write it?" but I kept my seat and listened to the instructions.

I thought about a few things that were almost silent: fingers through hair, a pen over paper, nyloned legs crossing, a feather drifting in the wind, tongue over teeth, a sigh, and leaves in the wind.

The first draft of the poem disappointed me. I had expected it to be much better than it turned out. The poem didn't flow.

An Approach To Silence

Fingers through hair
A deep sigh
Nylon legs crossing
    Whisper
Pen on paper

Tongue over teeth
Drifting feathers

After reading the poem a few times I decided it needed to be cut. The small words that carried almost no weight were gotten rid of.

Almost Silence

Fingers through hair
Sigh
Pen on paper
Drifting feathers
Crossing legs
Whisper

When I heard the movement of the poem I was again disappointed. I had expected more than what I had achieved.

Again I decided to cut the poem, to make it flow in almost silence. So many things were clouding it, giving it sound. I wanted silence, and so, as I sat at home, I cut the poem to three lines.

Almost Silence

fingers through hair
pen over paper
whisper

Deciding on these three lines was difficult, but each line fit. When your fingers are sliding through your hair it makes a sound, almost a sound. When a pen us running over the paper there is a small sound that only people who are listening can hear. The third line is only one word, *whisper*. The sound the word makes coming out of the mouth is quiet, almost comforting. Almost silent.

—Nickie Barnes

What You Should Eat
Before Reading The Poem

Before they read poetry,
cows eat seven pounds of
sweet clover, exactly
three days before it blooms.
Before they eat poetry,
carp taste the bottom
of the pond, savoring
a thousand textures:
silt, gravel,
intricate strands of old algae.
Before they eat poetry,
buzzards prepare
themselves by long fasting,
then gorge, in a crowd,
on dead possum.

Unfortunately, you are neither
cow, nor carp, nor buzzard.
Eat something clean and thin,
nothing fancy, nothing expensive.
A portion of common sense.
Filet of dream.
The honest salad of acceptance.

But not too much:
like the wary
streetwise cat,
come to the poem
a little hungry.

What You Should Eat Before Reading The Poem

Certainly the Poem and the Tall Tale are kissing cousins. What is most interesting is how obvious lies can suggest something of the truth. And even more: how truth and memory and all sorts of other things mingle in the event that is called a poem. Here is an essay about the long, complicated genesis and evolution of one of the lives of the poem.

From The Porch To The Page: Memory, History, And A Poem

My grandfather J. C. "Ironhead" Hague lived at 118 Logan Street in Steubenville, just three houses up from the Pennsylvania Railroad tracks and the Ohio River they ran along. From his porch, I could see across to the steep cliffs of West Virginia, wild and forested save for the raw cut into the rock made for Route 2, the Panhandle's river highway. A hundred feet below that road, on the shore just above the high water level, there stood a wooden structure, maybe eight feet tall and painted white. This was a daymark, a navigation aid for towboat pilots, and it was practically all that remained of a place called East Steubenville. The only other building nearby was a small abandoned house almost hidden by willows. I used to daydream about living in that house, so close to the water, and about having my own boat and getting up in the morning and going fishing below the Market Street bridge.

One evening, my grandfather and I were sitting on the porch swing, talking quietly and listening to the nighthawks. Noticing my gaze drawn to the daymark light and that dark house just beyond it on the far shore, he told me a story.

"Me and Doc and another fella was fishing just about this time of the evening, years ago. We was out in Doc's johnboat, anchored about halfway across, right off where that daymark is. In them days, the lights was kerosene lanterns, not electric like they are now. Women who lived along the river would make a few dollars a month contracting to keep them lanterns filled. Towboat companies paid them, and a couple of dollars wasn't nothing to sneeze at.

"We wasn't having much luck fishing, so when the woman who lived over there come out carrying a big can of kerosene, we watched her. Wasn't nothing else to do. She made her way down the path, then started to climb that daymark, the handle of the can slung over her arm like the handle of a purse.

"She lifted the thing—it slipped—and then, all of a sudden, there was fire everywhere. The woman herself was on fire, big orange fire, and the wood of the daymark was flames. And then that woman, still burning, climbed down, turned, and started walking toward the river. Her hair was on fire and her arms was straight out beside her, like she was trying to fly. Only she was burning up. And then we heard her screaming. It come out over the water, high and slow. Made your heart break to hear it. 'My God,' Doc yelled, and we pulled up the anchor and started rowing as fast as we could, The woman stumbles into the river and falls down, right on her face. The fire on the front of her goes out, smoke all around her like a skirt, but there's still flames coming off the part of her out of the water. And there's a terrible smell coming to us in the boat.

"Doc jumps out fifteen or twenty feet from shore, and scrambles in. We come in right after. He's got the woman turned over and he's kneeling with her in his arms, and he looks up at us and says, 'She's gone.'

"O my, that was a miserable sight. There wasn't nothing we could do. Up the bank, the daymark's burning like a bonfire, and Doc's holding that killed woman, and me and the other fella's just standing there, we couldn't talk or move.

"It was miserable, miserable."

I was ten or eleven when my grandfather told me that story. I thank him in retrospect for not treating me like a child, for not holding back the truth. It is hard to forget such a tale, and it is equally hard to continue to hold its vivid horror in mind. But it strikes me that it might be interesting to investigate what has happened to that story, how it changed over the 12 years or so that passed from the night I heard it on the porch at Logan Street to the time it became a poem in the early 1970s. Maybe in talking about what happened, I can develop a few notions about how a poem comes to be, and suggest something about what poetry is for.

First, the poem:

Burning Lady

Sometimes nudging on the bottom,
sometimes not, a johnboat
noses squarely up the slow summer current,
urged on in its slim-oared steady going
by a boy who thinks of fish.
He passes twilight, silence fogging down
off Steubenville,
and anchors over potholes in the bottom
where he's come to know the boulders
spinning in a flood dig out a likely depth.

Gazing idly at the West Virginia shore,
a flat and minnow-slivered hundred yards

away, he sees the daymark light, bright
within a quiet grove of trees. A woman walks
along the shore, fuel can in her hand,
climbs the hill of gravel
that the light's implanted in,
starts to fill the tank.
                              Suddenly, the shore is
bursts, exploding ovens, discharging into
air. The woman, blazing, screams along
a spit, arms waving, hair a ghastly
vapor. He hears her her screams seethe
over stock-still water, and anchor up, lays
his blisters to the oars to where
the woman lies, still burning,
black as oily logs on sand. His hands,
unattached from pain, comply with fire
and scorch, but roll the body
smoking into water, bald, unclothed, its
salmon, now unsighing flesh like blossoms
from beneath a crust.
                              Stench hauls his
trembling short, the bait of grief
sprouts barbs, and piercing, draws him in,
undone, broken, all his evenings
flashing by, until at last
he feels himself drawn up, weary into air,
and feels the first black smack of death
upon his sides, feels the eyes of shadows
measure up his weight, and gasps in air, air
that is not air, the johnboat bobbing, knocking
hollow on the stones.

The most obvious transformation the poem has enacted on the story, I think, is in its situation, the circumstances under which it occurs. The original story involved three adults. The poem reduces the fishermen to one, and it is clear that this new character is a boy. Is he my grandfather as I imagined him as a young man, or is he Doc, or is he the other nameless fellow?

No: he is none of them. *I* have become the witness, displacing the historical figures. Now I might discuss the possible reasons for the tampering with the facts of the matter; I might discuss the gain in immediacy the boy provides. But in terms of how the poem came, I can say no more than this: it happened to *me*. When my grandfather told me that story, I was somehow ripe for it; I had daydreamed about the house (the very one the Burning Lady lived in, though I did not know it then); I had been fishing dozens of times; I was young and impressionable, as the saying goes; and perhaps most importantly, I was frightened terribly by the story. It was so powerful, so close and so familiar to my own life and place that it became, for the purposes of poetry, a part of my own experience. No matter that it is historically inaccurate: it is nevertheless true in the way that poetry can be true. "Truth" should never get in the way of a poem, or, for that matter, a novel or story or play. Joan Didion touches on this phenomenon in her essay "On Keeping A Notebook":

> The point of my keeping a notebook has never been, nor is it now, to have an accurate factual record of what I have been doing or thinking . . . perhaps it never did snow that August in Vermont; perhaps there never were flurries in the night wind, and maybe no one else felt the ground hardening and summer already dead even as we pretended to bask in it, but that was how it felt to me, and it might well have snowed, could have snowed, did snow. *How it felt to me*: that is getting closer to the truth about a notebook.

And that is getting closer to the truth about the poem, or essay, or story, or novel that may well be conceived in the notebook. For I might as well have been in that boat. I could have been. And, as the poem came, I was.

This transforming of materials is a difficulty many readers and beginning students of writing seem to have with poetry, especially when it is poetry which has its roots in actual events or circumstances. The difficulty might best be illustrated in its obverse by studying what happens when a young writer reads her poem in a workshop and then hears it criticized. "But that's exactly how it happened!" she cried. "How can you say it doesn't work when *that is exactly what happened*?"

The problem is clear: the art has not transformed the reality, evolving it into something with the power and grace and heightening that distinguish art from raw material. The student whose poem was criticized did not understand the power of the *lie* to lift actual experience into the realm of the artistic. My father once defined Appalachian literature by jotting this down on a piece of cardboard: "Truths that are unbelievable, lies that are believable, and everything else in between." The poet James Dickey puts it another way when he speaks of the possibilities of asking "what if?" of an actual event, allowing the transformings of the imagination to take over. A remarkable example of what can happens when "What if?" is asked is his long poem "Falling," based on the true story of an airline flight attendant who was sucked through a faulty cabin door and fell to her death. What if she were conscious throughout that fall? Dickey imagines what it would be like, and invents her mind and heart and feelings as she plummets to the ground.

But now, let's play a little "what if?" of our own. What if I were the mother of that woman? Five years after my daughter's death, I pick up a book of James Dickey's poetry, and open it by chance to "Falling." I see the newspaper account which Dickey places before the poem; I know it's the report of my own child's death. I am appalled. I read the poem. I am shocked, outraged. How dare he claim to know what was going on in my daughter's mind as she fell? What audacity to invade her private thoughts and then to publish his sick substitution for the world to read! Besides, if he'd done his homework, he would have known she was unconscious all the way. This—all of it, every single word of it—is a lie!

Right—almost. True—but not quite. For the intelligent reader of poetry—or of fairy tales, for that matter—strikes a bargain with the writer. If it could be put into words, this bargain, this contract, might go something like this: "I, your reader, am no fool, and bear no grudge against you and what you do. I understand this partnership called literature; I understand my role in it. I will suspend my disbelief; I will let you do what you mean to do with your material, and I will give myself over to it. For your part, writer, you will give me something worth feeling, something worth seeing or knowing or considering in a powerful way. You will open my eyes and my heart. You will instruct my soul. In return for this delight and wisdom, I will not hold you to some small fact of history or the 'truth' (just as I forgive Keats for mistaking Cortez for Balboa in his sonnet.) I will not niggle and whine, but will understand that you have designs on me and on the world, your raw material. It is those designs that I am most interested in, not the raw material, however interesting it may be, and often is, in its own right."

Designs. Patterns. Shapings. These are what poems are about. Poems are not primarily or solely about history or mere facts. Thoreau may well have been thinking about poetry when he observed in his journal that "The fact will one day flower into a truth." Poems are about how the writer has experienced history or "facts"; about how they felt to him or her; poems are the flowerings of the writer's expression and connection of those truths in forms no one else could have unfolded in exactly the same way.

The second most notable transformation of the facts in "Burning Lady" involves the ending. What is happening in the final lines?

Stench hauls his
trembling short, the bait of grief
sprouts barbs, and piercing, draws him in,
undone, broken, all his evenings

flashing by, until at last
he feels himself drawn up, weary into air,
and feels the first black smack of death
upon his sides, feels the eyes of shadows
measure up his weight, and gasps in air, air
that is not air, the johnboat bobbing, knocking
hollow on the stones.

Briefly, "the boy who thinks of fish" at the beginning has become a fish at the end; the hunter has become the hunted; the witness has been transformed into the victim.

Death has become real to him; the burning lady's destruction has brought reality home to his heart. He feels the "first black smack of death," and like a shad or channel cat dragged from the water by a fisherman, he "gasps in air that is not air." What happened to the ending of the original story? It was, simply, no longer true, given what developed as the poem took shape. The truth of the poem is the boy's horrid awakening to the possibility of annihilation, and so the facts had to be changed for this truth's sake. The poem established its own rules; it created its own history; and the original story was left behind. This happens frequently, I think, for in poetry it is the design, the pattern, the shape of the experience best conveying the truth as it is felt to the poet that counts—nothing else.

Isn't there something arrogant and selfish about the poet's attitude toward the facts? Perhaps. But ends and means, the notion of *purpose* come into play here. If a poet knowingly distorts the facts for purposes which are immoral or illegal, then we must reject the work. But if the effect of the work is moral, if it is true that it presents life—or death—as it is, conveying the truth as the author sees and feels it, then, whether we agree with it or not, we must respect its designs, its patterning and shaping. "Burning Lady," I hope, does no dishonor to life or death, and the poet at least learned something from it, though painfully. Disaster is a part of the scheme of things, and so, paradoxically, its expression and re-creation may be good, and true.

There are other things to be said about the poem and its history, but I would like to end with just a few, a couple of which might suggest what I think poetry is for.

First, I do not want to overlook or discount the oral origins of "Burning Lady." It began as a story told to me. It was a part of my family's legend-hoard, and it took its place not only among other stories told by my grandfather, but among stories told *about* him as well, stories told by my father, uncles, and aunts, as well as by cronies of Ironhead's who leaked their tales slyly but deliberately to me during the two summers I worked on the railroad. So, if for no other reason, "Burning Lady" came to me as an opportunity to preserve a bit

106

of family lore. It was my small contribution—in my own way—to the maintenance of the meaning of my people. This is very important work that poetry can do, I think.

Secondly, I never tried very hard to publish the poem although it did finally see print in a little book called *Mill and Smoke Marrow,* made up of poems about growing up in Steubenville. I don't think it's as good as my grandfather's tale. The language of the original is more robust, less literary—more powerful, perhaps because I can hear my grandfather's voice in it.

But there is a final consideration concerning the history of the poem and the facts it has transformed. The retelling of my grandfather's original story is not a verbatim record. I took no notes when I was ten; I had no tape recorder (nor did Joan Didion). So the story, too, has been transformed. The first time it was ever written down was when I began this essay. It, too, is an artifact, not exact fact. Ken Kesey wrote, "It takes the past a long time to happen." This essay itself is one way the past is happening to me; memory and imagination are blended in its origins—in the shaping of my grandfather's story, in the poem that came later, in the remarks I make at this moment. History, like art, is a process, not a static set of facts and dates, or styles and subjects, and as time passes, what we call "history" or "fact" may itself be transformed, understood in new ways, reinterpreted in the light of new knowledge and discoveries.

So I have made the poem, and now willingly discard it; now, I give the story back. I return it to the river of time, after having been, twice now since that evening on the porch years ago, its temporary vehicle, its fumbling shaper. That's poetry: the shaped perceptions of things passed and passing on, recast in new forms, broken apart and reconnected, always changing, but still somehow orbiting the strange attractor, to borrow a concept from chaos science. In poetry, the strange attractor is truth, clothed in an apparent randomness and subjectivity, but which, nevertheless, makes designs, patterns, shapings. What goes around, however far and unpredictably away, comes around. It takes the past a long time to happen, but it happens. And it keeps on happening: the process, the happening itself, is one thing poetry is; it is one thing that poetry participates in and serves.

* * *

Write some lies that are the truth. Write some truths that are lies. Observe yourself at work carefully, and think about what happens as you do these things.

107

What Is This Business?

I heard a man say
with no malice,
"What is this business?"

He sat in the middle row.
For an hour, poetry floated over him
like an evening in the country.

Now and then it wrapped
him in itself, a fogbank
not uncomfortable, but damp

with condensation which
trickled down the clapboards
of his thoughts, leaving

moist lines there like writing.
As the reading ended,
the man stood, beside himself,

bemused. Away from where he'd been,
for a moment he studied those
water-scrawled walls, lit now

in an unfamiliar moonlight.
Then satisfied, I suppose,
that he'd read the message rightly,

he smiled, fingered a pair of bottles up,
and left. Where his beers had stood,
two dampnesses remained.

I watched them spread,
uncertain edges blending gradually
together, growing larger.

What is This Business?

If you've never read your poems to an audience, find one and do so now. Pay attention to what happens to your poems as you read them. Pay attention to how powerful and engaged in life you feel, underneath all the surface anxiety and pride mixed up with embarrassment. Know that the same good feeling awaits you whenever you do the work of the poem and bring it to the world.

Know that this is the alternative:

Dancing Alone In The Dark

"My poems hardly ever have bodies."
—Katie "the Red" DuMont

Lights out,
rain roaring outside.
It is January,
month of no sun,
Once a week
I dance alone
in the dark:
it is safer that way,
no feet to step on,
no conversation to make,
no body to distract me.
I could go on
like this forever,
turning beautiful
curves in the vacant air,
no music,
no one watching.

But this, as far as the lives of the poem go, is pointless and lonely.

The Poem's Choice Of Kin

There are dozens of dream-folk
it would love to have
haunting its pillow.
Its head
athwart the plated flank
of sturgeon, its cheek
nuzzling jackal's
pumping side.
It would love
to drowse in the kelpy scent
of coelocanth,
stiff uncle
of boiler plate and salt.

There are only a few
ways out of a stupid life
into a wiser one,
where the sun isn't made to lie,
where men don't kidnap
its innocent truth
to the sordid motels
of fact.

So to improve itself,
the acres of mystery
it's been given to till and discover,
the poem would love
to lie down (and it does)
within inches
of the teeth of sharks,
to turn its face (and it does)
into the dusty pelt
of a grizzly
as into the hair
of a sister
come to sing it
awake.

The Poem's Choice of Kin

> I think it is important to have some notion of what life is like when it is encased in a form different from our own. It is a major step to realize that the form we happen to inhabit is not the only one in which life dwells; life can come with wings instead of arms; with eyes more acute than ours.

I think it was Saul Bellow who said this; at least, it is in a notebook among notes on his work. Animals and plants are so diverse, so *other*, and thus so interesting that I cannot see how any poet could stay away from them for very long.

In the British Museum, in one of the Egyptian Rooms, there is a reproduction of a tomb painting featuring some god or other belonging to the Land of the Pharaohs' uncanny pantheon. It is characteristic in its blending of two or three or four animals and birds into one, a kind of chimera, a composite monster, a thing never beheld in the actual world. Similarly, our poems about animals do not have to be realistic; they do not have to be biologically accurate to have an effect. This is not a dismissal of accuracy in poetry—far from it. But the accuracy a poem pays is ultimately not only a factual one, as far as is possible, but perhaps more importantly, it is an emotional and aesthetic accuracy, too. In other words, we are free to invent animals, monsters, beasts of all kinds, as long as they are, somehow, embodiments and enactments of some truth—or of some desirable untruth, some delicious and fantastic fiction.

* * *

When you go to the British Museum, look hard at the Egyptian stuff, especially the gods and goddesses, and try to imagine a world in which they— not the Christian Jesus, for example—are in charge. What if the Supreme Being(s) we prayed to had teeth, claws, feathers, and seven faces? How would the world be different if the God or Gods were different?

This could lead to a series of poems in which the implication is that the world is governed not by the God we have all been taught to worship, but by other Beings entirely. You do not have to abandon your present faith to pursue such a series of poems. You just have to be willing to play.

* * *

Go to your own local museum; maybe it's your county historical society's museum, housed in some old mansion downtown. Maybe it's a specialized and exclusive enterprise, like the museum of dolls near one of my home places, or the Ohio River Museum, in Marietta, Ohio, or The Museum of Appalachia near Knoxville, Tennessee. There are places like these all over the country; find the one nearest you and adopt it as a source of poems. Write a little chapbook inspired by the museum and its contents. Learn desktop publishing and make a book of your own and see if you can't peddle it there in your local museum. Look up the origin of the word "museum," and see that poetry has as much right to be in such a place as do paintings or antique musical instruments.

Lives Of The Poem

Some are like women,
even when written by men.
They call out
to the birds within us,
heart's flocks like smoke
across the sky.
They see how our souls
expand and contract,
questant though delicate
as the eye-stems of snails.
They smell of rich leaves
and of childbirth,
of milk, and creeks
running seaward.
We have spent all our lives
to find them
that we may give them
all our lives.

George Bernard Shaw writes: "The artist's work is to show us ourselves as we really are. Our minds are nothing but this knowledge of ourselves; and he who adds a jot to such knowledge creates new mind as any woman creates new men."

That's pretty highfalutin, but even if it's only new knowledge of ourselves and our work, it's worth the risk. There ought to be something in our lives to which we give ourselves utterly, completely, and unconditionally. To live always holding something back is to live a cowardly life. Poetry obliges us to lose some of our self-consciousness and to live and write courageously, and yes, sometimes, even recklessly.

At the conclusion of our creative writing class, my younger son Brendan Hague wrote this letter of farewell to poetry. It is not only moving in its expression of some of the aspects of the lives of the poem, but it helped remind me that even those who do not have lots of success with the writing of poetry can still learn important things, and form important attitudes and habits of the mind and heart:

Dear Poetry:

What a ride it has been so far. At first I really didn't understand you, but now that I have more experience with you, I can identify the power you can bring to the table. I myself am not that great at expressing you, but I enjoy hearing others.

I will say this, you sure have put up with a lot from me. Maybe it was me trying to explain way too complex thoughts, or maybe it was just babbling about nonsense. Either way, you have consistently been there for me, no matter what.

I'm not totally sure if I will continue to try to speak through you, but hopefully if I do, I will become better at it. I think I have to. Because along with understanding you, I realize that poetry speaks to people. It speaks to people the way I like to speak to people. It impresses, identifies, and with serious matters, it forces you to think. I remember a poem we read as a class, "When the Towers Fell," by Galway Kinnell. Here's a quote:

> Some with torn clothing,
> Some bloodied, some limping a top speed
> Like children in a three-legged race,
> Some half-dragged, some intact in neat suits and dresses,
> They straggle out of step up the avenues,

Each dusted to a ghostly whiteness,
their eyes rubbed red as the eyes of a Zahoris,
Who can see the dead under the ground.

Now they say a picture's worth a thousand words, but how many pictures are painted after reading that passage? Poetry, you're like a tool for expression, like a canvas or sketch pad. A skilled poet is no different than your DaVinci or Van Gogh, except that they use the beauty and power of words instead of oils. I'm not going to say that I haven't created *any* good poems because you were with me when I wrote my semester final poem. It was maybe my first poem in which I said exactly what I meant to say. It had good flow, a strong meaning, and it earned me an "A." Thank you for that. It's one of the few things I have created artistically that I am proud of. See, I am a perfectionist, and if things aren't absolutely precise and perfect, I am not satisfied. Obviously you can imagine the frustration involved in a rookie poet. I have more unfinished poems than I have completed ones. But tell me, poetry, is a poem ever complete? Do we really ever fully, express ourselves? Our life is just one big poem that we will never be able to fully, completely write but we should attempt to write about things that are close to our heart.

It is time for me to leave you with a quote from my semester exam poem:

We need to be.
Just find a place and be.
And when you are truly being
we will find this "real world."
And, yes,
It will be wonderful and amazing.
And worries that we have today
Will vanish into the purple skies
And smoky mountains.
And we can enjoy being,
And love loving.

The Stupidity Poem

Coarsely autobiographical,
it struts from my fingers late at night,
its scatological diction
louder than I want.

But under my working hat,
that defunct kitchen I wear like a felt placenta,
feeding my head on leftover, bone-picked dreams,
I cannot escape.

I listen to its bumbling non sequiturs,
Bunkerisms crowded together like turkeys dying of the pip,
and I have to, I have no choice,
I greet it, shake its beery hand, and smile.

Who says writing is a profound and holy
loneliness of the kind saints enjoy?
There's a crowd here, a flatulent mob
who have gorged on garlic and Twinkies,

and I know every one of them like a brother.
They've gone bankrupt on credit cards.
They come with their hands out, scratching their palms,
guffawing like rubes at a sideshow.

The show's on me, and the laugh.
What brood is this my skill is unable to tame?
What dimestore tawdriness and hype
that clutters the church of my craft?

If this is writing, let me be blessed with stroke,
fall aphasic into a limbo of silence,
disarming these carny string bands, these bogus jokers,
these know-nothings rampant, these words with no work to do.

The Stupidity Poem

"If we had a keen vision of all ordinary human life, it would be like hearing the grass grow or the squirrel's heartbeat, and we should die of the roar which lies on the other side of silence. As it is, the quickest of us walk about well-wadded with stupidity . . . "

So wrote the English novelist George Eliot. She was right. The poem knows that its work is not to increase, but to decrease, stupidity. It feels so strongly about it that it would rather fall silent than to increase the inane babble around it.

But then its brothers continue to act up.

* * *

Can writing poems sometimes be disgusting, wrenching, and difficult work? Under what circumstances? What poems can you find that show this? What poems have you written that show this? Re-read them, and ask yourself, "Is this true?"

How refreshing it can be to jettison the useless or counterproductive baggage we lug along with us. Do not fear that your poems will shrink and become lean and will sound like actual speech.

Poem in Heat

Sunlight hums on the garden table,
fluttering this week's pages.
How far to where the poem lives?

I look at my morning's
writing, messy sprawl
trying to stand up and dance.

Wasps singe
the edge of air
with their whines.

Beetles flash
like small explosions
among stones.

Even leaves crinkle
and blaze or dry
to ashy runes—

Everything's afire
except these lines.

I wrote "Poem In Heat" as an exercise in slant rhyme, which my students and I were exploring. If you do not see or hear the rhyme, get yourself a handbook of poetics (there are many of them) and study up on slant rhyme, then write a few experiments yourself.

What Should A Poem Do?

for wild man poet Ethan Baker

A poem should
climb up your nostrils
and bump its umbrella open
inside your head.

A poem should talk back
to policemen, the pope,
its own several selves.

It should dress like a groom
and belch at the wedding.

It should answer
when called:
scofflaw,
berserker,
spy.

It should point its fingers,
complain, contend, accuse,

name names.

What Should A Poem Do?

Ethan Baker was a character. He was a bluntly built person with a big voice and a sometimes manic presence. He pretty much did what he wanted in school, (and, with equal intensity, didn't do what he didn't want to do). Year-round he wore a black trench coat that went to the tops of his heavy, high-heeled engineer boots, and a knit cap, three or four feet long, the like of which hasn't been seen since the Middle Ages. I have no idea where he got it, but he wore it, too, in all seasons.

He was an actor (his most arresting role was as the dentist in *Little Shop of Horrors* —typecasting, some believed) and there were people in our school, faculty included, who feared him. At first, I might have, too, but slowly I learned his talent, and gained some feeling for how he related to the world. (He was mostly agin' it).

At any rate, every teacher of poetry—or any of the arts, for that matter—ought to have an Ethan Baker now and then. Such a person reminds us how unpredictable and contradictory humans can be, how contrary and unsettling, and yet how full of creative energy and imaginative force. Ethan's enthusiasms almost successfully resisted criticism and coaching; the only real accomplishment I can claim in working with him is that I got him to finish what he started, to let me type his poems up for him, (his handwriting was a hellacious scrawl that looked like a jumble of broken tablets of cuneiform), and to build a body of work, which I remember typing up in one long five-foot scroll and printing out on deep purple paper and posting in the Writing Room. His poems were all of a piece, slangy, jazzy, in-your-face playful verbal aggressions; he was one of the most distinctive high school writers I have ever worked with. Here are a couple of his poems.

In Honor Of Your Wedding

Yeah, the Apocalypse, the Raganrok,
I'll dance barefoot and tattooed
with a sickle moon in one hand
a white dwarf sun on a chain (Lucifer my morning star)
in the other,
and the Christ's head around my neck.
Waitin' to play fetch with the Beast and the Fernis wolf.
Waltzin' to acid hip-hop or cocaine be-bop on a Sony.

Yeah, I'll be at your funeral.
I'll dress like a Hindoo unreal blue Shiva.
I'll bring a big bunch of orchids, tropical flowers and fruit.

I'll do mantras, holy self-sacrifices and bloodletting,
waitin' to grind orchid petals barefoot into your grave,
dancin' with a spurting neck stump torso and the skeletal jester
to the gnome's tin drum.

For your wedding my sweet,
we'll build a wicker man fifty feet tall
(we pagans and Picts).
Light the grass *FWOOSH crackle.*
Dance blue skins around flamyburningwicker.
To your cathedral we'll send
spectral cats   shadows of were-pit bulls   and shards of stained glass
to behead you on the altar.
And the gnome'll kick your head through
the muddy puddles to the party . . . *tap*
tap tapity tap
tap tap tapity.

March Hare March

Blueing light
from green green brush
on the country road, the twilight hare.
Careful now, wabbit.
Asphalt eggshell thin
one wrong thought
might shatter
into the hour before dawn
among stars so cool
freeze dry to the bone
fall . . .
fall . . .
fall . . .
until you're caught in morn's first web
invisible except for dew
mouth open in the quiet rabbit scream,
might shatter . . .
cwazy wabbit . . .
one wrong thought . . .
cwazy wabbit . . .

What to say about such creatures as these poems, which comprise as valid a presence in the lives of the poem as any others? I say we celebrate them; we try to learn the rules they seem to operate by, or seem to have deliberately discarded, and then we find what's good in them. Here, in "In Honor Of Your Wedding," we have a wild abundance of metaphor and allusion brought to bear on a situation that's full of tension. The speaker has learned that someone he calls, ironically, "my sweet" is to be married. This obviously is maddeningly unacceptable, and the poem builds a nightmarish vision of what the speaker will do at the celebration. It is violent, strange, powerful. I also happen to think it is funny, in a grotesque sort of way. I have said before that poetry is large; it must be able to include this kind of work.

"March Hare March" is full of wild verbal energy, too—I love the surprise of the Elmer Fudd language, and again the wild inversion of normal "reality" presented in the action of the poem. The punning imperative of the title I like, too. Ethan's poems in general remind me of Wendell Berry's " Manifesto: The Mad Farmer Liberation Front," in which Berry celebrates the possibility that poetry and life can confound our expectations, that making poems and making a life are human, therefore unpredictable and sometime wild enterprises. Berry's poem contains its own imperative, which it seems Ethan Baker heeds in his poems: "Every day, do something/ that won't compute."

* * *

Write a bunch of poems that "don't compute." Turn commonly held beliefs upside down, showing them to be mean, vulgar, or empty. Take a well-known poem and re-write it from its opposite point of view, or voice, or situation. Take on poetry itself, and see how far you can push its language or form or subject without it becoming something else—an essay, or a story, or a sermon.

Elsewhere in "Manifesto" Berry writes: "Be like the fox/ who makes more tracks than necessary,/ some in the wrong direction." Write some poems that deliberately go "in the wrong direction."

* * *

Another, entirely different student entered the lives of the poem a few years later. Mike Herring was in the class following Katie The Red's and Colleen's. He was—and is—a gentlemanly fellow, dark-haired and intense, on the quiet side, the nephew of my wife's business partner and the son of Marilyn Parks Herring, one of my wife's classmates in college. Marilyn is my friend and a fellow high school English teacher.

122

Like Ethan Baker, Mike gets a blue ribbon for brashness: here's the first poem he handed in for his first college creative writing class ever, at Washington University in St. Louis, to his first creative writing teacher beyond me:

My Poetry Assignment, Sir

I am spouting leaks
so full of inspiration am I.
Paralyzed, desperate to fulfill
your stipulations
your qualifications
your requirements.

Asking us to write
structured poetry,
<five repetitions
eight new images
and three contradictions>

is an oxyMORONIC
par a' docks
    like comfortable nails
    sincere religion,
    or spacious dorm rooms

it is poetry
    in shackles,
instead of some
azuresky
acidlisp
guitarswing
lovecord
chasmsplash
kneenumb
sweatylip
wordsong
    as it should be.

Because repetition should not be assigned.
Because repetition should be spontaneous,

Because repetition Because repetition
Because repetition is boring.

This poem is my rebuttal,
my opening salvo,
and my recipe.

Let's get cooking

—Mike Herring

Poetry is the one child in our lives on whom we wish a kind of incorrigibility. Remember that many saints were considered to be totally out of hand.

I wonder if Mike had ever read Langston Hughes's poem with much the same situation as his own? If not, then chalk another coincidence up for the lives of the poem; like the culture of Cincinnati, poems are not only gregarious, they're the social equivalent of incestuous—everyone knows everyone else.

* * *

Write some poems that talk back to your teachers, or poke fun at the great masters. Learn what a parody is and write one, or two, or a collection of them.

* * *

Steve Stricker was in the workshop in the Seventies. A quiet, tightly concentrated young man, he wrote little gems of observation and surprise. It was from Steve, early on, that I learned what high quality poetry high school students could produce, once disabused of their childish notions of what poetry is. (See The Big Poetry Mama Poems).

Peeling A Walnut

The black walnut's juice strikes
a tingle of joy
up the cut in my thumb.

My stained fingers grip tight
the sphere,
it screams a squeak
as the knife blade divides it.
A newborn,
round and wrinkled,
arrives.

Strong verbs. The surprise of "strikes/ a tingle of joy/ up the cut in my thumb." The arresting juxtaposition of "strikes," "tingle" and "joy" and its strong, unstumbling rhythms. And the surprise of the closing images—the freshly husked walnut, still damp, compared to a newborn baby—startlingly accurate. There is great delight in this small poem.

Here's another Stricker poem, another favorite of mine:

Ice

The stream froze last night:
not thick
to a rock hardness,
chipping, cracking,
but like a tissue floating
on water,
fogged window
to the bottom.

What I most admire about this poem is how steadily it keeps its eye on its subject. I am almost entirely unaware of an "I" in this poem; there is no self-consciousness drawing my attention away from the subject at hand, no temptation to "comment" on the experience the poem unfolds, no bothersome tizzies of the ego to deal with. The poem happens for me, directly and skillfully wielding metaphor, imagery, rhythm and syntax.

Believing that living fully the lives of the poem requires it, I wrote little sketches, sometime half-critical, of the writers in the workshop Steve participated in, inviting them to recognize themselves and to guess which was whose. Here first is the one about him; the others follow. Perhaps the personality types or the behaviors, are similar in workshops everywhere. They too show something of the variety of the lives of the poem.

Sees Small, Might Get There

Lives in a palpable world,
touches its bones,
knows the taste of its marrow.
Wears boots when boots are called for.
Falls to the ground
heavily, and often.
Knows the embrace of that woman of earth
who is ample and deep around him.

Sorry She Couldn't Do It

Really isn't.
Apologizes to anyone
but herself.
Thinks that's enough.
Forgets that no one but she can do it:
tell the light against her mother's face
when they drive to Carolina,
tell what it is she likes
about some person's brief and struggling poems,
tell what it is that makes her get her hair cut,
tell what it is that's right
in wearing pearls, or feathers, or black,
tell what is hard about being smart,
what's easy about being dumb,
what's hard about staying silent,
or being beautiful when no one knows.

Sorry she couldn't do it?
Maybe sorry she knew she could,
but wouldn't.
Maybe sorry she doesn't know why.

Maybe just waiting.
Waiting.

Couldn't Think Of Anything

Intensely aware of nothing,
she spoons in diamonds with breakfast cereal,
does not hear the low seethe of lava
building in the kettle.
Dressing, she does not consider
how her body's valleys and mountains
toss with her cells
in a sea of mystery and interest.

On the way to school,
she sleeps, or seems to.
It is a dead sleep, dreamless, bankrupt.
She does not see the gingko
making leaves along the road.
She does not name the forty
orphan poems waiting in the signs.

In homeroom
she blabs empty bubbles of talk.
Her knee-socks fall: she doesn't notice.
Gravity means nothing.

During class, she thinks of writing poems.
After school, she rides a bus full of novels.
She doesn't turn the page of her attention,
won't begin.

Only Knows One Way

Thinks misspellings won't last forever.
Thinks some miracle will cure
the tremendous gaps of high school.
Thinks the idea of reading is okay,
but the time it takes more valuable
for parties.

Hopes some girl will like his mind.
Wouldn't think of reading her some poems.
Studies up on skiing
so she'll like him.

Never thinks to write a poem
about stealing groceries from old ladies,
being black,
establishing an anti-butterflies society,
not eating for three days,
inventing a language
that speaks clearly to hummingbirds.

But has a lot of hope.
Thinks success teaches in college.
Thinks its voice can be rented.

Thinks fame lives down his street.
Thinks maybe they'll bump into one another
one fine day.

Is Only Here To Listen

Sometimes you want to demand
"Prove it:
how many tocks does the clock
make in an hour,
what is the sound of shoes
on the rug,
what word does the wind say
exactly at nine?

How many motors does this cat have,
how many knives,
how many dreams of small birds?

How does emptiness sound?
How deep can you go?
How long will you hold your breath?"

Does It Once In A While

You'd think she'd risen from the dead:
all that light, that song.
Easter roars from her words like heat.

Then darkness descends.
Months of emptiness pass.
Her fingernails darken like coal.

She cuts her hair off, or dyes it yellow.
She speaks a new language, dark,
baroque, inconclusive.

What will start it again? you wonder,
that sudden rising of meaning and heat,
that flush of color, that life?

Something akin to Steve Stricker's eye for the natural world, and his seemingly effortless metaphors, reappeared more than a decade later in the poems of Dan Striley, a student in my first in-school creative writing class. Dan was six-foot-five, gentle, witty, and for almost the whole year stricken with bouts of lover's melancholy. He experienced long, entranced spells during which he was incapable of little else than casting adoring gazes at the smart, gifted, wonderfully named, and psychologically angular Joanna Bach. Both of them wrote fine poems that year. My favorite of Dan's mixed his gift as a writer with his enthusiasm for the natural world. This poem won for Dan an Honorable Mention in the 1997 Ohio High School Poetry Contest.

Deep Trees

We follow shadow wings
To the corridors of the crows,
The pine limbs low with their dark bodies.
We call out, clap our hands,
Frenzying their wings into Baroque whispers.

There is much to comment on in this fine little poem. But before any comment, let's read it again, slowly, out loud. Here's the space in which to do this:

129

Now to allow the Critic a few moments: first of all, the aural qualities of "Deep Trees" are notable. In the first line, a long "o" sound is established: fol*low* shad*ow*. This is not gratuitous or coincidental, nor is it left behind: in line two, the long "o" appears again in *crows,* and then again in line three in *low*. (Read the poem again, aloud, and hear the effect of this pattern of sound.) Then, in the fine technique of "repeat and vary," the long "o" sound goes away, only to reappear, climactically, in the final syllables of the final line: *Baroque.* This effect is very beautiful, and gives to the poem a kind of aural architecture and movement of sound that appeals to the reader's ear and to her sense of harmony and wholeness long before it emerges explicitly in her consciousness. Further, *o*'s open-mouthed exhalation of wonder fits the emotional movement of the poem, which is one of a suddenly amazed attention to the powerful and silent presence of the crows, and their dramatically silent sweeping up all at once at the poem's end.

There is more to admire. Phrases like "shadow wings" and "corridors of the crows" and "dark bodies" create a kind of hushed mystery—just where are we, and what is going to happen?—that gives the poem a rich tone, sustained throughout. And the final paradox—baroque music being intricate, and polyphonic, and, well, often loud—juxtaposed with "whispers" is wonderfully in tune with the hushed mystery of the earlier lines. These crows do not cry out—it's the speaker making the noise—and their persistent and remarkable silence, even in flight after being alarmed, is powerful. There is great activity; the silence is broken only by "baroque whispers." Very nice, very, very nice. Such short lyrics, capturing moments of heightened perception, are remarkable achievements for young writers. They display a lot of innate giftedness, an ear for language's music, and a kind of discipline— "This is enough, I don't need any more in this poem." The Critic has been partnered with very effectively in this poem.

One final thing: I continue to like this poem in part because it has arisen from an earnest occupation of Dan's, bird watching. It is important to have passions which we pursue, hobbies we dedicate ourselves to in full concentration. The ability to be seized, taken up by, swept away for a time by some ardent interest, is a characteristics of all artists—and the happiest artists are those who are taken up and made happy by their art. Hobbies and interests which engage us deeply, and which place us in contact with the subconscious and with the shaping and inventing and wondering capacities of the imagination are all good practice for becoming a writer. Pursuits which bring us in contact with nature are especially fortuitous—both for the writer and for the planet, which needs attention and expression. Dan's poem is, among other things, an ecological act; it recreates something of nature's wonder and beauty, and in so doing, reminds us of what might be lost if we do not live lightly and respectfully on the land.

Here's the interesting history, at least as it began in writing class, of "Deep Trees." I had been reading the poetry of Mary Oliver, and admired especially her poem "Wild Geese." So I asked the whole class to read it. After we did, I invited everyone to take a word, or phrase or whole line from Oliver's poem, and to use it as the title of a poem of their own. We spent some practice time in class composing those attempts, then we shared them in a read-around—a no-criticism-one-right-after-the-other sharing of recent work. I liked so many of the poems, and was so struck with their variety and surprising takes on the original words or phrases or lines, that we deliberately went back and wrote a couple more each, revised, and then selected the most striking to include in a class anthology entitled *The Wild Geese Poems*. This class project, in which we set out deliberately to work up a theme or subject or exercise into a full-blown manuscript, is one of my favorites of the year. Here's a lyric from *The Wild Geese Poems* by the aforementioned Joanna Bach; it won Third Prize in the 1997 Ohio High School Poetry Contest, out of 260 poems submitted from all around the state, and judged by David Citino, now Poet Laureate of The Ohio State University:

The Desert, Repenting

When I was ten
Mother took me to Arizona;
We walked for miles
Into the desert,
The colors of the earth
Painted in the sky;
Grainy sand spilled
Hot autumn shades
Across the clouds,
The portraits of men
Stained, blood red
In the background.

Another exercise Joanna excelled in was one I call "The Story of A Poem" paper. The assignment: "Go back to one of the poems you have written this quarter (or semester, or year) and in as much detail as you can, explain its conception, gestation, and birth. Tell all and anything you can think of about its coming into existence. Show and comment on all of its drafts, and explain as well as you can why you changed what you changed. Think of your audience as people who are intensely curious about how a poem happens." Here is Joanna's:

Silence

Seconds
Past
An
Echo
Slipped
Away

The Story of Silence

Silence begins with skinned trees and ends seconds past an echo slipped away. At least that's how it unfolded for me when Mr. Hague announced the ominous writing topic of silence. In a hushed voice he stated, "Some believe the best poem is that which most closely approaches silence," and then more simply, "Write that poem." As a brainstorming session, I thought on those things which were silent, or had an essence of silence. The breeze, an echo, skinned trees, waters, and snakes all stuck in my mind as quiet things. And thus my poem began:

The
Breeze
Blew
Through
Skinned
Trees
Like
Watered
Blood
In
A
Snake's
Vein

At first glance it seems to work. The breeze was a quiet, sweeping image, and the skinned trees provided a picture of an empty forest.

The placement of the words almost looked like the long, thin body of a snake, or the branchless trunk of a bare tree. The poem appeared to be listening to itself. But something was wrong. I hadn't captured the feeling I had hoped to convey. I wanted my readers to experience a silence in themselves; to feel a bit of awe and speechlessness.

So I decided to attempt a whole new poem; one based on the collection of images, rather than appearances. I enjoyed the skinned trees, and I kept them; but I especially wanted to incorporate one particular thought that sent silence echoing throughout my body. I chose to use sound, ten seconds after an echo had faded away. It was a unique image that brought forth unusual ideas. As I thought on what an echo left behind, I felt a soundless ringing inside me. Like I was waiting for something tremendous to happen, or in still wonder after something magnificent had just happened. This feeling trapped me and I tried to reproduce it by writing:

Skinned trees
Blood on the battleground
Old dilapidated cars
Parked like scattered wildflowers
On a desert floor
Current on the underside of a river
Sound
Ten seconds after an echo fades away.

As I reread this poem, I couldn't help but feel disappointed. The blood image did provoke a sense of mournful solitude, but it just seemed to clutter the feeling I had hoped to achieve. The last two lines seemed to carry the greatest potential. When I read this image over and over again, I was convinced that it had dreams of greatness. As I looked at both drafts, I chose to combine their strengths. I enjoyed the silence of the first poem's form. With only one word per line, it was almost as if it were saying, "I am barely here." And since I had such hopes for my echo, I soon came up with:

Sound
Ten
Seconds

After
An
Echo
Fades
Away

From this version, I played with the idea of adding in a canyon to lend a more potent mental picture. The echo had bounced back from "stark canyon walls" several times before it died back down. Much like the second version of "Silence," those three little words crowded the image. Since I was so concerned with using words that did not clutter the poem, I looked for ways to say what I had to say as simply as possible. Thus I cut the lines "sound" and "ten." That accomplished, I read the poem again and again.

Unsure exactly what it needed, I turned to an objective critic. Dan Trevino and I spent a majority of class listening to the sounds the words made. *Seconds.* I liked how the "s" trailed off, as if it were, in itself, an echo fading away. In keeping with this, I changed "after" to "past," and based on the counseling of Dan (who insisted "f" was much too harsh a letter) I stuck "slipped" in for "fades." I left off punctuation to provide for a continuous, unbroken flow. Hence my poem simply stated: "seconds past an echo slipped away." I knew my work was complete when Trevino read the final version of "Silence" and sat for several moments in quiet contemplation.

There are so many wonderful things in Joanna's narrative: here is a young writer with startling sophistication successfully managing the Creator and Critic, really thinking, reverencing language, consulting with allies, standing firm on the shifting sands of creation, not losing her head or heart—in short, engaging fully in the lives of the poem. Just visualize her and Dan Trevino, hunched over in a corner of the writing room, saying words over and over to one another, listening to them and evaluating them as intently as two researchers in a science lab plumbing the mysteries of the gene.

Intensity. Attention. Devotion. Yes—the lives of the poem.

* * *

Sometimes, as was the case in another year's anthology, *The Ice Age Poems*, the writing requires research. Prior to creating that series, we studied The Ice Age in print, bringing in maps, articles, pictures of animals. Then we took a field trip (another, more whole-body kind of research) to the Cincinnati

Museum of Natural History, which has a wonderfully extensive and intricate walk-through Ice Age Exhibit, with panoramic murals, a glacier, landscape features like ponds and rock outcroppings, all populated with life-size models of Pleistocene animals found in the Cincinnati area about 11,000 years ago. Here you can see, up close, Sabre-Toothed Lions, a Mammoth at the moment of its death as it slides into a kettle pond, Dire Wolves, and my favorite, Jefferson's Ground Sloth. As you walk through the glacier, you can hear its low grinding across southwestern Ohio; as you enter the reconstructed landscape, which actually represents a place a few miles north of Cincinnati, at the glacier's southern terminus, you can smell the scent of fir trees and flowers on the air, and hear the songs of birds. In all of its detail and sensory information and novelty, it's like stepping inside a poem itself.

I asked students, even before we visited the museum, to write a poem that personified cold, that made it a character with a life of its own. Here's one of them, a poem that won Joe Dumont (yes—Katie The Fair's younger brother) Fourth Place in the 1998 Ohio High School Poetry Contest, and which he read on TV in the same appearance that featured Mary O'Connell's winning poem, "Angie."

Cold

He's driving down ol '55
smokin' a red and
groovin' to Neil Young
and his "Heart of Gold."
Crumpled wrappers of
half-digested burgers
crinkle like dried leaves.
Yeah, he's been this
way before.
He guides his
Chevy Impala with
its 450 mag and
whitewalls across
the flatlands, as
familiar as a lover's
cold shoulder,
he sweeps down
the plains,
turbo-charged Jack Frost,
and greets each new town

with an icy smile.
They all know him 'round here.
He's the telegram
you just can't open.
He's the quiet
that ain't supposed to be.
He's the smell of
mothballs
when grandpa's sick.
He's the sign of bad
things to come.

—Joe Dumont

Joe's poem is notable for its specificity, its textured detail, and for the voice it creates, and its colloquially urgent announcement of doom. In subject matter and presentation, it reminds me of a modern version of the messages that show up in ancient tragedies, news filled with ill omen, delivered breathlessly and with terrible seriousness by some unnamed fate-harried figure who then disappears. The last four sentences are where the surprises are; what a list of original metaphors for the icy finality the glaciers brought when they descended over continental expanses. And that "he's the smell of/ mothballs/ when grandpa's sick" is a wonderful example of what T.S. Eliot called "the objective correlative"—a physical image that powerfully evokes an emotion in the reader, that places the reader in the emotional experience the poem recreates. Archibald MacLeish presents the same notion in his poem "Ars Poetica" when he suggests that

A poem should be equal to:
Not true.

For all the history of grief
An empty doorway and a maple leaf.

In other words, instead of *telling* the reader how to feel, the poet, through the careful selection and arrangement of images, *makes him feel* that way.

The lines of "Cold" are in control, too, and there are some other fresh and apt comparisons—to the glacier, the landscape is, indeed, as "familiar as a lover's shoulder;" the glacier has been there before, in three major advances, as geological history tells us—and the qualifier that calls it a "cold" shoulder is punningly well-chosen, too.

I think this poem came pretty much of a piece for Joe; the Critic and the Creator worked hand-in-hand for him, and by the time he was finished with the writing, he had already drafted, revised, and edited, pretty much simultaneously. That happens sometimes in the lives of the poem.

To finish the story of the Ice Age Poems: we studied the prehistoric cave paintings of Lascaux and Auvierge, and we downloaded maps and print information on the Ice Age from the Internet. We clipped pictures of Ice Age art. I brought in a book I'd been given about Mammoths, entitled, appropriately enough, *Mammoths*, and featuring an introduction by Jean M. Auel, author of *Clan of The Cave Bear* and several other best-selling novels of the Ice Age. We scattered this disparate material on a couple of tables and pored over it as a group. Then, slowly, the poems began to come, listening to one another, growing out of the research. Finally, since as always there were graphic artists in the class, we used original drawings of Dire Wolves and Jefferson's Ground Sloth, as well as original prints of pine branches; in addition we added appropriate images from my library of clip art, and drawings of the houses made of Mammoth bones that had been described in a *Scientific American* article I had saved, and we published the book. Here's one more, by Mary O'Connell:

Echoes

Inside
Cave River runs cold
and out
where the short-faced bear
dips his mouth
where the passenger pigeons
cloud the skies with
wings and bellies
where the sloth's searing
claws strip branches
for gnawing
where a woodland musk ox
milks her baby
where owlet eggs are being
rolled and rolled away
then cracked, then swallowed
by hungry dire wolves
outside
the river runs cold

whispering past over
shell bottoms
over the coarse hair of the
giant beaver
discovering their secrets
to tell the sleeping cave.

* * *

It strikes me just now how important to this notion of lives of the poem is the fact of my staying put long enough to have taught brothers, sisters, cousins, then the children of my students. Much of the fun of the inter-relatednesses here would be non-existent if I had not, for a dizzying complexity of reasons, some altruistic, some selfish, and some merely lazy, stayed at Purcell Marian all these years. In my very first year of teaching, I had had an offer, in the middle of my Purcell contract, to join the faculty of Xavier University, my alma mater. It was one of those potential turning points in my life that I look back on sometimes and wonder about: "What if?" But I have not one regret; staying where I am, I have learned that life is a call, and that no matter how we ignore it, or try to transform it, the life we are born to will find its way. Just as the poem, in its unfolding through version after version toward its final one, wrestling with us, toiling against our ego, our id, our Critic, our selfish or self-conscious Self, nevertheless often makes it through and comes into its own life and fullness, so our personal and professional lives: they too go through many drafts until they come to some sort of completion.

Our culture is very nomadic, and not just in the physic\al sense. We are pressed by socioeconomic issues as well to "move up," to be "upwardly mobile," and all of these pressures may well be a threat to the kind of placedness that certain kinds of poetry thrive on. Without a kind of "village" to dwell comfortably and familiarly in, poets are just as lost as any other people, and maybe more.

But the creation of such a village requires discipline and diligence. Ideally, there will be a physical proximity created between the members of your village; you will live near enough to one another to become a part of the fabric of each others' lives. This is not absolutely necessary, though; Joe and I have worked on our friendship over a quarter of a century in time and a continent's breadth in space. Part of our relationship's longevity is, of course, just luck, but a significant part of it is that we continue to write to and for each other, even when the subject is far distant from our friendship.

* * *

Write a poem, or a series of poem, which personify such qualities as 'cold" or "hot" or "bitter" or "sweet" or . . . well, build your own list of possibilities. Play around with creating a variety of voices in them, some formal and elegant, some casual and slangy.

* * *

It is a deep kind of fun to "open up" a poem like Mary Oliver's "Wild Geese" with a whole group of writers. The exercise reminds us that life (and the lives of the poem) are abundant, vast cornucopias of images and ideas out of which we can capture or discover poems. Writing in the mid-1800s about composing essays, Alexander Smith says, mentioning the famous naturalist and essayist Gilbert White, whose literary output was fueled by his calm at-home-ness in the village where he served as minister:

> And just as the Rev. Mr. White took note of the ongoings of the seasons in and around Hampshire Selbourne, watched the colonies of the rooks in the tall elms, looked after the swallows in the cottage and rectory eaves, played the affectionate spy on the private lives of chaffinch and hedge-sparrow, was eavesdropper to the solitary cuckoo; so here I keep an eye and ear open; take note of man, woman, and child; find many a pregnant text imbedded in the commonplace of village life; and , out of what I see and hear, weave in my own room my essays as solitarily as the spider weaves his web in the darkened corner . . . The essay writer is a chartered libertine, and a law unto himself. A quick ear and eye, an ability to discern the infinite suggestiveness of common things, a brooding meditative spirit, are all that the essayist requires to start business with.

And later he says:

> The essay writer has no lack of subject matter. He has the day that is passing over his head; and, if unsatisfied with that, he has the world's six thousand years to depasture his gay or serious humor upon. I idle away my time here, and I am finding new subjects every hour. Everything I see or hear is an essay in bud. The world is everywhere whispering essays, and one need only be the world's amanuensis.

It is exactly so with the lives of the poem.

139

The Poem Starts To Start Over

It has come too far:
language all domestic,
a clever, polished game.
Fluent, all the easy rules
down pat, it wins nothing
of the world.

It wants again to be wild,
un-weatherproofed,
burdened with the dark weight
of the sky.
It wants to roam old places
alone, to hunker
shivering in a cave
where beasts live,
where fear is moving
among crushed bones,
where its winter meat
is lean and tough as leather,
and where, come some bright
day loud with birds,
spring hurts,
a seed inside its head
that wants to split.

The Poem Starts To Start Over

Perhaps a mid-life crisis sort of poem, this wound up in *Poetry* magazine. I do not remember the details of its composition, nor exactly when it sprung up, but it expresses a common American theme. Like Jay Gatsby or Huck Finn, the poem seems able to transform itself, to re-invent itself, and so survive hardship by a kind of magic; it is as adaptable as "many-turning" Odysseus, whose ability to survive the wrath and wiles of the gods remains a powerful reminder of the ornery toughness of humans and the geniuses of adaptation and evolution.

At the same time, it remembers the self-sickness alluded to in the exhange of letters between me and Jerry Wayne Williamson. And it acknowledges that the birth of the new self, with the help of the midwife poem, may be painful.

The Poem Admits It's Out Of Practice

Every day it engages in subtle retreats,
rationalized avoidances,
multitudinous evasions:
ignoring all it knows of Freud,
it climbs the chimney,
inspecting bricks and flue;
it studies a book on hieroglyphics,
sits smoking for hours in the john:

As if a forest in high summer
could cease photosynthesis;
as if the sea, at full moon,
could stanch its own swelling;
as if sex, at its height,
instead of cries and thrusts,
leaps up, crosses the room,
and answers blandly
survey questions on the phone.

The Poem Admits It's Out Of Practice

Fully accounting for the lives of the poem often requires contradiction. So as soon as I say that poetry is supremely adaptable, I have to say that it, like other things in nature, can get in a rut. Annie Dillard tells us about how Pine Processionary caterpillars will follow the leader in a circle around the lip of a flower pot or discarded paint can until they all starve to death, their instinct to conform even more powerful than their instinct to survive. Sometimes our poems, too, hold back, do not go where they might go, out of fear or laziness or just a kind of spiritual or artistic stagnation. It is not a happy thing to see. But the breaking out from it, which almost always happens, is a marvel, like the sudden blossoming of the Evening Primrose, which happens, literally, in a second. I have watched a whole section of garden be transformed in the time it took me to go into the kitchen for a drink and come back out—a hundred yellow blossoms, smelling faintly of lemon, where, a minute ago, there were none. So too with poems, if we keep practicing, working through the dry spells.

The Poet At Fifty Walks Away From Writing

No machine could accomplish
this grave and reverent
retreat: shank's mare's solemn spondee
the only way
to do it,
directionless save the direction
pursuit spells out
from behind.
There, all his life gathers,
a world tailing him—
hillsides, creekspins,
windfalls, voices
of buntings and foxes,
teachers and dead men
rustling like leaves
into gullies paved
with jugshards
and shale,
then swirling out again,
swirling and always coming . . .

Yes, regrets:
that he has softened
where once he was hard,
gone to punk
at the heart
like a beech
with a rotting trunk,
that he doesn't drop
his leaves anymore
without counting.
That his name is a
stranger
who lives like
a beetle
in old books.

Rewards?
A few students
going to bloom

in the yellow air
of their youth;
a few proud scars to show
for skirmishes
with the truth;
a few namings that may last
like old mileposts
along an abandoned
National Road.

Plans?
To keep walking,
to stay ahead
of those sleepless posses
that follow,
loading their nouns
every twilight,
jerked onward
by taut-leashed verbs
all ear and eye and hunting,
their panting
the confusion
he wakes weary to
each morning.

The Poet At Fifty Walks Away From Writing

This is the second, then, in a series of poems about the hardships and demands of the job of poetry. Yes, "job." It may sound ludicrous to speak of poetry as a job, as bricklaying is a job, or managing a truck stop, or being a nurse. But it's true: sometimes the life of the poem is not so beautiful, not so wonderful, and sometimes people can burn out on it, especially if they take it too seriously. And sometimes, as in the next poem, they can deny it. This speaker seems to have overdone it, seems haunted by his past, and seems to be suffering from a compulsion in which poetry hounds him, as if he is some sort of fugitive. What is he feeling guilty about? What, exactly, is he fleeing?

* * *

Write your own "flight" poem or poems. What would you flee, if you could? What would it be like to fly high above your troubles, looking down on them, shrunken, not so important any more? What things in life dog you most persistently? Does poetry dog you? Write a poem in which we feel it snapping at your heels. Write a poem in which poetry nags you, bitches at you, calls *you* names.

146

The Annunciation

The artist is a servant who is willing to be a birth-giver.
In a very real sense the artist (male or female) should
be like Mary . . . obedient to the command.
—Madeleine L'Engle, *Walking On Water*

At fifteen the voice came to him,
druid murmuring, a sighing
from the skull of a goat,
dead essay at husbandry on the slope
behind his aging uncle's homestead.
It was almost lost
in the clamor of his thoughts:
how the beautiful skin of his sister
swaddled nothing but what seemed
a stupid life of surfaces;
guilt over his mother's death agony,
which he suffered like a constant crucifixion;
the nagging plain-mindedness
of his plain and secular father.
In this din of self, at first
he thought it only wind,
searched high in the locusts and sumacs
above the house for its tremor,
found nothing.
                        Then, that night,
sleeping near his garden
to ward off the suburban deer
that trampled his corn and beans,
he awoke and heard it again, this
time closer, a kind of whistling
in the thin bones of his fingers.
From his sleeping bag's
damp flank
his arms arose,
the right a little higher
than the left:
he cried out in fear.
Thus did it begin.

147

Now he sits in a room
filled with horns, bones,
geodes, cosmologies—
the gathered Gabriels
he denies—
and in anger tries and tries
not to hear nor to name
this strange thing
growing and chanting,
this thing that struggles to say him
inside him.

The Annunciation

Some of the details in this poem arise from the actual circumstances of a very gifted student writer, Tony Ruter, with whom I worked in the Seventies. Madeleine L'Engle's thoughts on obedience to The Call I find to be true, and difficult. The theme of The Call is a very old one in human life and in literature, and it most certainly is operative in the lives of the poem.

Consider this remark by W. H. Auden in the light of the epigraph: "The poet is the father who begets the poem which the language bears." And this, in a letter from Maud Gonne to William Butler Yeats, explaining why she never agreed to marry him: "Our children were your poems of which I was the father sowing the unrest and storm which make them possible and you the mother who brought them forth in suffering and in the highest beauty, and our children had wings."

Wow.

Several years later, after the tutorial with Colleen Glenn and Katie "The Red" DuMont which I write extensively about elsewhere in these notes, I got the idea of putting together a chapbook of poems about working with women writers. I used the Maude Gonne quote as epigraph for the book, and adapted the title (*Neither Father Nor Lover*) from Theodore Roethke's "Elegy For Jane."

The poem is on the next page.

Neither Husband Nor Lover

Maud Gonne to William Butler Yeats, explaining why she never agreed to marry him: "Our children were your poems of which I was the father sowing the unrest and storm which make them possible and you the mother who brought them forth in suffering and in the highest beauty, and our children had wings."

   for Katie The Red

I have watched and worked with you
in a hundred forms
more clever and shifty than Athena's:
scholars, guessers, women with attitudes,
early mothers, late bloomers,
mute, shy, bodacious, lusty
madonnas, goddesses, princesses,
teases, wackos, drinkers, druggies,
judo-instructing woman warriors,
prim daughters and wild sisters,
straight and gay,
friends forever and
eternal wily standoffers,

All of you learning to make words
straighten up or do The Frug,
give birth or smack some devil down,
ranking lines in martial rows or
dancing red stanzas, hair flying.

You are my Americas,
my breaks, my Belle Isles.

Though there is between us
something like a treaty,
something like a vow,
with words, we build sacred bridges
sometimes across the divide:

We visit in the chaste ceremony of our work
a quiet dream in which we rest in lines
snugged to one another, drowsy with love,
or stir sweetly together in a singing dark,
blameless as divines.

Tony Ruter remains one of the more mysterious fellows in the lives of the poem. I have not seen him since he graduated from my school nearly three decades ago; I have not seen a poem by him in print anywhere; I do not know what he does, where he lives, if he ever went to college. How strange it is that such intensities can so fully drop out of our lives, as if we were to wake up one morning and, with no recollection of how it happened, discover that one of our arms is gone.

I remember Tony's presence in the workshop. He was a tiny blond fellow who came to us when he was twelve, fresh out of Montessori school. He was known around Purcell for being almost overwhelmed by his own bookbag, which he lugged alongside of him, straining against its weight.

But when he began to read a poem in workshop, a remarkable transformation came over him at once. His voice would acquire a heavy burr, or brogue; he would enter a trance of language and rhythm, and he would take us to such ancient places . . . I remember once seeing a series of drawings he did. They were incredibly detailed pencil drawings of old crones, women whose faces were a concatenation of wrinkles, and whose features looked more like parts of trees or barky shrubs than they did human noses or eyes or lips. His was a tense, private, haunted imagination, a dark rich past tangled inextricably into it, just as images and language and rhythms were tangled effectively into this poem of his, written when he was thirteen or fourteen years old:

Twrch Trwyth

Twrch Trwyth,
eater of acorns, father of hogs,
bursts from forest.
Holds the hunter in yellow tusks,
shakes, shatters, disembowels,
grinds guts into frozen ground.
The broad blade is useless,
the boar spear is splinters.

They go up the hill,
where hob herd.
Pole, ax, and knife glint in gray light,
while warm mist rises from sow stalls.

A blunt ax butt
falls hard.

Hard falls the hog.
Cloven toes thresh cold air.

The pig, pink from enforced incest
squeals through yellow teeth.
Eyes turn up in skull.

An ash rod honed hard
bites, bursts the jugular,
sputtering, spewing bright blood, bright life,
into the pan.
To the kitchen the pan,
to the bloodwurst the blood.
Some soaks into the stone icy earth.
Escapes the cycle for a second,
while warm mist rises.

Fruitless threshing slows.
Up steel, down blood,
buckets of bowels stand in rank.
Kidneys, liver, lungs
to be boiled down to pudding.

The boiling trough scalds hair loose,
while warm mist rises.
To hang sausage in the cellar
they kill hogs.

Cold hogs hang in cold light,
while blood drips warm
to clot in the snow.

What in the world is going on here, and when? The poem, though in parts
unfinished, creates a violently rich tableau of—what?—Anglo-Saxon or Celtic
life around the time when *Beowulf* might still have been chanted by some
mead-inspired scop? What in the world had this boy been reading? What in the
world had been mixing and chanting and churning and bleeding in his
imagination? I heard a rumor about him after he left school. He was, someone

said, on his way to Iceland or Norway, someplace in Scandinavia, in search of his roots.

His initials, which he always printed below and to the right of the last line of the poems he brought to workshop, looked like runes.

At any rate, my poem takes some liberties with the biographical facts. I did, however, visit him once after school; he was living in the cellar of an abandoned house on what I remember was his uncle's property; he brewed his own mead there, had a Nubian goat tied to a stake on the hillside, and grew a long sloping garden of corn, which he had to defend from deer and groundhogs by sleeping on the ground beside it.

I think the theme of the resistance to The Call sprang up when it became clear to us in the workshop that Tony did not trust his gift; he always seemed terribly reluctant to read his work aloud in the workshop, and we'd think that he must have written some bad poems. Then we'd hear something like "Twrch Trwyth" and be astonished. He won the College of Wooster's High School Poetry Contest one of the years he was in the workshop, and I couldn't even tell you with what poem.

Separating out the personal issues a student brings to the lives of the poem and the more public ones that are laid on by the teacher and by the dynamics of the workshop is difficult. Was Tony's reluctance to believe his gift the result of resistance to my coaching, or to the comments of the others in the workshop, or was it something more deeply seated and darker, some self-distrust that said to him, "You cannot possibly be as good as they seem to think you are. They are wrong, and you are right—your work sucks, and deserves nothing of your deepest and most reckless effort"?

Perhaps Tony's Critic had seized the upper hand in him, and talked him out of faith in himself. Tony was, as I remember now, an intense and serious boy, stand-offish at times from the escapades of his peers. I remember thinking how much of an old man he seemed even as a youngster. Perhaps it was this premature seriousness that made the lives of the poem in him less than an occasion of personal affirmation and joy.

The lives of the poem are not always happy.

The Poem Rends The Veil

One life's holocaust: a beautiful girl,
sixteen, a student dancer last year in New York,
now back at her hometown high school,
bra-less, svelte, wearing a long-sleeved sweater from Saks,
pale but powerfully-legged,
smiling at everyone, her loud red lips
ablaze beneath her black, cropped hair,

And looking at least twenty, chic,
the daughter of a rich handsome man
and a mother devout and calm,
her older sister a happy cheerleader
at a college in the South,

This child, this little sister, doing her chemistry homework
one night alone in her room, the plain sense
of the periodic table before her on the desk
next to her lipsticks and dance slippers,
this child takes up her scissors,
her eyes half-closed, her right hand
steady and strange, and lifts her
blouse, carefully, and presses the scissors
into the white flesh of her chest
just beneath her breasts,
drives the points there, then pulls them
slowly apart, opening a gash,
does not cry out, does not want
to cry out, is punishing herself
for something, knows this is not

Good, but then finishes, soaks the blood
up with a sock and hides
the sock, and next day in school,
sitting in chemistry, carefully again
reaches under her fresh shirt
to touch the wound, to make it
hurt again, it must not heal.

All of this, many times, over
many months, the scars lining her

stomach, her back, her thighs,
the pale forearms she never bares
unless in her private agony
as if to a lover only she can
ever know, and in her troubled
darkness, tense and say her Yes to.

The poem, like a survivor of Dachau,
Buchenwald, Treblinka,
learns the inside story.
Forced, a witness, it is dragged outside,
singing Kaddish,
into the bright light of an April morning
where it is beaten sullenly and long.
Later, bandages shrouding its face,
it hobbles to our door, knocks,
steps in, groans,
tells us everything.

The Poem Rends The Veil

This is one of the most problematic of all the poems I have considered including in *Lives of the Poem*. First, the subject matter is intense and strange, and because it is very loosely based on an actual situation, I wonder whether I am on solid ethical ground in writing about it. Is it an invasion of privacy, even if no one but me knows the facts? (See "From The Porch To The Page: Memory, History, and A Poem.") Secondly, it presumes to connect this single suffering, self-inflicted and the product of sporadic pathology, with the huge suffering of the Holocaust, certainly not self-inflicted and certainly not the result of the victims' disease. I'm on shaky ground here; I feel uncertainty. Third, the Holocaust, for as much as I can empathize and imagine, is not my story; am I allowed to presume to use it for the poem's purposes?

I'll be straightforward here and say that it upsets me to have to ask such questions. Writing, I thought, was not an overtly political act. But it seems it is, and if we expect to move freely in our writing, across racial and ethnic and ideological borders, we had better carry a passport, or at least be prepared to answer a few hard questions.

* * *

Now here's a redeeming, if unsettling, development: the very subject of the poem above—she and her newborn infant—sat just behind me in church one Sunday recently, years and years after we were in class together. We spoke, I goo-gooed the baby, mom smiled . . . I am happy all has turned out well. Sometimes what you see is not at all what you really get. As someone once said about Freud and the interpretation of dreams, "Sometimes a cigar is just a cigar;" so too the lives of the poem are sometimes just the lives of the poem—not actual life.

* * *

Commit a few politically incorrect poems, writing about another gender or race or member of an ethnic minority, uncovering your own prejudices and stupidities. Forgive yourself for them, if you can. Recall Whitman's words in his *Preface*. Then burn the poems. In your backyard. Then write a poem or two about what you felt, about what it must have looked like to your neighbors, about whether or not you felt any burden lifted from you as the smoke rose into the sky.

156

Writing During January Rain

In small rills, it inspects
the crystallized ground for entrance.
It wants to go down like roots.
All day it catches light from the sky,
but it wants to go down,
seeping among hardpan and pebble.
All day it wants to go down
but it wanders the stony earth
and does not touch the maple's foundation,
now thaw the balled hands of vine roots,
nor go anywhere deeper than it is.
Its failure, on toward dark,
gathers in sheets and freezes.

Writing During January Rain

Sometimes it just doesn't come; sometimes all the obedience in the world, all the openness and receptivity we can muster is not enough: no one's home, the Muse has vanished.

It happens to everyone. The key is not to panic. Be patient with the absence; practice acceptance and equanimity. Rage, depression, grief—none of these will overcome it. Sitting down each day at the writing desk and hoping— only this will work.

And sometimes—rarely, but often famously—the poetry goes away forever from the poet, never to return. Who said life has to operate justly and logically? If we are willing, on the one hand, to accept "inspiration," we must also be willing to accept, on the other, the cessation of it all. Will it kill us? I don't know. I doubt if it *has* to be fatal; I think some people may choose to die over its loss just as some people choose to die when their wife or husband dies. But who knows?

* * *

What does failure look like from your vantage point? Is it possible to write a poem that complains without whining? Try it. Now try it again.

Thinking To Make A Poem

Lost in thought, he finds an idea, blank
as snow on snow. How large he cannot guess.
He cannot see where it ends, or how it begins.
He only knows it exists, huge in the air before him.

If he listens closely, he hears its language—
beeps, hoots, drizzle of static, modulations
that sound like children laughing. He hears music,
birdsong, the complex clatter of weather.

He inspects its shape for an entrance.
However intently he looks, he finds nothing
like a door, or latch, or seam. It contains
itself completely, a conundrum, without clues.

Season after season passes. He grows hungry.
He thinks he smells smoke, the richness of fat.
He cannot possibly eat it. So he tries to starve
himself, to shrink small enough to find some

Subtle texture on its surface he can gnaw.
Soon he is as tiny as an atom, nervous, unable
to be still. Gravity pulls him, an orphan moon,
toward its world. He sees his shadow speed

Along its surface. Suddenly, as if breaking
through clouds, a landscape rises before him.
It is his former body, its moist interior rills
visible, pulsing, the nimbus of his lungs

Expanding toward the far ridge of his chest.
His heart roars like an ocean. His liver seethes,
bathed in a fragrant acid. Far off, he sees
the surf-washed shores of his brain, luminous fish

Sparking in its tide. And now he is not falling, but gliding,
a shuttle in re-entry, his surfaces heated,
the atmosphere grown thicker. Gently, he tries a turn,
finds it easy, banks toward a level darkness

On the horizon. He lands in a place that's familiar.
From behind a slight rise, two people approach.
They speak a pleasant English. They resemble
his mother and father, dressed in spirals of ribbon.

"Welcome to flesh," they say. "This is where you begin."

Thinking To Make A Poem

All through the commentary on "The Poem Braids Its Lover's Hair," I remarked on how things "came to me," or on how I didn't know what I wanted to say, or what the poem wanted to say, exactly, but just kept working until these things came clear. Put simply, I was saying that writing did not so much proceed from something I had thought, from some idea, but that the writing adventured *into* thinking. Here, from a very useful book, Peter Elbow's *Writing Without Teachers*, is a more thorough explanation.

> The common model of writing I grew up with preaches control. It tells me to think first, make up my mind what I really mean, figure out ahead of time where I am going, have a plan, an outline, don't dither, don't be ambiguous, be stern with myself, don't let things get out of hand. As I begin to try to follow this advice, I experience a sense of satisfaction and control. . . . Yet almost always my main experience ends up one of *not* being in control, feeling stuck, feeling lost, trying to write something and never succeeding. Helplessness and passivity.
>
> The developmental model, on the other hand, preaches, in a sense, *lack of control*: don't worry about knowing what you mean or what you intend ahead of time; you don't need a plan or outline, let things get out of hand, let things wander and digress. Though this approach makes for initial panic, my overall experience with it is increased control. Not that I always know what I am doing, not that I don't feel lost, baffled, and frustrated. But the overall process is one that doesn't leave me so helpless . . .
>
> Insisting on control, having a plan or outline, and always sticking to it is a prophylactic against organic growth, development, change. But it is also a prophylactic against the experience of chaos and dis-orientation which are very frightening.

Very good advice. The final line of "Thinking To Make A Poem" suggests that the way to poetry is not primarily through the mind, but through the flesh, the double-helix, ribbony stuff of DNA—that is, through the body, the senses. The stuff of poetry is not primarily intellect, but image: a poem is not so much *about* something, as it *is* something. For other adventures, see "Where Does The Poem Live?", "Chaos Poem", "The Poem Three-Railing Into The Mind", "During A Break In Writing Class", "The Poem Finds Its Poet", "The Poem Lures Her Along, Shows Her The Promised Land", "Poem Entering The House After A Winter Walk", and "Finding The Poem."

During A Break, First Day Of Writing Class

1

A girl named Darcy converses
with the cats.
She speaks to them easily,
in her own tongue.
They live in another world:
in their stomachs, the tiny bones
of birds
soak and soften.
But an ancient light
here binds them—girl and cats—
while the lawn beyond,
glazed with the slant fall
of sunlight, composes
soil and futures.

2

Turning away,
I hear, out front on the street,
above the buzz of neighbors'
mowers, music
of young women laughing.
I imagine them Egyptian,
three thousand years ago,
an invisible sand on the wind.
I try to forget
what I understand of words,
hear their sound
as the voice of another time,
the scents of myrrh and aloes
draped upon them
like gold light.

3

Let me approach
all truths
as explorers approach new tribes:
speech at first useless,
an exchange of gifts
in the place of words,

the silent wonder of both sides:

Who are these strangers,
Where are they from,
Why have we met,
How will they change
my dreams?

During A Break, First Day Of Writing Class

Isn't it odd and wonderful that sometimes the best or most significant things come slant, as Emily Dickinson noticed—sideways, at the corner of the eye? Here's a poem about the writing workshop—but more, about how taking a break from it opens up in ways unexpected. Not thinking about writing winds up producing some writing.

This was one of the workshops held at my home. There was always a good feeling there, because, in part, we were out of school. (The girl named in the poem, however, was being home-schooled at the time—she came to find a community of other students while still remaining outside the traditional school.) Just being somewhere other than the classroom changed things, and people could write things and say things that they might not have been able to do in the building.

It's good to get "out of the building" in our writing, and to vary the surroundings in which we write. Nature, married as she is to Chaos, abhors too much regularity and structure just as surely as she abhors a vacuum.

* * *

Go to a local cafe or market, plunk yourself down in a booth or at a table, and write for an entire morning. Look up for whatever passes by, and listen hard for snatches of conversation that might be suggestive. Do this several times, all the while making poems out of it all, and you may come up with a little pamphlet or chapbook: *The Cafe Poems, The Market Poems.* Send them off to your local newspaper, or your school literary journal, or one of the many e-zines that have sprung up. Or print them all up on a big sheet of paper and sell them during lunch at school. Or hand them out for free at the market or cafe where you wrote them. Frame a page of them and present it to the owner—I'll bet you he or she will proudly display your writing—it will mean something to the proprietor that a writer has paid attention. In the meanwhile you will have done something "out of the building," and will be able to testify to other writers about the value of such self-assignments. And maybe you'll have a story or two to tell your grandchildren. Certainly, you will have some poems to show for it all. And you will have lived in a way that only the writer can live, with that special alertness that is a kind of high, obtainable in no other way than in making the life of the poem an adventure.

* * *

Katie Schlosser was an all-league volleyball player at Purcell Marian, quite an artist, and just as outstanding academically, graduating as valedictorian of her class. Late one winter, a local business, Joseph Beth Booksellers, advertised a Love Poetry Contest for Valentine's Day. I feared that poems deliberately written about love might be, in the hands of amateurs (pun intended), pretty sappy affairs. I suggested to the creative writing class that we turn the contest upside down, and for kicks that we all write and submit anti-love poems. That way, I hoped, we would avoid the sickeningly sweet clichés, and maybe even come up with something that would catch the judge's eye, offer an alternative to the pap and pabulum the contest was inadvertently inviting.

It worked. Katie Schlosser won First Place. Here's her poem.

Lick

You are the sour taste cloud that staples my tongue,
the hair in my mouth,
the lemonade powder that prickles my nose . . .
You are the piece of gum
with the liquid center
that loses its flavor after three chews,
but I keep it anyway.

And Ann Case, another member of the class, won Second with this poem:

Tetanus Shot

Love is an argon balloon,
dense,
sinking to the ground,
scratching the rusty fence
and bursting.

Despite the students' success, there's a woeful footnote to all this. As we all were sitting in the little reading area of the bookstore while the judge of the contest was talking about the entries, I leaned over to Katie and said something about the last line of her poem, criticizing it, encouraging her to take another look at it. She stared steadily down at her hands. Her friend turned to me and said, "Geez, Mr. Hague! She's winning First Place, and you're telling her how bad her poem is. Lighten up."

It was at that moment that I once again realized the terrible power of an education, whose effects in some cases can look more like a trailer park after a tornado than a beautiful landscaping job by Olmstead. Remember, it was misapplied and inappropriate and unchecked knowledge that brought us the atomic bomb, eugenics, and any number of moral conundrums of the last century or two. So you've got to know when to silence The Critic, puffed up with knowledge and arrogance and attitude; you've got to know when to stop. There I was, messing up a perfectly good moment for a writer who had triumphed.

Several years later, Katie The Red, by then Associate Editor of *Writer's Digest* magazine, invited me to try out as poetry columnist. I sent a couple of sample columns, including this one, which I dedicate to Katie Schlosser as penance for my rudeness at her awards ceremony.

The Marriage Of The Creator And The Critic

(Part One)

There are two of us involved in the making of a poem, always two. One is hot and disorderly and mostly in a tizzy and says "Yes!" to anything we put down on paper, anything we dream up in our wildest visions. "Yes! That is good"—even when it isn't. "Yes! That is inventive and fresh," even when it isn't. This writing self loves us unconditionally, as the cliché goes; no strings attached: "Yes!" This writing self corresponds to James Joyce's Molly Bloom, famous for her Everlasting Yea at the dreamy conclusion of the novel *Ulysses*:

> ". . . he kissed me under the Moorish wall and I thought well as well
> him as another and then I asked him with my eyes to ask again yes
> and then he asked me would I yes to say yes my mountain flower and
> first I put my arms around him yes and drew him down to me so he
> could feel my breasts all perfume yes and his heart was going like
> mad and yes I said yes I will Yes."

This writing self corresponds to the Greek notion of the Muses, those female divinities responsible for the inspiration of —what else?—the musician. Also the epic poet, erotic poet, historian, astronomer, tragedian, and several others.

This writing self appears at the beginning of the creative process. Without her, nothing can happen. She is the heat in the fire, the soul in the body, the

166

wild in Natalie Goldberg's *Wild Mind*. If we cannot welcome her and the fertile chaos and nonlinear messes and disparate and disjointed bits she brings us, we may never discover anything new in our material. Even Leonardo, that master of Renaissance grace and orderliness, knew and praised her. He wrote,

> You should look at certain walls stained with damp or at stones of uneven color, the embers of fire, or clouds or mud. You will be able to see in these the likeness of divine landscapes, mountains, ruins, rocks, woods, great plains, hills and valleys. You will find most admirable ideas; from a confusion of shapes the spirit is quickened to new inventions.

The crucial theme in Leonardo's advice is being open to the ideas that arise from irregularity and disorder. Everywhere in his sketchbooks, the artist recorded his encounters with complicated confusions: deluges and fires, for example, or clouds and plumes of smoke. He knew they had something to teach him; he knew that "from a confusion of forms the spirit is quickened to new inventions." Despite being one of the most meticulous and mechanically adept artists of history, he knew that to the influx of chaos and happenstance he must say "Yes."

For many of us, this Yea-saying is very difficult. Brought up in an educational system modeled on the factory—the very epitome of linear efficiency—we have been conditioned to distrust disorder, randomness, nonlinearity. Many of our teachers have subscribed to the logical and linear model of teaching; very rarely, in our learning careers, have we been simply put down in front of the actual mess and mystery of the world, and invited to make sense of it on our own. Our job has not been to learn how to engage raw material—be it salamanders or the Civil War or memory—and to be playful and original in our discovery of its meaning. We haven't been asked to actually *do* history—or for that matter, to think about what history *is*, exactly. We have simply been asked to demonstrate, by proxy, mostly on paper, merely some knowledge of its content, some proficiency established by legislators and educational bureaucrats. It is revealing, for example, that there are no poetry-writing, or piano-playing, or oil-painting sections on state proficiency exams, the so-called High Stakes Tests. Can you hear the message clearly? Can you see what kinds of citizens the makers of these tests want? High stakes, indeed—the longer we fail to acknowledge, empower, and certify the imaginative and the extraordinary, the more imperiled our culture. "Their city died because they had no poet." But for the poet, it's a messy and more daunting—and, fortunately—an almost ecstatically satisfying adventure to begin a poem. Oftentimes, the poet does not know what is going to happen.

167

I'm sitting down and putting words on paper. I'm trusting that this process will *beget* ideas. I don't have to have an idea before I write. I know the process of writing is like fishing—I send out a line, I get a nibble (if I'm lucky) and If I'm patient enough, and wait for the idea to grow fins and gills, and to take my bait of ink, I'll pull it out and be able to see it clearly, identify it, name it.

That's the poet William Stafford. Luck, patience, the openness to the poem's surprise—Molly Bloom's "Yes."

But if this hot and messy self were the only one involved in the making of poetry, there would be no art at all. Poetry would indeed be Wordsworth's "spontaneous overflow of powerful emotions," but an overflow undirected, unchanneled—a mere flood of verbiage and emoting. It would be no more art than the strewn papers from an overturned wastebasket are a novel, no more than the colicky squall of an infant is a sonnet. It would be raw self-expression—something a surprising number of otherwise sophisticated people still believe to be the very essence of poetry—as if screaming were the very essence of singing.

So there must be the second writing self, who helps impose order on all this passion, who helps cool things down, and who takes a more considered look at the mess the Creator produces. This second self is The Critic.

* * *

This is important to the lives of the poem, and my notes on the revising of "The Poem Braids Its Lover Hair" offer abundant evidence in support of saying Yes to what we are given. But there is the other side, too, which The Critic reigns over, sometimes heavy-handedly, always autocratically, and often unforgivingly.

The Critic

He's bearded and Ivy-leagued,
buff, fit as a boxer,
knows all about wine
and economics. He lives high
in the city, his apartment
buttressed with books.
He's loaded, drives his Mercedes,

spits on the boys
he passes.
He's always right.

I hate him—
he's always right,
and wields his knowledge
like a flamethrower
which he turns on me:

He's got guns in his breath,
hammers in his glance,
sharking dictionaries
arrayed behind him
like a battalion of
revving Panzers.

He's coming at me
laughing and coughing,
smoothing his little mustache,
windmilling his arms,
punching the air
with insults,
whirling his gears
like a thresher—
yeah, come on, Bubba,

bite me.

Still, The Critic is an indispensable partner in the writing process. My essay on the Creator, by the way, failed to move the editor of *Writer's Market*, and I was not offered the job of Poetry Columnist. That was okay; I certainly had enough to do what with my own work and teaching. In the long run, it was best that it didn't work out; the summer of that rejection was when I nearly finished *Lives Of The Poem*. (Though of course they will not stop just because I have ceased writing on them. My friend Jim "Ski King" Webb once marveled about what happened to his stories when, embarked on some mock-epic of autobiography, he interrupted himself only to return and find out that his friends had finished the story for him—so too with the *Lives*: they can, and will, "go on without me.")

Here is an example of how the lives of the poem are, surprisingly sometimes, the poem's and not the poet's. My friend Pauletta Hansel read an early draft of *Lives of The Poems*. Months later (nine, perhaps?), she gave me a copy of this, her reply to the question repeated in its first two lines.

How You Know

How do you know
when the poem is finished?
When it no longer sings to you
in the car, on the street.
You sang along then,
testing each word
as if learning new language,
just to taste its voice in your
mouth. You turn
down the radio,
down and then off
just to hear.
Now it sits quietly,
hands in its lap,
your thoughts drift to new matters,
sift other words.
You flip between stations,
sing to new songs.

How do you know? When you wake
empty-handed, when you no longer clutch
this poem through the night,
always knowing it's there.
Turning softly in sleep
as to not send it tumbling
off into dark.

And yet you always do,
comes a morning you
wake without words,
done with it,
it with you.

And with every time
you see it then, maybe in some smoky
bar in some other hand,
perhaps you are alone, or clutching other words
like life itself.
You remember
once it was everything to you,
it was all you'd ever known,
you thought it might be all
you'd ever know again.

One of the phenomena of the lives of the poem which tickles me the most is when poets in a class or workshop begin to work off each other, when they begin to feed one another creatively, when you can see that their being together is responsible for the birth of poems.

Dave Cross, wrestler and football player, was a member of my creative writing class two years in succession. An intriguing, complicated writer, he was at first the boyfriend of Laura Scott, another member of the class. They sat together at a table, and even I, mostly blind to the little signs of romance that flower in classrooms, noticed that they were a couple. But something happened; Laura looked angry; then, one day, they did not sit together. Over a few months, Laura's writing explicitly detailed the demise of their defunct romance, and Dave drifted off across the room to sit next to Sarah Humble, a year older than he, a person of great confidence and a wryly affirmative view of life. One day, Sarah was working on her writing practice, and she leaned over to Dave and asked him something along the lines of, "What's really thin? I need some sort of comparison for something almost transparently thin." Dave thought a while, and pronounced authoritatively, "Yellow. Definitely yellow." Sarah put the simile in her poem, and when we had our read-around after practice, we all remarked on how surprising yet apt "thin as yellow" was in her poem.

Sarah's poem went on to place highly in the 1998 Ohio High School Poetry Contest sponsored by Ohio Northern University, and she told Dave at one point that when she graduated Purcell Marian, she was going to take him to college with her, a kind of portable muse.

The next school year, Sarah departed to Denison University on a writing scholarship; in the meantime, Dave had written this, which won Fourth Place in the 1999 Ohio High School Poetry Contest in which over 400 poems from students in nearly 100 high schools were entered.

Off To College

"I'm going to pack you in a suitcase
and take you to college with me."
   —Sarah Humble

Sea monkeys grew inside my head
And bubbled out my ear.
My problems tasted like blood
To a blonde shark who quickly
Swam through the human currents
Striking with a pen at my memories
Picking my brain from the Klondike
When the shark's day came to leave
I was found kidnapped
Placed in a box marked
"Fragile, this side up."
With the coughing of a car
I awoke moving the sweaters
From under my head
Only to be thrown backwards
Into a softball trophy
Then forward into white bras.

In the free time
Between the speed bumps
I remember the cows
That I ate in my Whopper
All bottle-fed in cages.

Silently I think giving her
"Thin as yellow" wasn't a good idea.

Beyond the story of this poem's conception, I like its wild-mindedness, its rich and detailed and humorous imagining of what it might be like if Sarah really had packed Dave off to college with her. Equally delightful (and instructive) is the underlying notion that poetry counts; that the making of it has ramifications; it can change your life.

The stuff in the trunk is humorously presented, and the leap from that to remembering the corralled cattle that wound up in his Whopper, and feeling akin to them (about to be devoured by this "blond shark?") is a continuation of the subtly consistent tone of this poem. The metaphors are a little mixed; with the shark and the Klondike so close together in the poem, I am head-spun a little as the reader. But this movement and surprise is what I have elsewhere called "dance" in a poem; this jitterbuggy one is no wallflower.

Sending poems out to competitions and for publications and recognition is not counter to the lives of the poem, nor is it the work of Phillistines. The whole point of this book is that poems live in the world, not apart from it, and that the process of raising them up and getting them ready for their own lives beyond our notebooks and portfolios is instructive. If we care enough about words to use them to explore and express our lives, then we care about them enough to do the creative and critical work necessary to good work. This is not to say that poems which never go beyond their writer's notebooks are not good, or useful. Clearly, Emily Dickinson's story (who hardly published at all) is as valid as Lyn Lifshin's ("The Queen of The Little Magazine") who has published thousands of poems all over the place. Dickinson only let a few poems escape her into magazines in her lifetime, and when her first collection appeared in 1890, the year the house I live in was built, she had already passed away. Still, for the purposes of discovering what good work looks like and demands of us, this submission of poems, this publishing of them beyond our own classroom, is an important experience.

This does not mean that publishing should be the single driving force behind our participation in the lives of the poem. There are warnings everywhere in the literature of creative writing against making publication—or fame, or riches—the end of the process. And indeed I have been depressed to find workshoppers whose only concerns seem to be where to send their work, and how much they should get paid for it, and how to protect it with copyright, as if it were first and foremost a commodity, some sort of gizmo that they ought to get patented. Their first and foremost consideration ought to be whether or not their work is any good, and whether or not they have faithfully lived the lives of the poem.

The fact is that with the lives of the poem, at least (it may be different for commercial novelists, for example), economic issues are never central. We're not going to make a lot of money at poetry, outside of a few minor explosions of good fortune here and there in the form of grants or honors or awards. These cannot be planned for, nor can they form a solid economic base of operations. I say all this despite the little voice in my head, that unreconstructed and habitual protestant, who says, "If someone really tried, I'll bet they *could* eke out a living as a poet. What with desk-top publishing, and doing lots of readings and performances and selling lots of stuff—chapbooks, broadsides, extra contributors' copies—and coupling all that with Poetry In the Schools programs, I'll bet somebody could patch together a kind of economically viable existence, at least for a while."

Truth to tell, if I had no children right now to send to college, I might be tempted to give it a shot. Who knows? Maybe it will be a part of the story of my retirement into the lives of the poem. But right now, it's just not feasible. So we have to make sure we have a day job that will help support the lives of the poem as they work out in our own circumstances.

* * *

Now and again in creative writing class, I try to set aside the time to respond in as much detail as I can to a student poem. We couldn't endure such a close reading of our poems every time we offered something to the class, but it is sometimes quite worthwhile to hear a full-blown response, if only to remind us of how much is going on subconsciously in ourselves when we write—and of how much we have to bring deliberately to consciousness as we revise and invite The Critic to help us. The acknowledgement of the power of the pre-verbal in the creative act is important; it keeps us from over-intellectualizing our development as a writer, and it pays homage to the complex mystery that underlies the creative process in all disciplines. The acknowledgment of the limits of the spontaneous and the subconscious in taking us fully into the craft of writing is equally important, and helps convince us that we need The Critic, and that we need to get him (not to stereotype, but I think the masculine habits of analysis and penetration and hegemony are solely The Critic's—for better *and* worse) as acutely educated as we can.

Again, I offer this in atonement to Katie Schlosser, whose moment of triumph I trampled with too much pedantry.

Is It Any Good? Katie Schlosser's "The Sensual Slug"

Here's a poem by a student in this year's (1996-97) Creative Writing class. She has graciously given permission for us to work with her poem, which follows, exactly as it was handed in.

The Sensual Slug

As patient as the sun that poses behind the edge of the earth,
this garden nomad glides from world to world, adventure to adventure.
Veined green meals are enveloped by this probing creature,
and in it's wake a crescent moon of color melts into a glassy river.
It writes the lucid language of the outdoors, and creates the gala opening

174

to summer's beginning, with it's calm and slick demeanor,
the well-traveled hermit dives in head first, and spreads itself
        throughout the golden sea.
This speckled wanderer is company to the hopelessly nocturnal,
And when the night has come and gone, the sensual slug has left
        a shimmering impression.

This poem is an exercise in Ugly/Pretty. After reading Maxine Kumin's surprising "The Excrement Poem," which presents manure as a pretty amazing thing (Kumin is a horse farmer as well as a poet, and would be one to notice), our challenge was to take something commonly perceived as ugly or disgusting or distasteful, and to present it in the poem as worthy, even beautiful.

Katie Schlosser's poem succeeds in this to a notable extent. The writer is very aware of words, and selects language deliberately to describe the slug with a vocabulary of beauty: *crescent moon, glassy, lucid language, golden sea, sensual, shimmering.* This word choice is effective, and combined with the poem's avoidance of an overt meter or mawkish rhyme scheme, helps create a calm reverence of mood that reinforces the poem's focus and purpose.

But even as the language helps create the mood of the poem, it falls in other places into a predictability that diminishes its power and beauty: *garden* nomad, *probing* creature, *well-traveled* hermit, *speckled* wanderer, *sensual* slug. Combined with other adjective-noun or adverb-adjective constructions like *veined green meals, glassy river, slick demeanor,* and *hopelessly nocturnal,* the poem falls unconsciously into a rut of predictability. In writing and revising poetry, we try to bring to consciousness such unconscious patterns and to bring them under control, the Creator and Critic working hand-in-hand to make the poem the most appropriately varied it can be.

While we're talking about words, there are two particular choices in the poem that seem a bit off-key: *slick* demeanor and *hopelessly* nocturnal. Though *slick* is accurate in this description of the slug, its connotations (subtle emotional shadings of meaning), especially when coupled with *demeanor,* are negative. *Slick* suggests "tricky" or "conniving," as in "Don't trust him, he's a real slick operator." So these connotations make the line inconsistent with itself: "calm and slick demeanor" doesn't quite work because the whole passage's intent is to celebrate, not criticize, the slug's rather elegant behavior:

It writes the lucid language of the outdoors, and creates the gala
opening to summer's beginning, with it's slick and calm demeanor . . .

Similarly, there is something amiss with the later phrase *hopelessly nocturnal. Hopelessly* suggests something negative—an attitude found among suicides or those involved in utterly lost causes. Such negative meanings do not fit the mood and intention of the last lines of the poem which again celebrate the beauty of the slug.

Lest this commentary seem too negative, however, I want to remark on the early-draft competence of this poem. In practically every line, there is something to see—something to sense—and there is hardly anything more important than this physical presence of the poem to its reader. Look at this, line by line, and you will see that the writer has taken pains to accomplish what John Keats meant when he said, "load every rift with ore." Keats was reminding himself and us of the intensity, the compactness, the physicality of poetry. He was talking about avoiding lines of abstraction, about avoiding merely telling, and about creating lines in which images abound—something to see, hear, smell, touch, taste. This poem is packed with things which help to incarnate its ideas: *the sun, the edge of the earth, veined green meals, crescent moon, glassy river, summer's beginning, calm demeanor, dives in head first, golden sea, speckled wanderer, shimmering impression.* Good—now make these images even sharper, re-cast a few as metaphors or similes—and the poem gets even better.

One final thing, a technical point, and one of those things that ignores the very important "Law of Distraction" which Robert Wallace explains in his fine book, *Writing Poems*:

> The law of distractions says that, in a poem, any stylistic feature that draws attention to itself and so away from the subject and feeling, is risky. Even though it allows a reader to be distracted for only the tiniest flicker of a second, a flashy word, an odd (or missing) comma, an ambiguous bit of syntax, accidental misspelling, or the like, risks a dangerous, albeit subliminal, loss of full attention. Don't leave clamps inside the patient.

In this poem one distraction is the improper use of *it's*. *It's* is not the possessive form that is called for here—*its wake, its calm and slick demeanor*. *It's* is always the contraction for *it is*. Always. It is never the possessive of *it*. Never.

So to sum up—this draft is strong in some very important areas—imagery, sensual detail, general density, accomplishment of its purpose, which is to show something normally perceived as ugly as being beautiful. Its slight weakness is in its unrecognized and unrevised predictability of adjective-noun constructions, which create a kind of going-on-automatic-pilot which is the opposite of what a good poem, conscious of itself and its moves, can do.

* * *

And, while we're at it, here's another one, from another year. The poem is by Kathy Rich, daughter of my principal at the time. (Kathy has since graduated—in three-and-a half years—with a double major from Washington University in St. Louis, where she plans to study for her M.F.A. in Poetry.) Kathy was among the most dogged revisers I have ever worked with, and part of my enthusiasm for the little poem discussed below is that it was, I suppose, the result of effective revision—perhaps even of a kind of miraculous shrinking, which made it better, as if poetry were something like a juice concentrate—which, come to think of it, it is.

On The Way Toward The Craft: Kathy Rich's "Sophie"

Lazy,
Outstretched on her couch,
The white tip of her tail
Hints at a wag
In the school morning's sleepy darkness.

1.

Let me begin by saying that this is an almost perfect little poem. It is not a great poem; it is a nearly perfect little poem, and it will take some time to explain why it is, and to explain why, though almost "perfect," it is not a great poem, thought the fact that it is not great does not detract from its near perfection.

Remember that the subject of a poem is only one small part of its interest to a careful reader. Many poems, taken at the most literal level, are about similar things: a summer's day, an animal, some emotional spot of time. What separates the good ones from the mediocre, the classics from the also-rans? In part, it is the craft of the poem. A bad poem about a coelocanth or an okapi is not redeemed by the interest or oddness of its subject matter. What it's about cannot rescue it from mediocrity if there is no craft.

So, if poetry is, as we have often said, "language listening to itself," then please listen to this poem's second line: "Outstretched on her couch." The *ou* sound of *outstretched* and of *couch* are exactly the same, and the *o* of *on* is close: language listening to itself. In the third line, "the white tip of her tail," the alliterations of the *t* sounds exactly echo one another" language listening to itself. And in the last line, "in the school morning's sleepy darkness" the *s* sounds shush us almost back to sleep: language listening . . . well, you get it now. The poet is really hearing her poem, and she has made good choices to create a sonic pattern, some symphony, in it. The pattern is artful, part of the poem's small perfection.

There's more: if poetry proceeds in large part by means of image—if poetry, as Archibald MacLeish says, "should not mean, but be"—then this poem is a success. There is no intrusion of a speculative or exclamatory speaker; there is simply the subject, happening—no telling, no explaining, no exaggerating. The reader does not have to fight his way past some noisy, preachy, or whiny consciousness; the dog is there, before us, accurately and sensitively observed:

"The white tip of her tail / Hints at a wag . . . "

And what a fine word choice that "hints" is. It's a surprise, and a poem ought to create surprises. Additionally, it links the idea with the concrete object, with the dog's tail's "tip"—sound and sense arresting our attention, focusing on the thing itself.

Here I must point out that technically, the first two lines create a distraction. They are dangling modifiers—though I understand the whole dog is stretched out on the couch, the lines grammatically say that it is only the white tip of here tail that is stretched out—a clear impossibility, unless this is the smile-tail of some Cheshire-cat-dog. I'm willing to overlook this, but I think it needs to be addressed in one final tweaking of the poem.

But of all the right little moves this poem makes, I think its closure is the most artful, the most effective and crafty. "The white tip of her tail/Hints at a wag/In the school morning's sleepy darkness." That final line, drawn out as it is, develops a sonic pattern that absolutely requires slowing down to say without slurring or wrecking the words—"In the school morning's sleepy darkness." The sibilance of the many *s* sounds goes with the hush of sleep, as I have already observed, while the arrangement of consonants requires, in the saying of them, a deliberate reshaping of the mouth, and thus a noticeable slowing down of the speed of the line. That, too, complements the drowsy sense of the line and the actual situation of the poem. And the transferred epithet, "sleepy darkness," is a deft touch, too, subtly shifting the focus from the dog to the speaker, and casting its tone and color across all of the poem, inviting us back up into it, and into its drowsy, just-after-waking situation.

"Poetry is language listening to itself." I know I have said this many times, too many times, perhaps. But see: here, in this little perfection, we have "lazy" leading to "outstretched" leading to "couch" leading to "morning" leading to "sleepy", leading to "darkness." In the back-and-forth of the reader's consciousness as the poem happens, there is a pleasing unity to imagery, sound, and situation. Not a false note is struck, not an unnecessary word left in; not an intrusive voice or word choice or lines break distracts us from the thing itself. Read the poem again. That's all there is. And it is just exactly enough. Perfect.

2.

But it's not a great poem. Why not?

Because deeply significant subject matter married effectively to masterful technique is necessary to poetic greatness. There are thousands of failures about really important subjects. We've all seen poems with titles like "Freedom" or "Love" or "Justice"—all very significant and worthy ideas—but the poems themselves have been vague or predictable, or utterly without surprise or freshness, or completely devoid of imagery, or God forbid, rhymed to death.

A great poem is not only exceptional in its technique, which may involve imagery, form, skillful rhyme, structure, diction, symbolism, or any of the dozens of other technical and imaginative achievements possible in poetry, but in addition its subject matter is of rich and deep human significance. So I am not disappointed to say that though many have written good poems, I have not yet had a student write a great poem. This is not important. What is important is that each time we make a poem, we are getting a little better, a little more skilled, a little more experienced, a little more self-aware. Here's a passage from *The Work Of Craft* by Carla Needleman, a book I borrowed from my wife, a potter:

> A craft is not its objects; a craft is how I am when I am making them (and eventually, one would dearly hope, how I am the rest of the time, as a result of what has been transformed in me through craftsmanship.) The objects of the craft are by-products, very essential by-products, of the way I work.

If I paraphrase this, substituting "poetry" for "pottery," Needleman is saying something along these lines: "Poetry is not poems, but it is the by-product of my working with language, self, intuition, intelligence, memory, and skill in the way that poetry invites me to work. Poetry is the by-product of my working at being, in as much of my life as is possible, a poet."

And on the page facing the one from which I have just quoted, Needleman says, "Crafts are about one thing: the secret of how to work." So is poetry. The "work" of poetry involves technique, yes, and knowledge, yes, but it also requires patience, diligence, listening, openness, solitude, experience, the willingness to fail, and the habit of picking oneself up after failure and starting again. My guess is that "Sophie" took more than one draft. My guess is that this poet spends lots of time revising and rethinking and reflecting on the various drafts of her poems. "Sophie" is one of the by-products of that way of being and working, rather than the product of any particular aspect of the poet's education or experience. To an important extent, poetry arises from an array of habits that are poem-friendly, so to speak. What exactly those habits are is summarized but not fully explored, above.

So it is life (not too easy or comfortable, we hope) and experience (broad and emotionally and spiritually daring, we hope) and practice (daily, and under the coaching of a good writer-teacher, we hope) and solitude (actively sought out and brought regularly into daily life, we hope) and the richness of our experiences with poetry (constant reading and discovery of new poets and new approaches to poetry, we hope) that all contribute to the growth of the poet and to the lives of the poem. It is not surprising at all that a technically adept poem by a young person may not be great—how could it be, given all the life and study and talent and grace that greatness requires? But it can, if the young poet is dedicated and diligent, be good.

Thus "Sophie," remarkable for its careful craft, and for its restraint—the poet never shakes the camera—is a good poem. At this point in the poet's life and experience, that goodness is plenty to have achieved.

What Can You Use A Poem For?

It all depends on what's broken.
If it's your head,
the poem is a bandage
that will hold it together
till it heals.

Or you can use a poem, if you have to,
in the place of love.
It gives and accepts,
expands and contracts,
responds to your attention.
It holds you tight
and whispers in your ear.
It loves your flesh as its own.
It reproduces you.

Or a poem is the wrench that turns
your mind,
the hammer that clinches the nails
in the house of meaning you're building.
It's a hoe that weeds your life,
a plough that opens your ground.

And if it's your peace that's broken
by work or care,
the poem is the old chair
you hauled way out in the woods
and left by the creek
for just such a time:
it's to sit in a spell and rest.

What Can You Use A Poem For?

A somewhat facetious though partly sincere reply to the impossible question. Many have agreed with the notion that "poems make nothing happen," that they are good for nothing but themselves, that they are, in terms of the "practical" world, "useless." Maybe so. But it may also be true that they share, as do all living things, some special purpose, however obscure, in the scheme of things.

I remember a statement by a famous scientist, something to effect that "the height of arrogance and ignorance is to ask of any organism, 'What good is it?'"

On that score, here's a poem in reply to a student who asked, in innocent curiosity, I might add, a similar question when we were studying Maxine Kumin's "Woodchucks." I was grateful for her question because it prompted a poem that helped me understand, too.

"What Good Does A Woodchuck Do?"

for Stephanie Conlon, who asked

1
Where we cannot go, it goes,
travels the landscape's subway,
knows the buried meteor,
the cache of Indian bones,
the tight-packed native undershelves
of our laxer, greed-drunk world.
Brings to light what was lost
to time and avalanche and glacier:
paves its small clay porch
with amethysts and relics.
Helps the earth to breathe and drink.
Harvest wild's abundance.
Feeds the fox and badger.

2
Offers us another way of knowing:
imagining the groundhog,
its fat loping gallop
across the road

from woods to field,
imagining ourselves in its flesh,
we see the world intensely,
scent in every turn of wind
the instinctive essences of things:
clover, berry, beagle, rose.
Thus creation, for the groundhog
we become,
is ever birthbright, fresh, renewed.

3
Even never having seen one
is a hint, an education: we've failed
to know our neighbors and our place.
Having never seen one
is a goad to live differently, and better:
slower, more open and alert,
walking dirt roads in the country,
chewing a stalk of grass,
remembering our older and other selves,
our own low-to-the-ground beginnings.

4
"For the humble shall be exalted."
The woodchuck rises haloed,
made a minor saint and martyr
in a poem's hard felt grace,
one vision of the treasure
we might build the wealth of mind on.

* * *

Poems sometimes arise in opposition to the standard ways of thinking of things, or of seeing and saying things. Much hay can be made (forgive the mixed metaphors) by listening to the world with an arguer's ear. Write some poems about things most people consider "useless" or "ugly" or "trivial" or "stupid," showing their beauty or function or inspirational qualities.

See also "From The Porch To The Page: Memory, History, and A Poem" in the Notes to "What You Should Eat Before Reading The Poem."

In one of the hundreds of wonderful connections in the lives of the poem, Stephanie Conlon, to whom "What Good Does A Woodchuck Do?" is dedicated, married Andy Hull, one of my favorite at-home workshoppers. Andy wrote several memorable poems, a couple of which were included in the Special Tenth Anniversary issue of *Hackberry: Purcell Marian's Literary Magazine.* Here they are:

Creation Day One

Wound up tight

I give it its freedom
sparkling darkness
uncoiling and spinning

but is there a point where it will all come back

still spinning and recoiling
no worse for the wear
wound up tight

again?

Here's a poem that has made friends with physics—with cosmology, actually, and is now playing in the serious way that poetry and science can play together. Notice the shape of the poem—how it resembles a spiral galaxy, seen on edge, the incredible dense mass of stars like a fuzzy ball of light at its center, then the narrow disk of stars pirouetting out in the arms.

Related to this, the poem knows one of the cosmological theories known as The Oscillating Universe. This model says that though the universe is expanding (like this poem as it nears its middle) it will once again fall in and collapse upon itself at the end of time (just like this poem as it contracts towards its conclusion.) The poem's title remembers that even at the beginning of things, the end is present.

Andy centered this poem on the page in the early days of word processing. The centering function is a danger to poets who use it indiscriminately, for the shape of a poem on the page ought to be a deliberately chosen matter, not merely a handy eye-catcher that can be accomplished with the click of a mouse. Some poems indeed, like this one, do call for centering. Andy wanted the poem to look like a galaxy. But think about whether your poem about a monkey, or about randomness, or about the river, should be centered neatly like this. Perhaps your poem's theme and subject suggest another shape, another structure. I hardly ever assume a poem is finished unless I have fiddled with its physical appearance, making stanzas where there were none previously, changing the line-lengths, fooling around in order to see if something I was not aware of might emerge. Beware the habit of finishing too quickly, and of allowing the machine to make decisions for you.

Here's one more by Andy; it is built of several oppositions and ends with a kind of gift—a piece of dialogue delivered directly to the speaker. At first seeming little more than a miscellany, it has a coherence built on irony, and its light touch is remarkable.

Sunday Best

I'm sitting in my Sunday booth
gnawing on the last biscuit
from the breakfast bar

a young black boy
by the windows
explains to an older man
the reason the U. S. invaded Panama

Mr. and Mrs. Grier
with their two children
sit to my right, against the wall

Mrs. Grier tells young Jonathon
he must do well in class
because one day he will be
Dr. Grier

He wants to be an astronaut

Mrs. Grier tells Cindy
she must practice her flute
because one day she will play
in Music Hall

She wants to be the doctor

A man and his lady friend
sit across from me

discussing their dream cottage

It will be in Rolling Meadow, Maine
it will have a leather couch by
a real fire place

A little girl walking by
on the way to her booth
stops to tell me

This is my Sunday best

The Poem Turns Back Toward Familiar Territory And Fails

Mingo Junction, George's Run—
they might as well have been Katmandu,
Algiers. In his absence,
they had changed on him,
and when he came back, pushing the new poem
before him like an empty wheelbarrow,
nothing fit. The mills had
crumbled, their mountains of rust
blown away like the years,
the river even sicker than before,
a furrow of red oxide through the hills
like the gouge a bad plow
cuts in a field.

He ate lunch at the old place under the bridge,
the troll he remembered
now a councilman.
Little Leaguers he'd run with
now played fusion rock in Chicago.

The nuns at his grade school
had grown younger, wore jeans,
shopped at K-Mart for bargains.

Along about dark,
two boys rode by in a pickup,
and the old poem suddenly revived.
Something they threw
splattered on the pavement.
He lit a match and looked:
a copy of *New Times*,
a pair of sushi salesmen
grinning on the cover.

So at midnight, lost and drunk,
the station a dream in dim light,
he hopped a bus for Wheeling,
leaving the new poem

talking to a blond with no teeth,
the mayor's wife,
the queen of his prom,
someone it never knew.

The Poem Turns Back Toward Familiar Territory And Fails

Here's one of those poems that caught an editor's eye. A very complimentary note accompanied its acceptance, and it made my day. I was doubly happy because it appeared in a journal in my native territory, the upper Ohio Valley, and I like to believe that it was accepted in part because it knew its way around there, and that the editor considered this important. There was no inkling of any bias against it because it was local, or because it was about poetry.

Don't be stupid about it: know where you're sending things, and have a working knowledge of the kinds of work they like. At the same time, be stubborn: maybe some people need to have their eyes opened, their horizons expanded, news brought to them from unfamiliar provinces.

The Poem Finds Its Poet

Hung over after a bad year of exile
in college seminars,
white wine muzak bistros,
arid gulags of graduate programs,
the poem wakes up mean.
It takes to the river bank back home
where it grows an eye
like a needle's,
then curls at its other end,
sprouts barbs,
sharpens.
It invents a line
and ties it through its eye.
Then it waits for high water
instead of high talk,
welcomes the blather
of stove-in doors, clorox bottles,
the fleet of old whitewalls
tumbled bald in the flood—
all disasters the poem loves—
and gets its line tangled
in a willow on the bank
exactly where it wants it:
man-high,
at just about the shoulder,
the hook of itself hanging free.

Soon enough
a fellow stumbles by,
breaking through brush
toward the fishing hole.

The poems snags him
like a trot-line in air,
stabs the meat of his upper arm,
right through his shirtsleeve,
catches hold and won't let go.

The man curses,
drops his tackle, spills
his cup of worms.
But then he settles down,
does what he knows to do:
he pushes the poem in deeper,
fights it on up and out of his flesh,
then clips its barb off,
pulls the shank
back through.

The full hurt. All of it,
but bleeding, clean.
He gathers his gear,
stomps off for the river.
Thinks his trouble's over.

Meanwhile,
the poem considers
this man: his history of beer and wives,
ripe bait and bad debts,
double-crosses and survivals—
just the stuff a poem needs.
And so it thinks of fish,
and fish appear:
yellow mudcats
with their poisonous spines,
slashing, saw-toothed gars,
heavy-jawed muskellunges
that know how to chop
the minnow of a finger—
all of them deep,
just upstream,
beginning to drift
his way.

The Poem Finds Its Poet

The discovery of the poet through which the poem may manifest itself—the word making itself flesh, so to speak—is one of the great adventures in the lives of the poem. It's even more dramatic when the poem escapes school and teachers by virtue of nothing more than its innate orneriness, and returns to its native territory to exact a kind of revenge.

This poem wants the common details of common life—the flooding creek, the trash that tumbles down it, the unsuspecting accomplice and all the failures and shortcomings of his life—and it will have them. There's no resisting.

* * *

Write a poem about something in your life that cannot be resisted, for good or ill. Write about it as if it has a life of its own. Make sure to give it a body so that it does not simply remain incorporeal ideas—poetry gets physical with us, doesn't it? Remember Katie The Red's "poems without bodies."

The Poem Turns Mean

All night it lunges
like a neighbor's pit bull,
thick-necked,
dark claws mauling
the earth.
If a chipmunk runs by,
it eats it,
smashing the skull
like the wings of a wren.

By morning it has chewed
its leash to feathers,
torn up the yard
like a backhoe.

Still, you approach it
kindly,
hoping the best,
feeding sweet verbs.
It rips off your arm.
As you bleed to death,
it fixes on you
its hard green eyes—

beautiful jades
grown warm
on the throat
of a queen.

The Poem Turns Mean

It was no less a poet than Shelley, in his "A Defense of Poetry" who wrote:

> [P]oetry turns all things to loveliness; it exalts the beauty of that which is most beautiful, and it adds beauty to that which is most deformed; it marries exultation and horror, grief and pleasure, eternity and change; it subdues to union all irreconcilable things.

Jewels, the throat of queen, a pit bull. The union of irreconcilable things! I encourage in my writing students a habit which I call "Poking The Possum." It is based on the behavior we humans exhibit of being attracted to horrid disorder—car wrecks, the scenes of fires or explosions—or to roadkill. How many times I have seen little kids get off a school bus and start walking home, only to bunch up around the smashed body of a possum or squirrel in the street. Inevitably, a kid will pick up a stick or grab a pencil from his bookbag, and to a grossed-out chorus of *oohs* lift the skull, or pry open the death-grin of the jaw to see the teeth, or lever the sticky tail off the blacktop. The natural disgust we feel over such sights of physical wreckage is overcome by something else even more powerful, and that powerful thing, I think, is linked to poetry—and perhaps to all forms of creativity. As I have mentioned before, if you scour Leonardo's notebooks, you will find drawings of all sorts of complicated chaos—smoke, fires, swirling waters.

It is a test of Shelley's theories about poetry to see if we can make a poem that is itself beautiful in some way or ways—in its imagery or patterns of sound, for example—despite its subject being gross or disgusting. Likewise, it is equally interesting to see if what is generally considered beautiful might not, upon closer examination, be in some way repulsive or ugly.

Cultivating the habit of Poking the Possum makes us more courageous in the subjects we are willing to explore in our poems. The habit of hunting out beauty is a good one, good for life, good for those who suffer from a lack of it in their lives. And the habit of discovering the ugly and irrational realities beneath apparent beauty or manners or good sense is also a useful tool in a society that needs constantly to guard itself from scams and ad-men, from abuses of language touting fraudulent bills of goods.

* * *

Write a few poems in this Ugly/Pretty exercise. Then turn it around, and write a few poems that are Pretty/Ugly. Below is one I wrote during a workshop on poetry I gave a few years ago. (What a high it is to "write in public" along with workshoppers, to put poetry on the line and hope that it will produce, and even what a highlow, if you'll allow the word, to fail in public as well). I admit that this poem performs some rather obvious sleight-of-hand (by simply positing that the wart hog can sing, for example). But if the world it creates allows the reader to suspend his or her disbelief, even for a moment, then, as far as the poem goes, a wart hog *can* sing.

Warthog

All who see it
for the first time recoil:
its strange recurving tusks,
its piggish snout, its squat
hairy ugliness, its habits of filth,
slobber, mud.

But it is the finest
singer among all things
pig-like and offensive,
finer even than the jackal,
dugong, and razorback boar.
It can dance beautifully
to Bach and Mozart,
raising delicate dusts
with its pointed hooves.
It can paint with
the cruddy brush
of its tail
all swiftnesses of blue wind,
deep green foliage
stirred by the storm;
it can brighten even
the gold spume of autumn
washing down
Mount Lookout's
brilliant sides.

— Cincinnati Public Library, Sunday, Sept. 6, 1997

What Could Be Going On

A boy writes the finest poem
in the English language
one morning
(who's to say he couldn't:
this might happen every day,
in every town,
one of life's dark jests)
and then abandons it
in his locker at the doomed school
just two days before
he knows the demolition
will begin.
All summer
he walks by in the dusty afternoon,
watching the headache ball
beat the building down,
his poem inside the debris
somewhere,
like a small white note or soul,
as he cheers the wreckers on.

What Could Be Going On

Despite the best efforts, some students are unreachable. It is as if they are somehow immune to education. When they are gifted, it is painful to see the years pass with no apparent growth of their abilities. But the world is the way it is, and I know for sure that there are good poets—and probably a great one or two—who will never write a poem, or only a few—which they will treat as they would a cluster of tumors—to be swiftly removed from them. See "The Annunciation."

* * *

And so the ones who do devote themselves to the work, and grow, and continue it even after school—they make up for the ones who deny or abandon their gifts.

Despite the remark captured in the epigraph of "Dancing Alone In The Dark" (pg. 109), Katie The Red DuMont went on to write a number of fully bodied poems, including some sexy vignettes set in a local night club and in some late-night restaurants. Here's one of my favorites:

In The Smoking Section

Lady night caresses
the corner of her booth.
One leg
Stretched out
In a black leather yawn.
The other pressed like a shield
to her chest.
She sits,
acting like her life
is as secure
as the cling in her tank top.
Pulling out a Camels hard pack,
she's reminded by the pyramids
of her dreaming Egypt,
of wanting to go there.
She takes a deep hit back to reality,
tosses the cigarettes on the table
and exhales a sigh of smoke.

There are some good things in this poem. After the personification and characterization "lady night," I especially admire the image of her "One leg/ Stretched out/ In a black leather yawn." Here we get a physical detail that helps us compose our picture of this young lady, dressed in her tight leather pants. We get an intimation of her fashionably cool ennui. Most of all, we are delighted by the surprising transferred epithet of "a black leather yawn" and by the contrasts between the sexy hipness of her manner and dress with the ironic conservatism of her lifestyle and its holding her as tightly as "the cling of her tank top." As the poem unfolds, we are impressed by all that goes unsaid—by all that is implicit about the woman's deferred dreams, and the many "hits" she has probably suffered from reality—because she's locked into her role of midnight diva, with no apparent possibility of getting to her "dreamed Egypt." No wonder she smokes Camels—it's the closest she'll ever get. What at first glance might appear to be a hard-boiled club person, aggressively dressed and holding the world at bay, really turns out to be a hard-hit vulnerable person whose dreams may well remain unrealized. There is at once in the poem a close, cold look at this person and yet a sympathetic understanding of her, a kind of pity for the predicament she is in.

Now, one more important fact about the life of any poem. Most of what happens in Katie's poem happens at a level that is at once more than, and less than, conscious. To put it most simply, more is going on in the poem than Katie was consciously orchestrating during the writing of it. And here's the hard part: the poet must be aware of this fact, and labor in a way so as not to frighten off the unconscious, the powerful forces that give us many of the riches the lives of the poem can provide.

Here's another Katie The Red poem literally embodying its subject.

A Poem About Writing Poetry

Straddling the dictionary
I punctuate metaphor
Pressing poetic thighs
Astride pages
Arousing the space
Between words
I slide skin
Slowly into definitions
Words merge
Poems
Spilling
Down
My legs.

198

In her daily life, Katie is modest and kind and in many ways, as conservative and proper as anyone could be. But the lives of the poem are not exactly our lives, and the rules may be very different in them. "A Poem About Writing Poetry" is certainly living its own life, not Katie's, wild and sensual and—despite her earlier disclaimer—completely incarnated. Our poems may, and will, go places we ourselves never would in actual life.

Speaking of actual life: "A Poem About Writing Poetry" had a life beyond the pleasure of itself. Katie submitted it to a writing contest sponsored by *Ohio Writer* magazine, in the "Writing About Writing" category, and won Second Prize. The other poem that accompanied it is this one:

About Purchasing A Poster of A Wizard Writing An Ancient Book During A Moment of Writer's Block

I tack inspiration
on the ceiling
right above my bed,
spreading smooth
its flames
and feathers
and cosmic wizardry,
then I fall,
flat onto my pillow,
pulling my pen
and paper
to me
like a blanket,
waiting for
candle-wax
and smoke
and ink
to drip
down dreams
that'll wake me
from my own
into the moment
of a poem's
rising.

The Poem Does Lunch Out East

The poem shows up
at the editor's office
during rehabbing:
bits of old plaster
pock the manuscripts
on his desk
where the windows were,
sheets of drywall
rise from floor to ceiling.
Overhead, an emergency lamp
glares as if lighting a disaster
or confession.

Meanwhile, out in Ohio,
the world glows like an angel
or a nova, and continually,
in every township,
lights and visions blaze.

Back East, during the noon brownout,
the poem and the editor do lunch
at the editor's club,
named after a blessed martyr
of the Ninth Century, where, left alone
for a few moments in a room
with a dim painting
of a deceased university president,
the poem begins
a long string of curses,
muttered like a mantra under its breath.

Scrod, broccoli in cheese,
a tinny white wine. The editor leans
confidentially across the table,
asks the poem (it is thinking now
of holy verses, sacred lines, the long
responsibility of itself in print)
if it remembers a Cincinnati
basketball game twenty years ago.
No, the poem lies, astonished.

"Well that's that then, isn't it?"

All the way back to his office,
cheerful in victory,
the editor advises the poem to change
its ways, calm its language down,
join a support group
or the Society of St. Jude.

Halfway up his broken office steps,
the editor turns to face the poem,
and waves, a smiling Nixon-like farewell,
incumbent,
minor salesman,
his soft white palm
the habitual flag
of surrender in the sun.

The Poem Does Lunch Out East

My first big-time literary lunch took place a few months after the editor had judged one of my poems as the best of the year in a Midwestern literary journal. He had been there at the reception for the winners, we'd talked, and he'd told me to send him some poems, and if I was ever out his way, to look him up; we'd have lunch. I did, I was, and I did.

It was not a success, and, unless you are dealing for some mediocre page-turner of a novel that people will read on the beach in the summer to keep from falling asleep with their faces in the sand, such sham ceremonials rarely are. Spend your time more wisely: take a shower, get a tooth fixed, go to confession.

Swayed By Critical Opinion,
The Poem Gets Its Posthumous Credentials

The poem knew its way around books,
but so what?
Anybody could do that.
Indices, tables of contents,
software and modems,
cross-references
like the blind leading the blind.
And all that dust!
Every time the poem opened a recent volume,
the words broke apart like ash,
the Lent of ideas.

It thought of making a living
selling insurance, driving a truck,
operating a mine.
Not for long.
It decided to devote its days
to themselves,
shape a kind of priestly existence
out of attentive hours.

Nobody around would hire it.
It slept under papers in the street.

People stepped over it on the way to the bank.

Then one day it died.
It was buried in an envelope
with no stamp by a couple of truants
blowing bad dope in an alley.

Shit happens:
ten years later it was famous,
the trash of its grave thrown back
by an obscure scholar's revisions.
Come to, the poem blinked its eyes:
professors and students,
computers and call-slips,
footnotes, footnotes, footnotes.
The poem cleaned itself up.

It revised its vita.
It bought a tie.
It learned to quibble,
studied doubt,
turned on itself
like a blinding searchlight,

then deconstructed,
hard.

Swayed By Critical Opinion, The Poem Gets Its Posthumous Credentials

Among contemporary literary theorists, there are some, called deconstructionists, (hence the word "deconstruct" in the poem) who believe that any literary text has no inherent meaning, but "means" only and all what any individual reader can make of it. Thus, it is useless to trust that the writer had any meaning in mind, or that the writer might have cooperated with the process successfully, so that meaning arose from the writer's engagement with the forms and patterns of the world. No, according to "deconstruction," the poem or novel may be reconstructed by any reader to "mean" whatever that reader wants it to. Such theorists, of course, are not very popular among writers, who try, for the most part, to clarify and focus what they have come to understand the world "means" to them. They resent theorists who come along and tell them, and their readers, that what you thought you were getting is not at all what you were getting.

Here is another passage from my notebooks, and I have failed this time to note from where I took it. Bad boy. Though in the heat of the chase, we might be distracted, or pressed for time, we must still note the details. I didn't this time, and shame on me. But this point is so well-expressed, and so germane to the poem, I have to quote it anyway.

"Deconstruction!" [the author and psychologist Robert] Coles exclaimed. "Craziness! Abstractions gone perverse . . . Envy of the storyteller. Let us not deconstruct. Let us celebrate and honor, and most of all, offer to others, hand one another along with these stories and poems. And respect ourselves. No matter the pressure from the theorists . . . Hold onto the message, the effort of a human being to understand this world and find some vision of its meanings. Our job [is] to understand for ourselves and understand with those we teach. If that is not the Lord's calling, I don't know what is."

See yet again "The Annunciation."

On Reading That The Little Man Inside The Poet Isn't Very Happy With His Life

Beg pardon, buddy,
but he's happy, that little man,
and if he isn't, he's a fool.
Plus, he's not so little
as you think:
a man of sandstone and fossil shale,
his spine is as long as the Appalachians.
Giant, he loafs
in hollows where every creek
roars down to him
like moonshine
filtered through hickory,
ginseng, old walnut.

Hell, he's drunk—
or something like it,
only better—
half the day, and the rest of his time
he invents: tricky ghosts
of fog,
whippoorwills that sling
music over the ridges
like silver vines,
hypnotic balls of foxfire.

There's no gap
in creation
he can't fill
with some putty of verb,
some shim of a noun,
some mitered, smooth-grained
image.

His wife wears
the skin of persimmons,
blushes with frost,
sweetens in hard weather.
His kids speak

the native tongues
that peel off
shagbarks in wind.

Not happy?
Lord, he lives where
he lives,
laughs, falls down, sleeps,

dreams the good dreams
and knows a poem
when he finds one—
the intricate knee
of a groundhog
killed on the road,
heaven's own light
in the hillside's quaking aspens,
the way water
gives up its secrets
to the net of his mind
like a handful
of tiny fish.

On Reading That The Little Man Inside The Poet
Isn't Very Happy With His Life

In 1987 a friend and local poetry scene colleague of mine, F. Keith Wahle, published the following poem in the first number of *Soaptown: A Magazine Of Cincinnati Writing*, edited by another of my friends and colleagues, Rick Stansberger. I helped edit the next two (the writing community in any city or county is probably a small one; many writers know one another. This is as it should be. It's lonely enough work; not to have some sort of community to commiserate with and to enjoy the fruits of the labor with is probably cruel and unusual punishment.) There were only three issues of *Soaptown*—many literary magazines are ephemeral; they are, as someone else must have said somewhere, the mayflies of literature.

Here's Keith's poem:

Autobiography Of A Poet

There is a little man
living inside me who just keeps saying,
"Write this poem!"
"Write that poem!"
I don't think he's very
happy with his life.

I think it was immediately after reading this that I was moved to start "On Reading That The Little Man . . ." Keith's poem well expresses one late Romantic and Victorian notion of the poet that still enjoys a wide currency. Poets are unhappy people, this notion suggests. And writing poetry is not a means of connecting with the joy of life, but is a burden, a kind of disease. Though it is true to some extent that poetry can be hard on the poet, that it can take him or her into uncomfortable places (see again "The Poem Finds Its Poet," or "The Poem Rends The Veil"), this concept of poetry and the poet really stems from some popular myths about poets fostered by the public lives of such Romantics as Byron and Shelley, and the unhappily complicated psyches of such modern poets as Sylvia Plath, Anne Sexton and John Berryman, all of whom committed suicide. Despite the hip attractiveness of ennui and angst and despair, it's simply not a requirement that poets be unhappy or strange or neurotic; that they sometimes are is no more true of poets in general than it is of baseball players, or McDonald's managers, or astronauts.

That said, it is nevertheless true that there may be a compulsive or addictive aspect to the lives of the poem. In her "Moose in Morning, Northern

Maine," Mona Van Duyn records a conversation she remembers as she sits waiting for a poem:

I am hunting for nothing—
perhaps the three cold pencils
that lie on the table like kindling
could be used to start the logs.
I remember Ted Weiss saying,
"At the exhibition I suddenly realized
Picasso had to remake
everything he laid his eyes on
into an art object.
He couldn't let the world alone.
Since then I don't write every morning."

Perhaps Keith's poem is about this sort of compulsion, and the resulting negative effect on the artist (although I don't see where it hurt Picasso, one of the most prolific—and playful— artists of all time.) Some interesting questions are raised by all this: Can a person write too much? Can writing become an addiction and bring with it some of the negative side-effects of any addiction? Can writing be a way of escaping life, rather than, as Robert Frost characterized it, a "pursuit" of life? Even more troublesome: can writing become a substitute for life? See "the Poet At Fifty Walks Away from Writing."

* * *

There is a long tradition of poems written in reply to other poems, and of poems written in imitation of other poems. Find someone to ask who would know where you might look for a few examples. Read them, see how they work. Then be on the watch for poems to reply to or to imitate yourself. In the meantime, cultivate a friendship with the person who helped you.

* * *

Sometimes, the poems are answered by other poems by the same poet. In many ways, these lives of the poem poems are a kind of conversation, now agreeing, now disagreeing, one spurring the other to another idea or situation. Here are two poems by Joe Patt, a quiet young man who wrote these finely

209

crafted little lyrics throughout his months with us. An effective reviser, Joe produced these in the period of December 1987–January 1988.

Night Garden

Off tempo lightning bugs
   rise from the garden.
   A dark path of wind
   will guide them to another palace of green.
Crickets chant about the hose,
   a still highway of current
   that bathes in the moon.

When water soothes the vegetables
   a robust river sighs.
   The settlers on the banks
   are night crawlers, wallowing in the roots.
The owl's eyes pierce the night's mystique
   and he recites a poem:
   "Moon Falls Like Snow."

Moon Falls Like Snow

Pale caresses plateau,
subsides, clouds cover,
resumes, clouds pass.
Twilight to birth of day.

Silver hums to the land,
whispers melody
through dark breeze.
Night's guard over sleeping body.

Glow melts in my hair.
Dreams of bottling moonshine
fall like snow.
Savor it on tongue.

210

Nice poems. I like the hushed quality of "Moon Falls Like Snow," created in large part by Joe's deliberately short sentences. Something happens, briefly, and then there is silence for a time . . .

Going back to Keith Wahle's poem: Is it really a "little man" inside the poet? Maybe it's really a "little woman." Or a "big woman." Or a "womanly man," or "manly woman," as Shakespeare played with gender roles in *Antony and Cleopatra.* Explore the possibilities in a series of at least five related poems.

* * *

My teaching life and the lives of the poem are inextricably twined. So sometimes teaching gets into my poetry, and poetry into my teaching: good things, both ways. Here are some comments and poems that arose one school year:

Fear And Ogres And Kissing Dragons: The Big Poetry Mama Poems

Last winter [this was written in the spring of 1993] I was invited by Kathy Ray, a colleague in the English Department at Purcell Marian, to visit her ninth-grade class and to introduce poetry to them. I soon learned that their ideas of poetry were either that it rhymed and had regular meter or that it galloped along wildly, reined in neither by punctuation or sentence sense or the tension of the line. It was always about confusion or freedom or justice or love, and it frequently contained puppies, butterflies, kaleidoscopes, and something pleasantly (as opposed to grossly) soft or squishy.

When I began to suggest some other ways of thinking about poetry— especially working with them on cultivating the happy and fertile chaos that Natalie Goldberg calls "Wild Mind," they backed away in disbelief and terror. When I asked them to share drafts so that we could talk about what revising looks like in poetry, no one volunteered. A great anxious silence prevailed.

Ornery, I let it prevail until it was absolutely uncomfortable. And then I let it prevail some more. Finally, the bell rang, and the students fled, as if there were some ogre loose in the room.

At the time, I was not very much aware of how personally students took their own poetry and the criticism of it. Wait—that's not true: I was very much aware of it, but had yet to let that awareness change my teaching. And so I just

211

blundered headlong into the whole mess, trampling the kids and probably poetry, too. I cringe a little as I read back on what I did that day, but forgive myself, because I know that poetry is so large and various that no one teacher can fully ruin it for anyone, at least not in most cases. (Maybe I'm just rationalizing here: I never had a teacher who ruined it for me; even looking back from a very critical fellow-educator's vantage-point, I think that the worst any of my high school teachers did was not to know very much about contemporary American or European poetry, though they might have recited Poe and Longfellow *ad nauseam.*)

The evening of that class, mulling it all over at home, I remembered Rilke's observation to the effect that sometimes the most frightening dragons in our lives are just princes (or princesses) waiting for us to kiss them. Was there some way, I wondered, short of removing myself forever from their presence, to defuse the fear and uncertainty, the unwillingness or inability to risk, that had so paralyzed the students? I began to think of poetry as that dragon, and of ways to get the students close enough to kiss it, and so see it transform. Right then I chanced to glance at a magazine containing the photograph of a woman who had donned the over-sized head of a gorilla. She belonged to a Chicago theater troupe; the gorilla head was some sort of costume. Her simple and elegant black dress contrasted startlingly with the head, and that gave me an opening. Yes, poetry might be frightening and challenging, but it can be encouraging and strengthening as well. It could be like the wolf that mothered the infants Romulus and Remus, the founders of mighty Rome—a wild but somehow simultaneously nurturing thing. That notion gave me a way to marry Wild Mind with Mama, and it was immediately clear that there were comic possibilities in the marriage that might help release the students' tension. They could talk back in their poems to the Big Poetry Mama, and so gain a little power and control, and maybe even exorcise some artistic demons.

The next day, I came in with a three-foot by two-foot cardboard shrine to Big Poetry Mama, covered with ancient and powerful images of women I had collected from magazines and encyclopedias and then enlarged and photocopied: The Venus of Willendorf, an Abyssinian sculpture, a bust of an Egyptian queen, a late nineteenth century photo of a Zulu or Wariri mother, and the woman from Chicago in the gorilla's head.

And I think it worked. The students were still reticent about sharing their work, but when I invited them to "talk back" to poetry, to open a kind of sassy dialogue with it that might lead eventually to lessening their fears and, perhaps, if they "kissed the dragon," might even lead to a transformation of their perceptions of poetry, their discomfort began to diminish. Regrettably, I did not save any of those student poems.

I wrote a few Big Poetry Mama poems myself, too, and I was pleased to find her as large and as powerful and as comic as I had suspected she might be. She is, after all, just the Muse in one of her thousand disguises, though more vigorous and ornery, perhaps, than many might suspect.

Big Poetry Mama Warns About Backseat Drivers

They'll steer you all wrong,
send you flying over cliffs
or head-on into disaster.
Better to drive yourself,
to need no one
telling you what to do,
cajoling, assigning,
threatening,
pounding the desk in anger.
Figure yourself where you want to go,
then go there.
Make your own rules,
draw your own map.
Love the journey.
Find yourself.

Where Does Big Poetry Mama Live?

In the dirt under your fingernails,
where the world seeds wait to sprout.
At night, your hands like strangers
on the quilt,
small tendrils feel their ways
from your fingertips
across your stomach,
down your thighs and calves,
spreading and branching
like green veins.
Toward dawn, what they spell
across your body and bed
        is her poem.

The Little Students Get Their First Glimpse
Of The Big Poetry Mama

Off on the horizon they see her,
a great cloud as from the Book of Job
approaching. She speaks gobbledygook,
revelation, locker room.
She'll kill them all like chickens.

This they have been told
by the Dog-Eat-Doggers, that tribe haggard,
hairless—that pack of cowards and dolts.
Sadly, the children believe them.

"Poetry is so big she will stomp
you flat," the Dog-Eat-Doggers shout.
"She will eat you up and
shit you out like ashes."

So,
when they feel her hugeness approaching,
when they feel themselves drawn to her
as the ocean is drawn by the moon,
when they feel her secret magnets
start to tug on their little iron words,
the children fall back and cower
like lemmings, fools.

They have forgotten all they know
about Superman, about She-Ra,
about Davy Crockett and Joan of Arc.
Except for one of them—
a tiny fellow with red hair and braces,
a Warrior of Dreaming,
courageous and wild about writing.

He stands up, waving his arms and shouting,
"Over here. I'm over here!"

Lightning strikes him, he turns blue,
he walks high across the air,
his feet spin like fiery propellers;

he is a hero and his name
is what the stars spell out
against the night,
which is Big Poetry mama's skin,
her voice, the names she makes
that stick to everything.

Big Poetry Mama Gives The Beginning Poets Some Groveling Lessons

First, get down on your knees.
Now try writing something, try.
See? The blood thickens, the sweat pours,
and everything you say is stupid, stupid.
So get up and apologize to me.
Say, "Big Poetry Mama,
I'm sorry. I didn't mean to butcher your song.
I didn't mean to dangle your participle.
I didn't mean to give you a bad name
with my juvenile silly rhymes."

Say. "Big Poetry mama,
forgive me for I have sinned.
I have written about a puppy.
I have written about a butterfly.
I have written about Love.
And truly, I don't know diddly
about it."

Say, "Big Poetry Mama,
I beg your pardon.
I didn't mean to choke you
with abstractions,
I didn't mean to tangle you up
in my grammar mistakes.
I didn't mean to make you look
ugly because I was too lazy to type."

Say, "Big Poetry Mama, if you
forgive me, I will let you take
my first child,

my happiest days,
my life, my life, my life."

Say, "Please, Big Poetry Mama,
O please!"

What Big Poetry Mama Thinks About Grammar And Punctuation And Usage And Such

I ain't never heard no crazier question
except the time the mountain asked, "What's rain?"
You really think I care about
commas and apostrophes?
They ain't nothing but flies in your eyes,
smoke in your ears,
foolishness for cowards and drudges.

You want to know about them things,
don't look to no book.
Just go ahead and write
and meanwhile listen to me.

Whatever I say goes.
Whatever I say don't, don't.
Period.

* * *

Write some poems in which you talk back to poetry—or to music, or painting, or photography, or any other of the arts. Or let those things have a voice, and let them speak to their viewers or creators. Listen for what surprising things they might have to say.

Spiel For Opening Night Of The Workshop

It's luck I wish you. Wake the happy words.
—Theodore Roethke

When I say,
"If someone knocks at the door
and you are writing,
don't get up; let the ghosts
keep dancing in the attic,
flailing their veils,"

I do not mean
give up everything, starve,
don't work, don't be wrong
and young and subject
to cliché.

I do not mean don't play,
nor stop your troublesome
silliness,
nor give up your crazy
warpings of the language.

I do not mean
be serious.

I mean for you
to grow toward
what you are
in the easy summers of your laughter,
the trees of your thought
flush with leaves
and fruits as weird as pawpaws.

I mean for you
to turn water into
wine, and to stagger
drunkenly from every faucet.

I mean for you
to ignore the truth

217

and believe your dreams,
so that, someday, waking,
you might find the world
what you have imagined.

But if it is not,
I mean for you
to tell riddles
to all the sleepers,

to wake them up,
to give them your
fresh eyes
made of roses,
your magic rubber gloves
that play punch-line music
on pianos,
your haiku
made of flies' wings
that explode
like fireworks
in their pockets.

I mean for you
to turn over
the carpets in their
high-tech living rooms
to show them
what beetles write
in floorboards,
and to translate
for their roaring Hoovers
all the homely epics
of the dust.

Spiel For Opening Night Of The Workshop

When I first began teaching, I thought my job was to maintain a great distance between myself and students (to be fair to myself, I was only four years older than they were, dangerously close, and this in the late Sixties, a wild and risky time. My instinct to keep some distance then was correct, I think.) Now I know, however, that the kind of teaching and learning together that takes place in a classroom or workshop cannot be conducted at much distance; trust and respect need to grow quickly, and they can only do so when a certain closeness and shared experience is cultivated.

Writing And Place

I'm again harping on the close-to-home, the what-you-have. I hope it is understood that this is one angle, just one approach, to the lives of the poem. I trust (though I find it difficult to imagine for myself) that it is possible for someone without a sense of place, or home, to write beautiful and enviable poems. Part of the lives of the poem is that they are multiple: *lives*, not *a* life. Look at some evidence:

> I've been a foreigner for the past twenty years. I don't have roots anymore. My roots are in my memory and my writing. That's why memory is so important. Who are you but what you can remember? I have a very bad memory, so I invent my memories, all the time, and I remember things that never happened. Now I'm called a narrator because I make a living with my lies, but before I was just a liar.
> —Isabel Allende

> . . . No life and no place is destitute; all have possibilities of productivity and pleasure, rest and work, solitude and conviviality, that belong particularly to themselves. These possibilities exist everywhere, in the country or in the city, it makes no difference. All that is necessary is the time and inner quietness to look for them, the sense to recognize them and the grace to welcome them.
> . . . Any way at all of joining and using the air and light and weather of your own place . . . is a making and a having that you cannot get from TV or government or school.
> —Wendell Berry, "Family Work" in *The Gift Of Good Ground*

Wasn't it hard for the writer to have to live in exile, he was asked, and isn't it a pity so many writers are exiles? [Joseph] Brodsky

219

found it not so remarkable. 'You have guest workers and boat people, not only exiled writers. This takes the orchid out of the writer's lapel. To live elsewhere is a norm in the twentieth century. There's nothing significant about it. It's just more palatable when it's a writer than with those possessing other skills.' There was something to be said for the writer packing his bags. 'The further away from his homeland the writer is, the better for literature.'
    —Jim Forest, "Writes Poems, Will Travel," *Commonweal* 6:22
        May 1992

Such history as my family has is the history of its life here. All that any of us may know of ourselves is to know in relation to this place.
    —Wendell Berry

Geography aside, there are pervasive pressures to remain relatively rootless. We are rewarded with money, prestige and success for pursuing nomadic existences, for our ability to pull up, take leave overnight, plug in quickly to new situations and size them up swiftly. We are rewarded for the exploitative grasp of new circumstances, the almost predatory reading of people and places. The kind of knowledge valued is utilitarian, and being that, disposable. We re-tool. There's little demand for the kind of knowledge that comes of living a long time in one place, knowledge gained slowly with the turning of the seasons, in daily intercourse with neighbors. As a country storekeeper would say, 'We don't get many calls for that.'
    —Jim Wayne Miller, "A Felt Linkage"

Where I was born and how I have lived is unimportant. It is what I have done with where I have been that should be of interest.
    —Georgia O'Keeffe

You do not need to leave your room. Remain sitting at your table and listen. Do not even listen, simply wait. Do not even wait, be quite still and solitary. The world will freely offer itself to you to be unmasked, it has no choice, it will roll in ecstasy at your feet.
    —Franz Kafka

The bird sings the way it is beaked. There are resonances there [his native South Africa], rhythms there, sounds, smells, spaces there, the way in which you see the world and perceive yourself and others, that are learned in a nonverbal way in the place where you grew up.

It is perhaps the only place that I could allow myself to be blind in and I would not be lost.
—Breyten Breytenbach

There is a time in every man's education when he arrives at the conviction that envy is ignorance; that imitation is suicide; that he must take himself for better or for worse as his portion; that though the wide universe is full of good, no kernel of nourishing corn can come to him but through his toil bestowed on that plot of ground which is given him to till.
—Emerson, "Self-Reliance"

It's an old problem and there's no satisfactory solution. People have been drawn away from the place of their birth since Catullus went up to Rome, ever since German boys joined the Roman legions as mercenaries. And surely for centuries before that. If the writer of Genesis had been a sociologist, he would have noted there were unemployed men living down in the boondocks who got word they were hiring on at the Tower of Babel and so they struck out with wives and children and lived in a tent-jungle near the construction site. Living in London in the late 19th century, Arnold Bennett, the novelist, commented that he knew hardly any native Londoners. Almost everyone he knew had, like himself, come up from the provinces.
—Jim Wayne Miller

* * *

"The bird sings the way it is beaked." How are you "beaked?" What enters your poems from the place you live in, from your family, from your memory and personal history? If you had to leave, what would you miss the most? What, do you imagine, might rise up of it in your dreams? Or imagine never leaving. Would you be happy? What would you dislike the most about staying? What parts of your self and your childhood surroundings are permanent, and could not be cut away without disfiguring you for life?

* * *

See again "Where Does The Poem Live?," "Entering The Poem", "The Poem Turns Back Toward Familiar Territory And Fails."

The Advocate Speaks In Defense
Of The Poem's Rights

Not everything you'll meet
is a meek squirrel,
or a birthday puppy
eating from your hand.
Truth is not fish thrown to seals.
Not everything is nice.
Not everything is easy.
For example the poem,
that badger, that grizzled
squat beast
of claws and grumbles,
often seems mean
and strange.
It digs under the door
of your notions,
wrecks the tidy room
of your truth,
bucks you out of the nursery
of your ideas,
rolling you angry and cursing
into a life as strange
as metamorphosis.
It wants you to think,
sweat, wrestle with angels,
bleed words, change
your ways.
It wants you to be delivered.

But if you don't want to be delivered,
don't want to burst new
into the world
like a great poem or idea,
a shower of meteors
lighting some novel way
through the dark,
then here's what to do:
Hide out.
Skip town.

Close the blinds
of your fugitive motel
like the shutters of a mind.
Live on Pepsi and trivia,
drown in "Santa Barbara."
Give up.
Believe what TV tells you.
Whine when it isn't true.
Uselessly complain.

Then you'll be
you own life's helpless infant forever,
the false nurse of ignorance
clutching you close,
the twin who's your fear
holding you back.

But if a good life
is worth it,
if adventure is the point,
and the shape of your life
is not a fixed course,
boring before it begins,
but is a river of many bends,
a new world at every turn—
mystery and confusion,
discovery and possible glory—
then live like the badger,
badgering.
Don't think straight
like everyone else,
but think around all corners,
think clear through things
head-first, full-speed, knowing they can't stand up
if they're generic, cheaply gained,
or lies.

Climb an idea
further
than anyone else,
be stubborn and relentless,
see from the top of it,

scout ahead of the rest.
Or travel down it,
burrow and explore,
tracing its roots
deep into the ground.
See for yourself if they're healthy.

Study dirt.
Know Earth.
Dig gardens.
Scorn money.
Eat books.
Show your teeth
to the enemy.
Find work that
does good for many.
Love truth
like a beautiful sister.

Grow large,
travel strange roads,
president of the world
that you rip and praise,
question and upend,
the world that you wander
to know;
find the self
that you're born
to come home to.

The Advocate Speaks In Defense Of The Poem's Rights

Michael B., an edgy and strong-willed student of mine in 1987 or 1988, used to get quite angry when I pressed him to think beyond the first thought that came to his mind, or when I declined to answer the questions I thought he needed to answer for himself, or when, in the spirit of Whitman's *Preface*, I challenged his views of life, school, character, and so on. Like many students, he must have thought that school should be a place that confirmed all his views about life, that always gave him positive strokes, and that was generally a psychological haven, a sort of social-therapeutic-educational rest home, where no challenges would arise, and where no opinions would be examined.

One day during an exchange between us, he blurted, "When are you going to stop badgering me?"

For a moment, I was shocked. I saw, there in my place, a squat powerful beast, claws scraping away at that poor student, shredding his flesh and psyche and self-esteem, all the while emitting ferocious rips and growls. I saw blood smearing the floor, the looks of terror on the students in the room.

And for a moment, I almost believed. Thankfully, the hallucination passed; I came to my senses and saw that Michael was projecting on to me a problem that had existed long before he and I ever met. Life is hard. Life is complex, a mixture of glory and injustice. Life is disorderly and chaotic, and it requires us to reassess, review, reexamine, and to change our minds and our ways when necessary. It requires an intellectual toughness bred of argument and skepticism and self-knowledge. And sooner or later, it penalizes us if we don't achieve some measure of these things.

And so this poem began, taking off from Michael's metaphor of the badger—a metaphor that I saw a more positive side of and went running with as the poem invited me to.

* * *

The lives of the poem evolve in directions impossible to predict; niches open in the fluid landscape of Creation, waiting for the proper fauna to fill them. This poem is a life that found its environment years later. The school I teach in is growing famous for its mission of educating everyone who would like to come to us, regardless of race, socioeconomic status, or learning disability. As a result, there have been two books written about us, the latest of which is *Adolescents and Inclusion: Transforming Secondary Schools*, edited by Anne M. Bauer and Glenda Myree Brown. To make a long story a bit shorter, this poem appears in my chapter entitled "Joining Up: Becoming A Member of an Academic Department." The context of the poem's appearance

225

there is a discussion about the relationships between teacher, student, and subject, the necessity for argument, and the consistent challenging of unexamined assumptions.

The lives of the poem are always interested in such complex interactions and interdependencies. I love those Rube Goldberg cartoons that present an absurdly complicated way of, say, emptying a bucket. There will be seventeen odd items involved, each one tipping over or firing off or overflowing into the next, until the payoff arrives. As it is with all humor, a serious truth underlies it all: things are connected in ways we might not at first discern, and complexity is one of the ways life has of reminding us what kind of universe we inhabit. We have to be on our guard: there's more going on than we expect.

There's more in the little episode in the lives of the poem, of course: Annie Bauer's daughter, Tara Humler, was a member of one of my first Creative Writing classes, and wrote a handful of quite memorable poems, filled with sharply observed domestic detail and a whimsical self-evaluation that was charming in its frankness. Her poems and my poem and Annie Bauer's and Glenda Myree's book: in the *Lives of the Poem*, there's a whole lot of shaking going on.

The Poem, Rejected By A Seventh Editor, Tries To Go Back Home

But meets Oedipus,
young, handsome, his chest
agleam with sweat,
jogging down the road
toward Thebes.
Ahead, the Sphinx,
mom, dad, sons and daughters—
the full catastrophe.
Even the man with breasts.
So the poem,
friendly,
omniscient as usual,
tries to warn him.

Nothing doing.
You know Oedipus:
headstrong,
hoarding his own mind.
Off he trots
in that odd rolling
gait of his,
that pedagogy
of his own doom,
his tunic fluttering
out behind him
like a soul
coming unattached.

At this very moment
the poem looks up from the page,
catches the editor's eye.
The poem, smiling,
offers him its brooch,
the sharp-pinned one,
the one polished as a mirror,
the one that fits
the hand exactly.
"Go on," the poem says.
"You know what's coming.
Do it."

The Poem, Rejected By A Seventh Editor,
Tries To Go Back Home

Here's one of the more soap-operatic chapters in the life of the poem. "The Poem, Rejected . . . " along with many of the others in the collection, really has been rejected many times, beginning with an editor from North Carolina, my friend mentioned in connection with "Talking Together." He was the first to say to me that he had "sworn off, several hundred poems ago," poems about poetry. I got mad at him and started a letter, but never sent it. Instead I sent the poem, along with some others from *Lives Of The Poem*, out again. In June of 1990, I got a letter from Ron Schreiber, editor of the handsome magazine *Hanging Loose* which regularly publishes high school age writers alongside emerging and nationally known writers. Several years before, Phil Horney, a student I had worked with (and a school chum of Tony Ruter's), had published a poem there, and I thought it would be a natural place to submit. Mr. Schreiber's note follows:

Dear Richard Hague,

I'm afraid we've decided not to use these. Especially not a pleasant response after your words about the magazine.

I don't know whether I should be encouraging or not, but we do, I think, have a bias against poems about poetry (I know I do), and to receive a group of poems about the poem doesn't really give you a fair reading with us. (Had the group been different, and only one of these about a poem, would the reading have been better? Don't know, of course.)

Thanks, nevertheless, for letting us see these. Send others if you like.

Then, in February of 1992, I sent this letter, along with some of the same poems, plus a few new ones, to *The Journal: The Literary Magazine of the Ohio State University*, in which I had published occasionally in the past, and which was edited by David Citino, whom I'd known since Bob Collins and he edited the old *Ohio Journal* at Ohio State in Columbus:

Dear David:

Hope this finds you well. I'm enclosing some poems from a manuscript I've been fooling with for a couple of years now, entitled *Lives of the Poem*. Though several of the poems have been published, I'm meeting resistance from editors all over who simply "don't publish poems about poetry," no questions asked, no reasons given.

Just what the poem needs! Something to complain about, something to get the juices flowing.

I'm reminded of Henry James's rejoinder to someone who claimed that a novel without "bold action" was impossible. "Why without adventure, more than without matrimony, or celibacy, or parturition, or cholera . . . ?" James responded.

Why no poems about poetry? As easily not about bats, or Mike Tyson, or sacraments, or kielbasa.

So here, by God, are a few for consideration.

Best to you . . .

Months passed. There were new editors by then. At last came a rejection slip with names I did not recognize. Not even "We don't care much for poems about poetry" scrawled on it. Not even a "Hello, Dick: Gee, this is about as rotten a group of poems we've ever seen from you (and it doesn't help that they're about poetry, too.") No. Nothing. Silence.

You know what they say about paranoia: you're not really paranoid if they really *are* out to get you. Soon after, I ran across this ad in *Poets & Writers*, in the January/February 1993 issue:

Call For Manuscripts Books

Bennet & Kitchell, publishes books of poetry. No free verse, no off rhyme or rhyming on a secondary accent, no blank verse (unless enriched with assonance, alliteration, or the like), humor only if broad, erotica only if in good taste, no poems about poets or poetry-making. P.O. Box 4422 East Lansing, MI 48826

So it went: a submission on October 19, 1993 of "The Stupidity Poem" and "The Annunciation" to *Indiana Review's* special issue on "Anger" received this reply on Nov. 13: "We don't care much for poems about poetry." Naturally, on Nov. 18, I shot off "The Poem, Rejected . . . " and, for good measure and just so I wasn't misunderstood, "The Poem, Swayed By Popular Opinion, Gets Its Posthumous Credentials." Nothing. *Nada.*

Now any writer will tell you that to receive a comment—even a negative one—from very busy editors is a rarity. Yet here we had, among the silences, several notable disses. Did these editors all study together? Did they all read the same essay on being an editor? Did they all, in graduate school, have to sit through so many effete poems about poetry that they developed the same allergy? For people supposedly interested in poetry, to have "a bias" against poems about poetry and poets is, to spin the metaphor from "Dead Poet's Society" around, to hold a plumbing convention, then ban all talk of pipes.

But in truth I have gotten quite a kick out of all this. There's a kind of perverse delight in sending a poem out not with the usual hope and uncertainty, but with a cordial and knowing despair. And I am certainly not laying it all on editors; after all, I myself have been one, off and on, since the mid 1960s. As in everything here, I'm trying to display as many aspects of the lives of the poem as I am familiar with.

And there is this: all the rejection makes the the occasional acceptance even sweeter. "O, there are geniuses out there!" the poem cries." O, there are such insightful characters! O, there are still people with a sense of humor!"

All of this makes the lives of the poem that much more unexpectedly textured, unpredictably fringed and curved, unabashedly delightful.

* * *

One of the things I like about this poem is that I can change the pronoun referring to the editor in the last section from "him" to "her" as the occasion warrants. It's adaptable, and I am sure it will one day take care of itself quite nicely: it has the orneriness of a survivor about it.

* * *

And here, by way of therapy:

The Poem Writes Some Rejection Letters To Editors

Dear Teufelsdrock:

If you can't understand me,
read my lips:
the trouble's in your set.

Dear Witless:

Though you are Republican,
yet still I might have saved you.

Held Hostage In A Late-Night Seminar, The Poem Answers Some Questions

1: Who Invented Poetry?

Poetry was not invented,
though the idea is a good one
and deserves a dozen myths,
a couple hundred stories.
Poetry, like any place, was discovered.
A woman, long ago,
noticed that she rhymed with the moon.
After that, she became quite powerful,
a kind of queen.
"Look," she'd say every four weeks or so,
and point at the blood on her legs.
They killed her after a year,
but every month she came back,
tugging at all her sisters,
drawing them into the fields
where they planted
what everyone needed to eat.
Those who invented the garden
discovered the poem.

2: Are You Now, Or Have You Ever Been, Popular?

Do you mean like a basketball star or a rock singer?
Bodies wear out, voices crack.
Beyond all ruin and decay,
beyond all blown knees and cancerous larynxes,
I remain,
O yes, indeed, as popular as eyes are popular,
as ears and penises and breasts and fingers
and minds are popular.
Popular as honey on the tongue,
there to be tasted.
Popular as truth like a briar,
there to be pushed against
and awakened.
Popular as dreaming well,
which is what I am:
dreaming when you're awake.

Held Hostage In A Late-Night Seminar,
The Poem Answers Questions

These unfinished fragments (at least they seem that to me, who is even now fighting off the urge to expand and do variations on them, and, in my mania, to make a whole series)—these fragments, then, are preliminary explorations more than anything else. If the poem really were to be interrogated by authorities, what questions would they ask? What answers would and could the poem make? Would the poem have anything to hide? Would the poem have anything to confess? If Keats's "Ode To A Nightingale" were brought in for observation and questioning, what would its questioners notice about it and what would they hear it say? What questions would *you* ask of it?

Make a poem that arises from these issues. Make a poem that is a whole series of questions directed to your favorite—or least favorite—poem. Make a poem that confesses itself.

Poems: Do Not Fold

*"So . . . like I'm going to fold them up four times—four pages of them—
and like stuff and send them in that little envelope?"*
　—Mary O'Connell

1
Only guys with bad poker hands
fold.
Only old bridges, their backs broken,
fold.
Only wallets emptied of their dollars
fold.

2
There's folding money,
folding tables,
folding chairs.
But these poems?

Do not fold.

3
The chef folds eggs into batter,
birds fold in their wings,
you fold your legs under you
at the Roman banquet
Latin students hold.
But these poems?

Do not fold.

4
Keep them flat,
pressed as sheets
on an unused bed,
perfect virgin sheets,
kept from all creases, spots, rips.

5
Fold your hands
in prayer,
but these poems—

do not fold.

Poems: Do Not Fold

I first read this at the Purcell Marian Open Mic Poetry Reading & Coffee House in November of 1996. Poetry Slams and other forms of public performance were highly popular at the time (as they continue to be); students asked if we could come up with something public, and thus arose the Fall and Spring Coffee Houses.

And wasn't that first one an education! Paul Spaite and Na'im Muhammed brought irreverence and a wacky scat-singing style to their impromptu riffs, and Dan Trevino, Jeannie Sanders, Joanna Bach, and others read their street-wise urban stuff, their rap be-bop, their hip-hop love lyrics, their heartfelt hearthurt, their nature loving stuff, their true confessions, their essays in verse, all of it. Since then, the readings regularly draw a hundred or so students and parents and teachers to the school's Centre For Performing Arts, and have become an artistic and social fixture in the life of the school as well as the lives of the poem.

Mary O'Connell, to whom this poem is dedicated and who speaks its epigraph, is a tall, quiet, intellectually and physically striking young woman with high-energy writing genes, and a student in my initial in-school Creative Writing class. When for the first time she had gathered some poems to submit somewhere, the epigraph is the question she incredulously asked me. Smart aleck that I am, I wrote this little poem in reply to her.

Mary, by the way, is the daughter of Dan O'Connell, who was a participant in my earliest writing workshops at home sometime in the Seventies. He was one of a handful of guys who came over to my apartment every Monday night to smoke cigarettes and talk and read their poetry. So when Mary showed up on the scene, it was a good sign: a blessing of continuity.

She's a talented poet. She took Creative Writing for a second year, and this is the first poem she offered, in late August, early September maybe, to the class:

Angie

Propping herself up on the stool behind
our Customer Service desk she laughs and calls out,
"Hey there sex pot! We've been missing those gorgeous legs!"

and I smile like always
admiring her crab-like body
the dyed halo of balding brown curls
standing on staticy end

bifocals dangling 'round her wobbly neck
and her deep laugh

"The men are banging down my door you know!"
she says with a wink
then helps a handsome customer
loud-mouthed voice, full of fun

and I smile like always
noticing the limp when she walks
teetering side to side to side
under her dark eyes circles and
lines that crinkle when she smiles
and tells me how she loves to live;
because of this I know the world is holy.

"Angie" is an accomplished poem, and it went on to win First Place in the Ohio High School Poetry Contest sponsored by Ohio Northern University. Over 300 poems from 93 schools were entered, and this one was selected as the best. There's a videotape of Mary and her classmate Joe Dumont, who won an Honorable Mention for his poem "Cold", which we have appreciated earlier, being interviewed on a lunchtime news program in northern Ohio, and then the best part—each of them reading their poems. There are all sorts of surprises in the lives of the poem.

* * *

The challenge here was to write a poem about work, including in it actual speech, and some perhaps triumphant surprise. If they wanted it, I offered students the last line, hoping that they would invent a way to get to it. What I admire about this poem, beyond the effective play of its title (Angie-Angel), the connection of that playful-seriousness with the imagery ("halo of brown curls"), and the connection of those to the final line—beyond all this, I like that the poem mixes the sacred and the profane. On the one hand, there is the mention of the sexy legs and the mildly randy attitude of Angie; on the other, there is the serious coupling of this with the final line. Poetry does, indeed, link the sacred and the profane; it does, indeed, do as Shelley insisted it could do: see again the Notes & Divagations on "The Poem Turns Mean" above.

In fact, here is another poem arising from a similar assignment. This one is by Colleen Glenn, the other member of the tutorial with Katie The Red. It arose from an assignment that in part asked for a poem in "real spoken language," and which was suggested by Jim Daniels' poem, "Short Order Cook," which I ran across in Robert Wallace's *Making Poetry*.

Cashier

Old man comes in—
tosses a pack of Kools at me
then tries to be cute
and scan it himself.
Runs it over the laser
       nothing
Again
       nothing
I snatch it and
run it over with a
beep and I laugh.
"Takes practice," I say.
"Dollar seventy-five."
He slaps the change
on the counter—
I wait for him to put it
in my hand
before I ring it.
       —*click*—
Drawer pops open
and I lay the quarter
in his hand
with his receipt.
"You have a good day."
And he says,
"Yeah, you too, baby."
Sure, mister, whatever.

* * *

Here's another of Colleen's poems, this one an exercise based on a set of words given to the writer one at a time. The fun is to try to somehow fit the words into the poem, and to keep everything moving forward, and coherently. This poem was one of the 60 Finalists out of 30,000 entries from all over the country in *Read* Magazine's poetry contest.

Perspectives of A Woman And A Man

The svelte woman smiles innocently,
handsaw in hand as if it were a doll,
looking like a girl ready to frolic in the park.
She rakes her fingers through her spaghetti-hair,
takes a hit off her Marlboro—
a cowboy ready to spit.
Her tongue caresses her lips, kissing
the lingering air, and suddenly
seals her mouth as if it were
an envelope and the package smoke.
Then, without her saw she severs a radish from the garden,
chopping it with a hideous laugh,
juice on her hands like blood from a sacrificial lamb.
She tells me:
"The Pope is a killer, too, you know."

The obese man leans over the fence,
fatty flesh oozing through metal pentagons—
running hose in hand
like he's taking an eternal leak.
He stares until I can see
the veins in his eyeballs straining.
I let the edge of the saw scrape my thigh
and imagine empty black sockets in his head.
He rubs his hands over the smooth green rubber
and picks his ears,
and I can't help smiling.
He bends to help a fallen tulip—
bald head shining with perspiration,
then looks up with a grin—
the smile of a slaughtered pig.
As I continue my work in the garden,
he leaves our border—
the fat rolls jiggling hurriedly
back to Safety,
shaking his head, muttering,
as if I'm the strange one.

* * *

I like this poem for its strangeness: it is almost exactly wrong to think of a poem as being good because its subject and similes and metaphors are immediately explicable. If you have written a poem about something, and if you read it to your friend, and your friend exclaims, upon hearing it once, "Yes! That's it, exactly!" you can be sure the poem is mediocre. The Russian film maker V.I. Pudovkin said, "To show something as everyone else has seen it is to accomplish nothing." Look again at Colleen's images, at her surprising similes, at the strangeness of the situation.

At the base of this poem is what I call the Layering Exercise. I ask students to write a simple narrative at first, perhaps capturing a small domestic or neighborhood scene—or I ask them to write a narrative about a journey, real or imagined. Beforehand, I make a list of several random categories—colors, fabrics, place names, animals, kitchen utensils—and after the first draft of the poem is finished, I invite students to go back and layer in, wherever possible, something from each category.

What often happens is that an interesting strangeness enters the poem, and the metaphors and similes or surprising verbs students come up with to incorporate these items make the poem an unpredictable adventure rather than a routine exercise. Get a partner to make some lists and an assignment for the framework of the poem; you do the same, and write together.

* * *

And one final Colleen poem, written during the time of the tutorial with Katie The Red, and capturing the glitzy fast-track brightness and intensity of a section of downtown Cincinnati filled with dance clubs and bars.

On Vine

Ego-trippin
under neon lights on Vine:
moshpit victories
bounce and ricochet
off headlights,
flashing intensity
with bursts of adrenaline;
bass reverberating—
pounding rhythm
haunts the head,
wired to electrocute;
generation screams

238

with energy—
a thousand dreams
floating through
the air like smoke—
hazing just out of reach.

* * *

Speaking of energy and intensity, there's a collection entitled *Coffeehouse Anthology of Poetry*, published by Bottom Dog Press, which gathers together around a hundred poems and a few dozen statements about the coffeehouse poetry scene. In 1996 I began going with students to various coffeehouses and poetry readings around Cincinnati; I wanted students to see what poetry looks like outside of the classroom, in some of its natural habitats. Here's a little commentary of mine which appears in the anthology, yet another minor note in the lives of the poem.

Mixed Blend: Coffeehouse Poetry

The whoosh, hiss, and final sputter of the espresso machine punctuates—actually, *obliterates*—the punchline of the poem I'm listening to at Kaldi's, perhaps the most lively of several coffeehouse and bistro venues for poetry in Cincinnati. The waiters and waitresses (O, all right—the w*ait persons*) are hip urban types. Though punkish or grunge-ish in couture, they are young and good-looking beneath their paleness and their jeweled dog collars. And they are all business: if you're leaning against one of the bookcases, trying to hear around the corner to where a sweating dude is rapping about his lover's "midnight ecstasy humongous thing" with all the subtlety of a blitzkrieg, and you don't want to miss even one detail, one sally or thrust—well, too bad. The wait person with the pierced nostril will say, "You can't stand there, sir," and you'll have to go loiter out back on a kind of big patio overlooking an alley until the crowd shifts and thins, and you can get a seat.

His wad of hyperboles shot, the sweating reader gives way to the next. And I ask myself again—what kind of poetry can stand up and survive in such an atmosphere? It's always dangerous to generalize anywhere near poetry, but I think that, at first, coffeehouse poetry has to be accessible, with some sort of narrative line, of such outrageous or controversial or humorous or erotic subject matter that it will arrest the attention of the patrons. Or else it has to be so cleverly vulgar, camp, obscene or any combination thereof, that it will seize their sensibilities like the Ancient Mariner seized the Wedding Guest—and I also think that, whatever else, it has to be *loud*. If it's long—and this is true no matter if it is traditional poetry or what is called now "language" poetry (how unhappy and uninformative a term is "language"—what poetry *isn't* language?) it had better achieve the incantatory quality of the epic, perhaps the original coffeehouse poetry. If it's short, it has to have something of the quality of the punchline and the athleticism of the fly-weight—it has to hit hard and hit fast.

But isn't this healthy for poetry? Didn't Dana Gioia in "Can Poetry Matter?" call for the restoration of a "vulgar vitality" to American poetry? Who knows—maybe the next Walt Whitman is that fellow you heard last night, sounding his barbaric yawp over the beep and crash of the cash register, or the next Emily Dickinson that purple-haired young woman in clunky black plastic glasses who whispered huskily into the mike for seven minutes of perfect (and most immaculately safe) aural sex.

This too will pass. But when it does, I have to say I will be sad to see it go. Poetry can get pretty stuffy and the poetry scene become arid and almost lifeless, populated only by a few weirdly adapted Galapagos academics. The coffeehouse rejuvenates, invites the hybrid vigor, mixes the classes. I'm going to enjoy it while it lasts.

Found Poem: Titles From The Notes Of Jeannie Sanders (after Sei Shonagon)

Things That Look Too Good To Touch
Things That Leave Crumbs
Things That Take Your Breath Away
Things That You Do In Front Of A Mirror
Things That You Have To Look At More Than Once
Things That Would Be On Your Shopping List
    If You Were Shopping For Your Heart

Found Poem: Titles From The Notes Of Jeannie Sanders (after Sei Shonagon)

Jeannie Sanders is the younger sister of Kadie "The Gold" Sanders, a cohort of Colleen and Katie The Red. By the way, all this business about nicknames arose from the fact that simultaneously, the following girls were in the Creative Writing workshop or on the staff of *Hackberry*: Katie DuMont, Katie Dumont, and Kadie Sanders. Katie Schlosser followed a couple of years later. If I'd say "Katie," three girls would simultaneously say "Yes?" To distinguish them, we agreed on nicknames: since Katie DuMont has curly red hair, we called her "The Red." Since Kadie Sanders has blond hair (well, sometimes it is blond; I have seen her in recent years with bright red hair, and with multi-colored coifs startling in their variety) we called her "The Gold," and since Katie Dumont was the younger (and no relation whatsoever to Katie The Red) we called her "The Fair," in remembrance of beautiful Arthurian damsels. (Katie The Fair is the daughter of a fellow, Frank Dumont, I taught in my early years. In mid-life he left his profession and went to medical school and became a doctor. Katie also is in medical school; when she finishes, she and her father might practice medicine together. What a great alliterative shingle they will hang: Dumont & Daughter, Doctors.)

There was similar confusion about names in my own family. I am the third James, that being my father's and my grandfather's first name, too. But from the beginning I was never called James or Jim or Jimmy—I went by my middle name, Richard, Dick. But to complicate matters even more, my father was not called Jim or Jimmy all the time, either. Instead, he often answered to the household nickname "Firp." My grandmother had the habit, which I have inherited, of having to run through a whole list of names before she got the right one. "Come here, Jim er, Dickie, er Timmy, er—*Firp*! Come here!"

At any rate, Jeannie is Kadie The Gold's younger sister, and she took my British Literature and Culture class as well as creative writing. One day, fooling around in class, I assigned a poem whose subject—and form—might be "long and skinny." Jeannie threw herself down on the floor—she preferred to write lying down, her long dark blond hair spilling about her on the carpet like splashes of honey tea—and this is what, after some revisions, she produced:

Long-Skinny

Long-skinny is a supermodel
wrapped in a bedsheet
on the highway

eating a banana
and combing a horse's mane.
Her face is
a crescent moon
with earrings
in the shape of a teardrop's tail.
She wears a wedding gown
that follows her
like a tall, narrow shadow.
Her math professor's behind her
with his tapping yardstick.
All the while
she thinks of brontosaurs' necks
and trees,
not those long division problems
and pencils.
And the highway goes on,
blending with the landscape,
stretching,
narrowing in the distance.

—Jeannie Sanders

I am fond of the dictum I've already spoken about at length. "A poem is language listening to itself." This poem illustrates the principle very well. The metaphors inform one another; there is a "common denominator" to them as they deploy throughout the poem, one unfolding after another like the parts of a tent that goes up easily once you've got the rhythm. Other poems, of course, work differently; other poems "dance"; rather than listening to themselves, keeping an eye on their own movements, they answer some call from beyond, so to speak, leaping and pirouetting toward their conclusions with surprise at every turn. We can practice this dancing, too, just as we can practice helping poems "listen to themselves."

Another little excellence in "Long-Skinny" is the use of the participles at the end, with their ever-going presentness, and with their falling-off rhythms that are exactly right for a description of something becoming less and less distinct as it gets further and further away. Again the question arises: Did Jeannie know this was going on when she was writing the poem. And the answer is, frustratingly, but wonderfully, "No." And a further question is: After she was finished and the poem stood before her, did she then know all that was going on it? Could she have said why she used those participles at the end? Again, probably "No."

* * *

What, exactly, is the point of such questions? Please try to answer right now, before you do anything else. See again "Breaking Its Own Rule, The Poem Attempts To Answer The Question, "What's A Poem?" and "What's A Poem For?" Go wherever the answer requires you to go, and write it all down, maybe even make a poem of it, and let it become a part of your own personal *Lives of the Poem.*

* * *

If it's fair to ask the questions above, is it also fair to offer a few critical quibbles about the poem? Is it fair to allow the Critic equal time? "Yes," and "Yes." There are some things that Jeannie might have been more consistent with. For example, the participial phrases at the end of the poem are punctuated accurately and helpfully; too bad they aren't at the beginning. The rule is that such sentence elements usually get separated from the rest of the sentence by a comma—so it should have been, if she's going to be consistent,

> Long-skinny is a supermodel,
> wrapped in a bedsheet
> on the highway, eating a banana
> and combing a horse's mane.

And while we're at it with the Critic, Jeannie might also have tightened the poem by dropping the *and*, replacing it with a comma:

> on the highway,
> eating a banana,
> combing a horse's mane.

There are other places in the poem, too, where some minor tightening could have been accomplished with no loss of beauty or rhythm: "her math professor's behind her,/ tapping his yardstick." Wherever we can, we ought to inspect the poem closely for unnecessary words, and for constructions that might be tightened or made parallel. The poem needs our help in this; it will meet demanding adversaries in the public, and it needs the Critic to keep it in fighting trim.

Jeannie sent "Long-Skinny" and a handful of other poems written during the first semester to The Overture Awards, a city-wide contest in the arts.

244

Though she did not win, her portfolio was excellent, a consistent and surprising group of poems, and all well done.

"Found Poem" is another favorite Jeannie Sanders poem—though it's really, as a result of the sometimes magical movements in the lives of the poem, my poem, too. It came as a result of our looking at passages from *The Pillow Book* of Sei Shonagon, a young woman who lived in Japan in the 10th century, and who kept a journal which she stored in a drawer in her wooden pillow. Sei, according to the editors of Laidlaw's *Composition and Grammar: Steps In The Writing Process,* "made up categories to nudge her mind to interpret and connect her experience." Jeannie wrote down a list of categories for sharpening her own powers of observation, and when I saw it in her notebook, I thought that it was, itself, a beautiful little poem.

* * *

Found poems are an interesting phenomenon in literature. As Alexander Smith claimed for essays, so it is for poetry: it's as if the world were whispering poems under its breath, everywhere and anywhere—in advertising billboards, in the copy on the backs of cereal boxes, in scientific texts. The poem lurks there, hidden. Its finder, a poet cruising the world to see what will pop up, discovers it and pulls it up out of its camouflage of prose or mundanity, and says, "Look here. What I've found! Is it not interesting? Beautiful? Profound? Absurd to the point of delight?"

Surf some unlikely texts—newspaper articles, the lists of songs on a CD, a page from your history textbook. See if you can find a poem. Copy it down and bring it in and tell the story of your finding it, and why you think it's a poem, and if it's any good, and what its existence says about poetry.

* * *

Isn't there something artificial about all these exercises? I had a literature student once, Chris Woodard, who, after I had carefully laid out all the artifice in Shakespeare's "That Time Of Year Thou May'st In Me Behold" complained to me: "I always thought poetry comes mostly from the heart. But Shakespeare's really planning all this—every sentence exactly four lines, exactly the same number of syllables. It seems he must be insincere—he can't really be *feeling* what he's writing." This is a common belief among beginners in the serious study of poetry. The Creator—that hot, spontaneous, emotingly explosive force, is certainly crucial in the lives of the poem. But, as I hope we have seen, so is the Critic, that designing, cold-blooded engineer of a being,

245

directing the poem's craft. Eventually, I hope that Chris was able to marry his feeling response to the poem to his understanding of its intellectual structure, its marvelous technique, its absolutely expert craftsmanship. The aesthetic response to any work of art engages not only our feelings but our intellect as well. Great art nourishes us from both realms.

But now to return to the question of exercises. Do exercise poems merely engage us intellectually and imaginatively? Can we become committed in every sense to an exercise? Can we write out of our fullest being?

Yes to all—sometimes. As we have seen more than once (see the notes on revision about "The Poem Braids Its Lover's Hair" again) writing can be an act of discovery, ("mind traveling, destination unknown" Donald Murray says in one of my favorites descriptions of this kind of writing) as well as expression of the already discovered. And sometimes these little exercises simply provide the occasion of such discovery. Because they often stretch us out of normal ways of thinking and feeling, they provide avenues into unexplored, as-yet-unexpressed areas of feeling, intellect, and imagination. Give them all you've got, and you may get more than you expected back. The lives of the poem are generous, abundant, multitudinous.

Questions I Asked Christi Ryan's Prose Poem's Leg

Who shaved you so smoothly? Were you ever touched by the ocean? Have I mentioned my mother and her cold blue eyes? Which angel has discarded you, and is it true that resurrection is easier without the burden of the flesh? If so, where will the rest of your body have gone?

If, like fish and visitors, you start to stink after three days, will you forgive me if I bury you? Will you mind if I don't mark the grave?

Questions I Asked Christi Ryan's Prose Poem's Leg

Some critics and theoreticians decline to recognize the prose poem as a valid form of poetry. Let them go ahead and argue among themselves; it's much like a clutch of medieval monks having an intense philosophical argument about whether fire is a living thing or not while their abbey is devoured in the blaze. Whatever a prose poem is, it is art, and it has its own peculiar characteristics, though its borders—its definitions—are *in*definite, like an amoeba's.

Nevertheless, I have found it to be a liberating form; in it, you can, as one of its practitioners claimed, "fall through he cracks" between sense and nonsense, between form and amorphousness, between, at last, poetry and prose. It offers an environment of edges and sudden descents and ascents, of intricate borders; it is one of those places where, as James Gleick observes (see notes to "Chaos Poem,") "life blossoms." The prose poem inhabits, in its versions of the lives of the poem, what the historian Daniel Boorstin calls "The Fertile Verge." (Jim Wayne Miller, after hearing me speak tentatively of being a "border Appalachian," sent me a copy of Boorstin's essay. Later, I ran across its ideas again in Gleick.)

This poem is a reply to one by Christi Ryan, a student in my A.P. British Literature class; I do not have Christi's prose poem which inspired it, sad to say. But in the lives of the poem, there are other connections: she is the daughter of Steve and Carol Ryan, my son Brendan's state championship soccer coaches.

You cannot—nor, I think, would you want to—escape the filamentous intricacies of connection in the lives of the poem, even when they unfold away from the page.

Questions They Kept Asking Him

for Katie The Fair, who asked

"Why Do You Always Wear Black?"

So I can hide more effectively in unlit rooms. Grandmothers and other strange species also live in them, lying awake in terror all night, which is good for the circulation. It is not the years that make people old; it is decades of lassitude, years of noxious tranquility. Another reason is so I will not be tempted to cross busy highways at night. It's dangerous to dart out into the four-lane when all you are is darkness:

truckers regularly drive right through big shadows, as airlines fly through clouds. When the drivers realize the shadows are us, at first they want to smash the brake pedal to the floor, or duck down below the windshield. But after a time, they get used to it. Everyone gets used to it. Then they can ignore even the screams of the shadows they run down, or the scratch of our fingers as we try to catch their door handles. Other reasons: Hamlet. Laziness. Ineptitude when shopping. Because I love you. To keep you talking, asking questions, so that you won't die.

"What's Up?"

For years I have watched the sparrows at the window feeder. They are raucous, well-dressed. They look much more alike than all of you do; this is something of a comfort when one of them dies. They become more animated in winter, when the dark clouds of starlings rush back and forth among them and the wind is brittle, and when the pond freezes to the bottom and the carp are like jewels in the muddy ice, and when at night the Wild Hunter reels up from the ground and lights his own bones afire to find The Bear. Leaning back to see him overhead: that is up.

"Is That Really You In The Picture?"

For the longest time I could leave my body.
I could drift quietly among the leaves and
I could be all of any star except its fire:
I could be its distance, its roundness, its magnitude,
its power, its planetary genesis,
its blue-white light but not its fire.
I could be as cold as the first nothing.
Then one day I woke covered all over with death,
death like skin and hair and fingernails and teeth.
All through me, it was death,
all over me, it was death.
Since then I have been imprisoned here
in this temple of decay.
The picture is nothing.
Ignore it.

Questions They Kept Asking Him

The "him," of course, is me. Katie actually did ask me the first question one day in class. The second is made up. (I think it was George Ella Lyon who once told me that after she had presented a reading, a student came up and asked, "Did you really write those poems, or did you just make them up?" I wish I had been there to pursue the questioner's notions—they may have led somewhere delightful, opening weird and unlikely avenues into the lives of the poem.) The third question and the poem following it—which is not a prose poem, notice (I think I was reminding myself and my readers of the indefiniteness of the distinctions), the third one takes a big step out of the playfulness of the second into a serious confrontation with mortality. Poems are like children in that they may ask big questions mixed in with little ones—though to the child, and the poem, all questions and all things may be of equally large importance and interest.

* * *

Write some poems that are made up mostly of questions. Can a poem that does not answer its own questions nevertheless take the reader somewhere?

Or write some poems that mix big questions and little questions, big issues and little issues, and see what happens.

Or write a series of at least five poems, each of which has as its title an interesting question.

Or write a series of poems called "Interrogations," in which, in each, you put some big idea on the witness stand and grill it: "Sin," for example, or "Capitalism," "Virginity" or "Success."

See again "The Poem Approaches Physics."

Not Long After Jim Wayne's Death,
I Remember That Frost Once Called Poetry
"A Momentary Stay Against Confusion"

Not here.
Wind spins my pages and days
like litter and leaves in a field
where earthquake chops a pond into
three huge waves
that smash against each other then leap out
like slops flung crazy from a bucket:
nothing left but stinking mud
choked with strangling minnows,
rotten frogs, bad bait.

Base of my head like that,
mess, hockers, upchuck.

So much for building word-huts or walls,
little tree-shack philosophies.

Go naked and blind in rain and grief and to hell with you

the poem says to me right now.

Not Long After Jim Wayne's Death, I Remember That Frost Once Called Poetry "A Momentary Stay Against Confusion"

I first met Jim Wayne Miller in August of 1978 or '79 at the first Appalachian Writers Workshop in Hindman, Kentucky. He had come there to share what he knew with some aspiring writers and with a lineup of colleagues that, as I look back on it now, was the most accomplished company of writers I'd ever been among in one place until I was invited to attend the Bread Loaf Writers Conference as a scholar almost a quarter of a century later. Albert Stewart, the founder of *Appalachian Heritage,* was there at Hindman. James Still, the laureate of Appalachian literature, was also on staff. Still's skillful poetry, his emotionally rich novel *River of Earth,* and his stylistically amazing stories had made him known to a national readership thirty years before. Gurney Norman was on staff, too, the former merry prankster with Ken Kesey during his days at Stanford on a Wallace Stegner Fellowship and author of the novel *Divine Right's Trip*, which was published in the margins of *The Whole Earth Catalog*, one of the counter-cultural icons of the Sixties. There too was Harriet Arnow, author of the classic novel of displaced Appalachians, *The Dollmaker,* which was about to become a movie starring Jane Fonda. Betty Payne James, Barbara Smith, Cratis Williams, the "father of Appalachian Studies" whose 1962 doctoral dissertation at NYU put Appalachian Studies on the academic map, and Mike Mullins, director of the Hindman Settlement School—they were all there, too, and Jim Wayne, of course. Last but not least, I met and befriended Jerry Wayne Williamson, the young editor of *Appalachian Journal.* Fellow participants included Pauletta Hansel and Anne Campbell, then the Appalachian librarian at the University of Kentucky, and a whole glory of other people, including Jim "Ski King" Webb.

I mention all these folks because they, too, are a part of the lives of the poem. In one way or another, I have learned from them all. But it was perhaps from Jim Wayne that I received the most important psychological and artistic encouragement and confirmation. Besides his accomplishment as a writer, teacher, and scholar, Jim was also a great late-night partier. Many were the nights over the 20 years I knew him that we would swap stories and literary anecdotes and teaching lore. Jim had a European sense of personal space, which is to say, when you talked with him, he leaned closer to you, as an Italian or Spaniard would. Even his jokes seemed intimate confidences, delivered as he held in one hand a smoke and in the other a drink. I will always confound the smell of cigarette smoke with the memory of him.

When we learned of his cancer and its ravaging intensity, we found it hard to believe. I think I simply didn't heed the evidence of my own eyes, even though I saw him more than once in his last year, saw that he was losing weight and heard the cough that lingered long after he'd given up calling it just a cold.

When he died, I was stricken. For me, powerful emotions—fear, and grief, for example—more often take a form that looks like anger. So it is in this poem. It is almost vulgar in its details, and seems more about me than it is about Jim—and so it is. I was furious that he could die so young and so quickly, and that I had been in too much of a hurry (or was it too frightened?) the last couple of times I saw him to be more attentive.

Confession over. In the lives of the poem, death is a permanent presence. To forget it is to underachieve the love and gratitude and connectedness we can express, best and most preciously, alas, only in life.

The Poem, Breaking Away

It has endured and accumulated
a hundred baggages: work, the plotted hours,
the dyspeptic, hurried lunch, a habit
of calm politeness, a wickedness
of docility.
Now it wants to leave it all
in the great terminal, Grand Central
of change,
walk away, ditch it
like a dump of second-hands
behind.

Ahead, the road of many turns.
The poem's own hands in its pockets.
Wind like a goddess
all around it.
Its eyes open.
Its own tongue ready to speak.

The Poem, Breaking Away

There are things, like the death of a friend, or parent, or spouse, or the loss of a job, or displacement from our native land, that sometimes cause permanent changes in our spirit. Though in the short run these changes may appear to be absurdly useless, in the long run, they may take us to new places in our lives, and so turn out to be quite useful— they are, to paraphrase the poet Rilke, the dragons in our lives which only need the kiss of the maiden to be transformed into princes of delight and good luck.

Sometimes all the poems we write begin to sound alike. There was a stretch of time in the late 70s and early 80s when it seemed all I could do was to write a variation of the same poem. My wife especially sensed their staleness and similarity. I suspect there's some sort of mental or psychological effect similar to that in intense physical training: you reach a plateau, and no matter how hard you train, your performance remains at pretty much the same level. Later, there may come a burst of incredible progress, but the maintenance of the training schedule throughout that plateau is difficult. I think it might well have been the advent of these lives of the poem poems that broke me out of that rut. The varied voices and tones they took were refreshing and renewing, and opened up new territory for me. I was able to deploy knowledge and instincts that had not been accessible to the poems I was stuck in earlier. Jim Wayne once said, praising a miscellaneous knowledge: "You never know when something you know will come in handy in a poem."

Finding The Poem

An old man tells the temperature
by the cricket's tick.
A boy counts the scales
of a minnow.
Nine voices sing a madrigal.
An architect wonders
what she can build in an evening
of dry ragweed stems.
A Cherokee and a Russian
sit down to talk of physics
in a bar in Copenhagen.
Uniform buttons dug up
at Little Bighorn.
A carved heart on a box turtle's back.
How dark it is in basements.
Wind's slender fingers.
The blond hair of a prairie.
Why someone's father is named Boyd.
Fifteen names for snow.
A letter mailed to the wrong address,
opened, read, and understood
by the person who just moved there.
Water, just as it freezes.
Glass, cooling to a mirror.
All China suddenly hearing Beethoven.
A church, empty on a winter's night in Pittsburgh,
and a woman, driving slowly by,
thinking of zucchini bread
and Greek,
and of her grandmother,
dead for thirty years,
and of her two children
home in bed,
named Paul
and Annie.
Two stones, close as lovers,
lying side by side.
All that is here,
now.
Here.

Now.

Finding The Poem

What a pleasure this poem was to find. I just let the details in the catalogue build up and out in whatever way they cared to. Who can account for the juxtapositions of things? Writing often is a letting loose of thought and logic, trusting that some deeper sense of order will take command, steering the poem (or essay, or novel, or story—whatever) in the proper direction.

And though it is among the final poems in the series, it is not the final word on the lives of the poem. There is no final word. Poetry continues. It does not stop.

Remember "the Poem Wakes And Receives Visitors." Remember "Where Does The Poem Live?" "Trying to catch up." "Ready to help you sing."

* * *

Speaking of letting loose of thought and logic, here is a poem by my son, Patrick Hague, written when he was a junior in my Creative Writing class. It is of course difficult for me to be objective, but I admire the verbal ingenuity and thematic interest of this poem.

Bar None

There is a place where
a geometric blueprint of Willy-Nillity
comes for a drink every night.

A place where Scattered and weather-beaten Disorder
stop in for their nightly delineation.
A montage of Mystery sits with a configuration
of Disorganization and they discuss black holes.
Repetitious Disarray flirts with Scheduled Craziness
and they hit it off.

Hap-Hazard and Format are in a booth
with their newborn, Helter-Skelter.
They always were hippies.
Psychedelic Swirl steps in, walks to the
bar and asks for a scotch, plaid.

Whimsicality and Ridiculosity exchange
numbers and they promise to call.
The bartender, an old mess of blue and brown
cigarette smoke, wipes their glasses clean,
peers into the tip jar and begins
to count his poems for the night.

"Bar None" won First Place in the Ohio High School Poetry contest sponsored by Ohio Northern University. It has been published already in four different places: in *Polaris*, Ohio Northern's Journal of Literature and the Arts, in *Hackberry, Purcell Marian's Literary Magazine*, on-line at *Poetry.com*, and in the brochure circulated to every high school in Ohio by Ohio Northern, with the poem and a photo of Patrick receiving his award from the judge Will Wells, poet and teacher.

"Bar None" has much energy and wit. It came about in part through an in-class exercise in which I asked everyone to help fill one chalkboard with every word they could think of for disorder, chaos, wildness. We then filled the other with words in the realm of order or pattern. I then invited students to make a poem in which chaos and order come together, and, if possible, to make it a poem about poetry or writing poetry.That tip jar in the poem, by the way, looks suspiciously like the one in the Aglamesis Brothers Ice Cream Shop in Cincinnati where Patrick worked for several of his high school years.

Spinoffs

1
 My rubber poems bounce
as high as the moon.
For fuel, they use coal
and uranium.
Furnaces, reactors,
they fuse and smelt my words.

2
Moon poems glow
like uranium.
When they fail,
they are faint coals
at the bottom of the universe.

3
Drafts are coal moons.
Poems are uranium planets.

4
At first you think they are beads
he's wearing like some surfer dude
or some zonked-out aging hippie.
But they are his poems,
private Chernobyls he cannot clean up
or contain,
strung on silver wire
around his neck.

They touch his skin here and there,
sizzling like poisonous tattoos.

5
Her eyes are as strange as uranium.
She doesn't know any words.
When she opens her mouth, only moons appear,

yellow, pale blue, one less green than the grass.
You want to travel there,
be the Neil Armstrong
who brings her words back
like alien rocks to study night after night
but you can't.
After a time they
fade to the same color as her silence.

6
O America,
despite your census,
despite your networked ATMs,
despite Big Brother's universal T.J. Eckleburg eyes,
despite Walt Whitman's *omnes* catalogues
like octopus tentacles
hugging all to his heart,
you remain ungatherable.
Your uranium poetry glows, goes critical,
then decays, diversifies,
morphs rubbery into new species,
shoots particles into new niches and orbits,
new hybrids and mixes
like elements transmuting, coal to
poetry, metaphor to flesh,
love to thundercloud.
On your zip drive every day
you load and abandon new bodies,
fresh habitats, strange tongues:
Mike Fink, Monica Lewinsky,
Larry Flynt, Lil' Bow Wow.
You have a million channels.

You speed thousands of rubber
coal uranium moons
around some hungover red-eyed
Jupiter of madness and democracy
and fine words, and then,
kicking and screaming
with preposterous delight,
drag your poets along for the ride.

* * *

I've mentioned before the notion of poetry being an on-going conversation; here we see that again. Simpson's poem addresses American poetry, and my poem spins-off from Simpson's. Poems beget poems beget poems.

One other little delight in the lives of the poem. I've inserted Lil' Bow Wow in here at the risk of mystifying many if not most of my readers. I couldn't resist, though: when he was in eighth grade my younger son Brendan was running with a crowd that included a gifted young girl singer who performed at his eight-grade graduation. An explosion of self-confidence, she informed her audience that she would see them in a few years, when she was famous. My son was with her once at a gathering when she was talking to a friend whose cousin was the rapper Lil' Bow Wow, and Brendan was handed the phone to say hello. For a time after that, he and two school friends rehearsed raps in his room, the deep bass of their backup rattling the pictures on the walls throughout the house.

"American Poetry" Revisited

Whatever it is, it must have
A stomach that can digest
Rubber, coal, uranium, moons, poems.
    —Louis Simpson, "American Poetry"

The shark, gaffed and
horsed aboard, lay
on the deck, its gill slits
gaping, its silver eyes
seeing all, calmly neutral,
unaccusing.
Then it vomited forth
the first of its surprises:
a rubber man, perfectly
detailed, hair combed, delicate
eyelashes, lips a little
bluish from the cold of the
sea, a stub of pencil
in his hand. As we watched,
he scrawled a poem
on the deck,
a text far too tiny to read.

Then the shark, trembling
in its death,
vomited forth its second
surprise: a serpent
of coal, all black,
eyes, each of its ten
thousand scales,
even its bones
and bladder—
beautiful.
The third
surprise:
before we knew
it bit us
its poison
burned like
pure uranium

in our veins.

Too bad, but it took
all that
to learn to read
the poem.

Kiss, O kiss if you dare
such a shark.

Spinoffs and "American Poetry" Revisited

Two poems sharing the same poem as the source of their epigraphs. There is more than one set of issues raised by Simpson's poem, so the lives of the poem respond multiply. Of course, a lot of what happens in both poems is just playing around, but again by giving free rein to my imagination (the metaphor suggests that the imagination is in some way like a horse—in how many ways?—and what other things is it like? an egg? a machine?) I am led to a poem.

The second one is a warning. Again—sometimes the news the poem brings to us is not pleasant. People whose notions of poetry—or of any art— make them expect that art's vision is always of the uplifting and the "beautiful" are sadly mistaken, and the riches they will earn from art severely limited. Think of Picasso's "Guernica" or of Goya's "The Execution of The Third of May, 1808" or of the Sam Shere photographs of The Hindenburg disaster or of Nick Ut's Vietnam photo, "Children Fleeing An American Napalm Strike." These images are most definitely not uplifting, in the shallow sense; they are horrid, disastrous, wrenching, revolting—and they are powerful because of it. Poetry too can address the issues of war and oppression and torture—it can hold the view steady for its readers, who otherwise might never see such things, or too quickly turn away from them. Or not:

Poems When Nobody's Looking

Poems,
like sunsets, conceptions, secrets,
happen best
when nobody's looking.

When you glance away,
the pronghorn poem leaps
the backs of fifty bison
and lands in another country,
an astonishment of dust.

When you do not notice,
the afternoon sudden
subway poem appears,
in which a small girl's face
is Christ's crucifixion,
all Holocaust condensed.

When nobody's looking,
the assassin poem flicks the knife
across the unsuspecting throat
that gushes at once
its hot bib of blood.

But looked at too closely,
things clam up,
hunker down.
Looked at too closely,
embroidery dissolves into knots,
paintings into blobs, specks, smears.

Eclipses blind us.
Torture burns our souls.
Fearlessness flinches, blinks.

All day, watched pots of secrets
never boil.

* * *

Find some photographs that move you deeply, and write a poem or a series of poems about them. They may be family or personal photographs, or great masterpieces collected in some museum or book on the art of photography. Think of your poems as companions to them, not mere commentaries. After you have written your poems, mount them next to or beneath copies of the photographs. Consider whether you might want to publish them, or to do an "exhibit" reading of the them somewhere. Set such an exhibition reading up, select appropriate music to play in the background, and invite your friends.

The Poem's Brother-In-Law,
A Doctor Working On A Chapter For A Book,
Calls Asking For Lines About Blood

Macbeth, the poem says. More
filled with blood than your body
or mine. *All the seas incarnadine.*

Then suddenly it remembers a boy
from its childhood, hemophiliac,
freckled, wanting to play football
on the schoolyard.
Remembers how Sister Malachy
cried out to see him laid out
for a pass, how he dove
and rolled in the asphalt end zone
by the front steps, how he
stood then, grinning, holding
the ball high
as the red ran down his arm,
spiraling like the stripe
of a barber's pole
or one strand of the double helix
that twined his doom,

but beaming, king for the moment,
bright and triumphant
in the last crown of sunlight
he might ever wear.

The Poem's Brother-In-Law, A Doctor Working On A Chapter
For A Book, Calls Asking For Lines About Blood

Every collection of poems involves, after the bulk of the writing, a lot of thinking and messing around. For example, I lay all the poems in a new collection out on our big dining room table, shifting them around, rearranging them, trying to see how they ought to be sequenced in the final manuscript. Inevitably there are poems that for a variety of reasons are cut, and so become the orphans left behind. I thought it might be interesting to look at a few of these *Lives Of The Poems* orphans (though putting them in here really makes them a part of the collection, doesn't it?) In addition, I thought I'd try to explain why they were initially left out, and to say a few things about the process of making a book out of a bunch of poems.

At one point in the growth of this book, this was the most recent poem, actually finished while I was working on the revision of the *Notes & Divagations*. It started with a phone call from Tom Preston, my brother-in-law, that got me up from the desk while I was writing.

New poems are very dangerous, for me, at least, and I distrust my feelings toward them. Because writing poems is such an iffy business to begin with, every time I take a break from them to work on something else, or simply to rest and recover, the certainty that I'll never be able to make a poem again grows strong. And it increases in strength in proportion to the time away. One of the key skills in living the life of poetry is to learn how to deal with such wildly unconscious treacheries. At any rate, working on the Notes & Divagations had consumed a great deal of time; I hadn't committed a poem in a while. So when this one came, as a lark, really (you can't take poetry too seriously, and so sometimes you have to sneak up on it by acting as if you're not really serious, just having fun, or merely exercising, giving yourself an assignment for kicks), I was pleased. I hadn't thought of that boy from my childhood for years and years, though I do recall now that a few days before this poem arrived I was looking back through my high school yearbook and saw his picture. Maybe that sowed the unconscious seed; his hemophilia must have entered the stewpot in the underground workshop and when my brother-in-law called, something cooked up. I don't know; I don't know if anyone can explain these things. By the way, the poem is a fiction; the boy never did that.

But the recklessness which it celebrates, I see now, is akin to the recklessness that I have to go through to try a poem again after a long time away. It's worth the risk.

Is it any good? That's what I mean about new poems being dangerous: I don't know. I'll have to let it sit—and then, someday, I'll have to read it to an audience, and even, perhaps, send it out somewhere. Even then, even if it's accepted, I still might not know.

* * *

Years later, the poem *was* published, in a literary journal devoted to works connected to medicine and health care. It's called *Mediphors*. What a great idea! There should be literary journals, publishing poems and essays and memoirs and fiction and bagatelles and verbal knick-knacks for every discipline, every area of work and play. Anne Endress Skove (see her poem below) wrote me a few years back from Virginia; she works in the law, and was thinking about starting up a literary journal featuring creative writing about legal issues and ideas, or simply featuring lawyers who also are creative writers. Excellent! Or how about a literary journal for entomologists—day after day they study the astounding structures of dragonflies or beetles or chase rare morpho butterflies in the Amazon, or know more than anyone on the planet about a single species of ant. They must be bursting with things to say that won't fit in scholarly articles! Let them write poems about those dragonflies and beetles; let them shape memoirs around the incredible blue of those endangered tropical wings. Or a journal called *Buildings*, let's say, which focuses on carpentry, architecture, and design—and understands the word "Buildings" in the broadest possible senses, and publishes poems and essays and stories about any kind of "building" or any act that resembles the act of building.

* * *

In January of 2001, my school began construction on the addition of a new Arts Wing and addition to our gymnasium. My classes were almost literally inside the construction; the windows of my basement room, high on the wall, opened onto the excavation. When my colleagues asked how bad it was trying to teach in all that noise, I joked that the noise wasn't so bad—worse was the fact that whenever a worker dropped a hammer, my class would have to duck.

Inevitably, the lives of the poem noticed. Here was a complicated and exciting event unfolding, historical, and impossible to ignore. So out we went into the cordoned-off schoolyard, or up into the old stairwells whose handsome and huge Palladian windows overlooked the site, notebooks and pens in hand. We drafted and workshopped, producing poems that we collected, along with photographs of piles of pipe and welded girders and hard-hatted workmen, in a broadside called "Building Me A Building." Here's are Patrick Hague's "The Pit" and C.M. Kellom's "Memories of a Bobcat."

269

The Pit

Dropping from the crane, the concrete
slabs, impaled by rusty rods of wrought iron,
crash against the winter debris, leaving
a dent in the piles of smashed cinder blocks
and old, rotten wood.

Shiny new metal panels and brand new pieces of steel
are welded together, the side of a new building.
A better one. One without the bitter memories of
lost basketball games, without the ancient decaying
corpse-smell of the weight room, without the ring-worm
infested wrestling mats, without the cold concrete floor,
slickened and stained by the sweat of teenagers running
endless loops, without the concession stand, without the
basketball mothers serving up hot dogs and popcorn
and collecting money, without the guaranteed possible
winner split-the-pot-seller, without the grandparent ticket
sellers, without the old black ladies, without
the bellowing fathers, without the side-
line-never-miss-a-call
you-need-glasses, always-behind-the-play-officials,
buzz-cut hair, leap-frogging, high-jumping
nuts-and-bolts-tormenting, always booing,
offensive foul-calling, face beet-reddening-whistle-screeching-officials,
without the 1986 curling newspaper articles of the state champ
basketball team, without the 5-foot tall paintings of
Ron Beagle and Roger Staubach, without the grainy photos
of the 1955 baseball team, led by J. Ciccarella and T. Wholwender,
without *No Eating or Drinking in the Gym,*
without the Buddy LaRosa's athletes—
a building in need of a soul.

Memories of a Bobcat

I remember being at Career Day,
third grade:
playground mulch drops into a crater
from the mouth of a Bobcat,
black
white red
and a touch of orange.

I remember walking home,
last week;
a Bobcat sleeks down Paddock Road,
stretching its gums.
The man looks at me and nods in
greeting.
Bobcat,
its strength is beast, its movement
regal.

I remember walking past routine pipe
replacement
today;
behind the truck he waits for me,
crouched down, door open,
inviting.
I wonder if I could make it to my house
and back?
They shouldn't leave the key
if they don't want you to take it.

As I stand on the third floor and watch him
sleep,
Bobcat knight of the castle-like foundation,
I remember a part of me,
happy,
imaginative,
silent and sleek,
more so than I am today.
Imagination reflected in our creations.
What kind of name is Bobcat?

* * *

Start up your own little magazine, understanding that it may not live very long, but that its life may be as hot and illuminating as it is brief: a magazine like a little nova. You can either solicit poems and stories and essays for it from the public, or you can make it a one-person enterprise, doing it all yourself. See if it's possible. But try this, too: make sure you have ten subscribers before you start it up. The very work of talking it up to potential readers will be a good thing. Who knows—maybe you'll meet your future significant other, and live happily ever after—or maybe you will become entangled in the life of some beautiful tragic being whose woes and passions may forever overwhelm you, leaving you torn and disabled, human wreckage on some alien shore. There are many such startling stories in the lives of the poem.

During War Time, The Poem Dreams Up A Few Disguises

Desert Storm then, February 2003 now

I will go as an infant
into the insensible green networks
of battle lasers in the desert
and I will intercept
all their missiles and shells
and shit them out like honey.

Then I will require the generals
to clean me,
their own newborn.

And to smell my milky hair.

*

I will enter as a storm
the heart of the saint
and destroy everything I can.

What's left
I will give the name *holy*.

*

I will go as the green
that inhabits the chloroplast.
I will bring with me thinking.

All my leaves will have voices:
thought will compose the air.

*

I will go as Christ
into the bowels of Vishnu and Allah
and there I will rest,
even amid destruction,
thinking of new words for peace.

*

I will go as a mason
among the desert people
and make the bricks
of grief.

I will fire them
under long plumes of smoke
like the funerals of air.

Course after course,
I will build my own Baghdad.

During War Time, The Poem Dreams Up A Few Disguises

This is again a troublesome poem. It could be read, I suppose, as unpatriotic. But here, briefly, is the life of this poem: Patrick Hague's first-grade teacher, Linda Adler, a woman whom he and my wife and I came to love deeply for her dedication and skill and genuine love for the children she worked with, is a Messianic Jew. Part of her immediate family still lives in Baghdad. During the Persian Gulf War, seeing the attacks on TV, we wondered how she must feel. It made us sad and angry; we could not put the fact out of our minds that this woman's kin, undoubtedly as innocent and as kind as she was, might be dying there. So this poem, an attempt to make reparations, to give something back.

Of course, it also takes a stand, something which poetry must do. If poetry is for peace and against violence, it must speak up.

* * *

Find the poem or poems in yourself that speak up for peace and against violence (or vice-versa) and write them. Find other poems on the same subjects and read them and learn from the dialogue they invite you to have with yourself and your own poems.

* * *

Other possible poems to write or finish include "The Poem Wonders If It's Reader-Friendly," "The Poem Surveys All That It Sees," "The Poem Attends A Slam," etc. etc. With my other books of poems, once I was finished with them (which really means once I could do no more myself and had to send them out to see what others saw needed to be done) I was over them, distanced from them psychologically. I let them go, and they let me go. But with *Lives*, it is different. I know it will continue to grow as I keep teaching and writing and learning about the lives of poetry. I envision occasional new editions, each one larger than the last, new poems joining the college and a few old poems retiring, the whole book shimmering and evolving, busy and ceaseless, as full of energy as a well-stocked farm pond in high summer—or one of those cosmic blue-purple clouds photographed by the Hubble Space Telescope, in which stars are continuously being born.

275

She, Imperturbé, Cosmologique, Composes Her Body of Work

Dear Terri Ford:
These poems keep oozing over the top of their containers, like the
cover of the August 1997 issue of Harper's. *"Armory Square" strikes*
me as the most successful, as well as the least attention-grabbing, of
the bunch. All we require is a momentary stay of confusion, you
know, not a fire siren.

Sincerely yours,

Peter Davison
Poetry Editor

for Terri Ford

Galaxies throw their swirling arms across
space for hundreds of thousands of years,

and all for you: they brush your face, feather boas of light
flung stunningly around your neck.

The cores of a billion suns focus
 themselves in your pupils; comets

clench like curlicues
between all the objects of your lusts and lists:

asteroids, meteors, black holes;
between dust, angels, all the scattered

parts of God hidden in plain sight
in oceans of dark matter

which you gather unto
yourself, devour and digest, then

work out writhing poems
in which each participle

is the beginning of a new universe,
in which every noun is the name

of a world, every adjective
progenitor of the thing it modifies:

"languorous" begetting
the striped cat stretched on the windowsill

in the light of twin suns,
"heliotropic" giving birth

to hydrogen-yellow tendrils of time
fruited with pods of blue space—

then bursting into children and moons.
You invent everything—planets,

zeniths and zodiacs, zeugma
and Zoroastrianism.

You rest, merely thinking
of dancing, and become the Big Bang

beginning, the world its word made flesh—
language yourself, craftily

twisted and stretched, a system
of writing, your own legs dashes,

your eyes sidewise colons,
your lips pouting parentheses,

your heart the original predicate,
your heat the seed of all tragedy and redemption.

Wherever and however you move
you compose the epic of self!

Ink! Adverb! Paper! Hair and purses!
Freud and footgear! Redness everywhere!

O origin and creation!—among us enthroned,
regnant, at ease, you thumb your galaxies

as casually as pages, revise whirling quasars,
jot Coal Sacks loaded with dust,

sling around the universe like hot bodies
your swinging undulous gravity's ever-unreeling waves.

She, Imperturbé, Cosmologique, Composes Her Body of Work

If the differences between The Creator and The Critic have not been fully clear, this poem and its comments should nail it down for you, dear reader. For several years Terri Ford and Jim Palmarini coordinated the monthly poetry readings at The York Street International Cafe in Newport, Kentucky, just across the river from Cincinnati. At one point, in 1997 or 1998, my students and I were invited to present the reading, the first time, I believe, that high school students had been featured there. Sarah Humble read successfully, among others. Terri Ford is a fine and risk-taking poet, and in 1999 won a publication prize from Four Way Books for her collection *Why The Ships Are She*. I have often played a tape ("Six Deadlies And One Sorry Ass") of her performing her poems in my writing class, and a perennial favorite is "Your Sorry Ass," a catalogue or list poem, which engenders lots of discussion about what a poem is, and what kind of language a poem can speak, and the kinds of subject matter a poem can address. It's just like what would happen in a discussion among parents as their children go out further and further into the world, making mistakes, saying things wittily appropriate or wildly inappropriate, the parents having to teach and react and revise their own notions as life presents itself in all its unpredictable glory. Incidentally, "The Glory of the Continent" is Terri's latest handle, printed with the return address on all her letters.

This poem came as the result of Terri sending me an essay entitled "Excess" that she had written for the annual reunion of her cohorts at the writing workshop at Warren Wilson College. The essay is directly linked to the issues of Creator and Critic, as well as to a number of other issues, including the still-warm tension between the Ancient and the Modern, between Classicism and Romanticism (if you're not familiar with these terms, take some time to look them up in a dictionary of literary terms, and then read the most famous representative poems of each tradition. Whether you know it or not, you're involved in this argument, and the lives of your poems and your own writing habits need viewing in the light of the arguments' main points.)

The poem also tries to capture the spirit of Terri's essay and her poetry, which both owe much to Whitman, his voracious and all-embracing digestion of things, his benign orneriness in the face of censure and custom and convention, his expansiveness of spirit and expression. Her work is an embodiment of what Louis Simpson says in his "American Poetry," which provides the epigraph for both "Spinoffs" and "'American Poetry' Revisited."

Coincidentally, the last time I saw Jim Wayne Miller alive was in a Northern Kentucky workshop, where he was commenting on "American Poetry" in a point he was making about metaphor. We spoke briefly and hurriedly before I left, and those were the last words we exchanged.

At any rate, I couldn't have asked for a juicier comment than the one Peter Davison sent to Terri in his rejection. I think Jim Wayne would have been as delighted as I am, and as Terri was, with the opportunity it presents.

One final note: this is another poem whose language and ideas owe almost everything to science, this time to the field known as cosmology. It seems inevitable in our time that the lives of the poem will intersect with some realm of science—medicine, genetics, agriculture, ecology.

Just the other night I watched the President speak to the country about stem-cell research. I could recall few occasions in my lifetime when, during prime time, the entire network-watching public was addressed solely on an issue of science. Perhaps the last time was in the Sixties, when President John Kennedy announced the commitment that Americans would go to the moon before the end of the decade—and they did.

So do what you can to get to know your way around the general landscapes of the science; the lives of the poem will be richer for it. Along the way, you may become a better-informed citizen, capable of useful concurrence or effective dissent when the time comes for action.

* * *

Look back at Peter Davison's letter to Terri Ford at the beginning of "She, Imperturbé . . . " Davison complains about the poems "oozing over the tops of their containers." What exactly are the containers poems can come in? Obviously, the first "containers" that come to mind are set forms, like ballads, sonnets, villanelles, and so forth. But ever since the time of Whitman, it has not been necessary to contain poetry in traditional forms—and even the so-called "free verse" of Whitman is highly organized and contained, if you will—by cadence and anaphora and epiphora, and by opera-like structures that do not resemble the previous shapes poetry conventionally took. "Forms, constraints, containers"—what a promising set of ideas to pursue! Is it possible, for example, to make a poem whose constraints might include never using the letter "s"? What kind of poem might relentlessly have exactly three lines in which all the words are alphabetical in order? Is it possible in modern times to write a poem in the old Anglo-Saxon way, heavy with alliteration and with every line divided into two halves, the alliteration bridging the gap between them?

Equally interesting might be to speculate on what could cause a poem to "ooze over the top" of its container. Is there something akin to baking soda in a poem which, when mixed with the vinegar of language, reacts almost explosively, increasing a hundred-fold in size and power? Or is poetry like a liquid which, when potted over fire, heats and seethes and dances? ("I was simmering, simmering," Whitman reported. "Emerson brought me to a boil.")

Furthermore: is the phenomenon of the poem "escaping its container" a bad thing? Or is it an interesting and characteristic quality of poetry, reminding us that like the raptors and the Tyrannosaurus in *Jurassic Park*, life and growth will not be contained? There is a powerful, adaptive and energetically evolutionary drive to poetry; it is always trying out new shapes, forms, adaptations, and experiments, crowding every niche, however small, obscure, or oddly-shaped, sprouting variations and camouflages and complexities that proliferate, then, sometimes, startlingly die out.

True, there is always the tension between wildness and control, between mindless freedom and artful restraint that every artist contends with. In a review of *Isadora: A Sensational Life* by Peter Kurth, Robert Gottlieb writes in the *New York Time Book Review*: "[Isadora Duncan] is an extreme example of the American spirit of self-reliance that believes only in itself and refuses all limits. For Isadora there were no rules, there was only the Song of Herself." He also quotes Duncan's friend, Max Eastman, who was troubled by the fact that "she had made a cult of impulse and impracticality, rapture and abandon . . . She had confused caprice with independence, heroics with heroism, mutiny with revolution."

But ought it to be said that the poems Terri Ford submitted were similarly capricious and artless—or is Mr. Davison really just indulging himself in some sort of paternal slap-of-the-wrist on this upstart young woman? Some of the very poems he declined to publish are included in Terri's award-winning *Why The Ships Are She;* let's hope that Mr. Davison reviews the book, showing exactly what he found distastefully excessive about them, and in so doing, contributes his little bit to the lives of the poem. Or will the poems themselves (as they often do) have the final word in all this?

* * *

The Creator Workshop

In November of 1999, Kosmos here for an extended visit, I decided to host an adult workshop at home, inviting him as special guest along with some other writing friends. I wanted to build the workshop around The Creator rather than The Critic. I thought of how much energy my workshops and classes had devoted to The Critic over the years and realized that the other writing self, The Creator, deserved attention, too. Terri Ford's poems and her essay on "Excess" reminded me again that there is as much glory in expansiveness and liberty as there is in critical intensity and control.

281

The participants included Pauletta Hansel, my long-time friend and Southern Appalachian Writers Cooperative colleague. And Marta Donahoe, another friend and an organizer of Clark Academy, one of America's first public Montessori high schools. And Jason Haap, a young progressivist and agitator in my English Department at Purcell Marian High School, along with the sisters Sally and Katie "The Red" DuMont, and Scott Goebel, head of the Riverbank Poets Project in Hamilton, Ohio, which is about a half-hour drive from Cincinnati. Scott was also editor and publisher of *Red Crow Review* and of Redbud Hill Press. Through a friend, Steve Grieser, I had met Brian Volck, a young doctor, father, husband, and writer who had published a couple of things in national magazines, and who was looking for a workshop to enjoy. Another of my former writing students, Carl West, just graduated from Earlham College in Richmond, Indiana and back in town, rounded out the group. So on the first evening, the group included Hague, Enzweiler, West, DuMont and DuMont, Goebel, Volck, Donahoe and Hansel—sounds like the roster of a Notre Dame football team, or a particularly unwieldy law firm. We decided to meet for two-and-a-half hours every week for six weeks; I would provide them with a surprise field trip or two, and a concluding feast, and the whole point was to sit down together, play off one another's remarks, asides, off-handed comments, and poems, coming up with prompts and possibilities and then reading, without criticism, and purely for inspiration's sake, the new poems each week.

We had, of course, to start somewhere, so I copied Wallace Stevens's "Disillusionment of Ten O"Clock" and we struggled fruitfully with the poem. It's about the imagination and the costs of conformity. "All the houses are haunted by white nightgowns," it begins, and goes on to point out how "none of them are strange." Here, *strange* is used positively, to mean that which is unexpected, a surprise. "People are not going to dream / of baboons and periwinkles." What a great juxtaposition—and how true! The poem concludes grandly with the image of an old sailor, drunk and asleep in his boots, "catching tigers/in red weather." That final image is one of the most remarkable metaphors for the creative act that you will ever find. It "doth tease us out of thought"—and how fittingly in a poem by a man who said that a "good poem resists the intelligence almost successfully." That "almost" is the difference between the Creator running wild and the Critic bringing his fullest powers and sharpest restraint to the making of the poem.

So "Disillusionment of Ten O'Clock," read a number of times, got us started. We talked. Things began to cook and seethe. Possibilities began to emerge. Its final image, of an old sailor, "drunk and alseep in his boots," catching "tigers in red weather" gave us the title of the workshop and of the chapbook we published after it.

Here is one of the many interweavings of the lives of the poem that ensued. Earlier in the school year, Jason Haap decided to investigate the theme of chaos with his literature students. As he and I brainstormed the idea, coming up with words and ideas and readings related to it, I remembered Thomas Hardy's "Hap," in he which he evokes what my *Funk & Wagnall's* calls the "archaic" meanings of the title: " a casual occurrence; happening; chance." It is related to *haphazard* and *happenstance*, and of course is homonymic with Jason's last name. During the banter that first night in the workshop, Jason was bemoaning the fact that oftentimes he missed the point of jokes, or that the points of jokes missed him. At any rate, this poem evolved from that talk, and I brought it to the workshop the next week, and contributed it to the communal stew we were stirring.

Random Acts Of Haap

Knowing Hardy's poem,
he zigs when other zag,
so as not to end up
like the *Titanic*.
Dicing Time
works in the chili parlor
he goes to,
chopping onions.

If he laughs,
he throws salt
over his shoulder.

Whenever there is applause,
he sneezes.
Jokes dog him
like private eyes,
wanting to know
what's so funny.

Are ditties like these merely in-jokes? Maybe. But I remember reading, decades ago, an essay on the avant-garde in art by Paul Goodman, husband of the poet Denise Levertov. Goodman said that it is avant-garde to write poems with and about your friends, and to exchange yours with theirs. We all want to be cutting-edge, don't we? Wendell Berry would agree that writing ought to have a social function and connection; it ought to build community and it ought to occur where you live, and be useful to your neighbors. This is not to say that your poems can't be wildly imaginative, gallivanting all over the universe of places and ideas in the space ship *Enterprise* of their words—remember the poem about Terri Ford above. But it *does* says that sometimes, your poetry should pay attention to the closest and dearest corners of its environment—to your own lives and heart, and the lives and hearts of your friends, and the common wealth and welfare of your own town or county or city. "A man can be provincial only by being blind to his own province." That's Berry again. "The context of literature," he writes in "Writer and Region," " . . . is the household and the community—that it can and does affect, even in practical ways, the life of a place—may not be recognized by most theorists and critics for a while yet. But they will finally come to it . . . "

One example of this local-ness is a poem Jason wrote during the *Catching Tigers In Red Weather* workshop. Our conversation had turned to list poems or catalogues, and that led to us wondering if you could write a poem that resembled a set of directions. Just a few weeks before the workshop began Jason and I had volunteered to chaperone a dance at our school. We'd shown up in the cafeteria around nine o'clock one Friday evening, entering a pandemonium of strobe lights, sweat, acute hormonal excretions, and din. Gyrations, leaps, huddles of communal and solo booty-shaking clogged the dance floor. Kids with flushed faces and soaked armpits ran up to say hello to us, then reentered the whirl and veer. It's called "freak dancing," and even our Catholic high school's generally well-behaved population had caught the fever. Jason and I spent the evening stamping out little wildfires of lust and exhibitionism, retreating now and then into the hallway to gasp, laugh, or go pale. Of course, one of the jobs of the chaperone is to put a lid on such wildness, to keep it from oozing over the top of decorum's container, and the school's administration had had several complaints from parents and teachers about the shenanigans at its dances.

This all entered the life of the poem Jason brought the next week, the result of the juxtaposition of an impromptu workshop assignment to write a "checklist poem" and his experience of the dance. As he read it in workshop, line by line, in as authoritatively scowling a tone as he could muster, and its mock supervisory imperatives unfolded, we began to chuckle, then grin, then snicker, until by the end of his reading, everyone in the group was in full howl.

Checklist For Moral Dancing At A Catholic High School

__ no groin to groin friction
__ no hands on buttocks
__ no buttocks in another's groin area

__ no buttock(s) emphasis
__ no testicular/penile emphasis
__ no breast(s) emphasis
__ no skin contact (hands on facial cheeks excluded)
__ no up/down, in/out groin area motion with contact
__ no rapid right/left groin area motion with contact
__ slow rhythmic right/left groin area motion and contact acceptable with
    no groin to groin friction
__ breasts to chest contact acceptable when not emphasized
__ facial cheek to facial cheek contact acceptable with no kissing
    suggestiveness (i.e. puckers and lip licks)
__ no kissing

Now it so happens that Jason is a member of the Discipline Team at our school; the subject of freak dancing had come up in one of their meetings, and Jason, functioning as Trickster? Poet-Lawmaker? offered a version of his poem, straight-faced, as a piece of legislation. To his great delight, it was discussed, seriously, by a dozen teacher and administrators; something of its language entered the official discipline policy of our school. Too good: a tongue-in-cheek satire becomes policy. The lives of the poem go everywhere, and in a hundred disguises. Remember Shelley calling poets "the unacknowledged legislators of the world."

So sometimes, at least, poems can make something happen. Years ago, I brought Jim Wayne Miller's poem "Cheerleader" to class, and spent a couple of days helping students take a close look at it, as I did so myself. Here's the poem and the sample explication of it I offered my students. (Good poems like "Cheerleader" respond well to close explication; they have depths and riches and interesting niches which are rewarding to explore; mediocre poems offer us very little, and we soon find ourselves without anything to notice or pursue. Learning to explicate is yet another doorway into the lives of the poem.)

Cheerleader

Seventeen and countless times French-kissed.
her body marbled milk and honey, bread
and wine on tongues at half-time Eucharist,
she takes the floor to be distributed.

Jammed bleachers all at once are smitten dumb.
Deliciously she sways; her metered cheers

285

ricochet off girders in the gym;
they fall like sibyls' leaves over the tiers.

She spins; her skirt, gathering speed, whirls,
floats off her dimpled knees slender thighs
snug red panties—stands, falls.
The sweating crowd speaks tongues and prophecies.

Jim Wayne Miller's "Cheerleader": A Study Of Metaphor

One of the constant and universal joys of poetry is effective metaphor. A metaphor that works does more than merely juxtapose, placing two apparently unlike things together. In a sense, it overlaps things in such a way that what might have been a confusing mixture of images becomes, through the power of metaphor's recognitions, a resolving into one image, clear, new, direct. Poor metaphors only push things together, and though we may be able intellectually to account for their likenesses, something is amiss in the emotive realm. *This* doesn't quite go with *that* on the feeling level, and so the metaphor doesn't work. Or things don't fit together, as in this example of a poor metaphor from a student:

My mother's smile
spreads like the plague across her face.

It's just wrong—a mother's smile is a positive thing (in the context of the poem this is taken from, at least); it has no relationship to the horror of plague. What's intended, I think, is the completeness and the quickness of the mother's smile taking over her face, but here, the negative implications of "the plague" completely overwhelm the other idea. The metaphor doesn't strike us with the full force of double-sightedness made single, unified into one image.

Jim Wayne Miller's "Cheerleader" is a poem in which the metaphors work, and powerfully: we not only understand the cognitive relationships of the things compared, but we also feel the appropriateness of their emotional content as well. His metaphors have power because they resolve apparent differences into similarities that are true, that advance his theme, and that are not merely contrived or ornamental. And the similarities he discovers are, in this poem, often shocking.

In the first stanza of "Cheerleader" we learn that the girl of the title is seventeen and has been "countless times french-kissed." Of the possible thousands of details Miller could have chosen to begin with, he chose these. Clearly, the girl's youth and her passionate, perhaps even promiscuous nature, are meant to be our first impressions. This is further reinforced when we learn that her body is "marbled milk and honey." The phrase is pictorial, describing her youthful, unblemished, sweet skin. But a note of incongruity enters with this metaphor, for "milk and honey" sets up an association with quite another realm of human experience: the religious. Milk and honey, the alert reader recalls, were the foods associated with the Promised Land of the Israelites, starved for years in their Egyptian captivity. Thus the metaphor suggests not only the lush sweetness of her body (prime beef is "marbled" with tasty fat), but also the desirability of her body as a kind of nourishment to famished onlookers. The next metaphor confirms this food connection; her body is "bread and wine." Forthrightly religious, this comparison in turn introduces the next, which speaks of the girl as participating in a "half-time Eucharist." Finally, we learn that she comes out on the floor, this "Eucharist," to be, as communion is," distributed."

Pausing to collect the movements of the metaphors so far, we see that Miller is deliberately "overlapping" physical sensuality—even carnality—with religious ritual. This is a startling development (some might even say blasphemous). But herein lies the power of Miller's opening metaphors; their startling quality rivets our attention. We *must* notice them; we *must* work to resolve them, understand how those different-seeming things are really one. We may as yet not be comfortable with the metaphors and their implications, but we at least have some feeling (even if based on shock) for the connections they forge.

Miller then begins his second scene. Stanza one has introduced the principal actress in this little drama; stanza two presents her in action, and shows us her audience's reaction. Her physical attractiveness affects the crowd: "Jammed bleachers all at once are smitten dumb." The word "smitten" is effective here because it carries multiple connotations: "the enemies of God in the Old testament are "smitten" by his power and glory; a person can be "smitten" by love—or lust—for another.

Literally, we may suppose that the cheerleader's physical charm, coupled with her role as leader of cheers—and her almost priestess-like presence (more on that shortly) have for a moment silenced her watchers. They are intent on her, preparing to follow her dance and to respond to her exhortations.

Her effect on the audience is further specified, however, by the allusion to "Sibyl's leaves" in line eight. The Sibyls were ancient Greek priestesses (many of them young virgins) whose intercessions between the gods and mortals were inscribed on leaves which the priestesses scattered at the entrances of their caves. If the wind dispersed them before they were read, they turned to gibberish. Here, the intercessions of the cheerleader, her "metered cheers"—presumably to the gods of victory—are likened to such mysterious supernatural communications. Here, too, we find the religious metaphors of the first stanza further developed. A "eucharist," the cheerleader is also a passionate priestess dancing, delivering ritual chants, the power of her presence a potent mix of the sacred and the profane. Her enthusiasm is to be "distributed" among her devotees. Further, the literal distribution of communion—an eating—may be seen as a metaphor for the sexual appetite at least some of her audience feels toward her as well.

The third stanza is the climax of her appearance as well as the climax of her presence on the audience. Three lines are given to a description that is frankly voyeuristic:

> She spins; her skirt, gathering speed, whirls,
> floats off her dimpled knees slender thighs
> snug red panties—stands, falls.

It is clear that here, at least, the principal attraction is her physical being. The rising speed of of her whirling and the comma-less catalogue of movement captures not only the rapid dance of the cheerleader and her skirt, but as well the breathless excitement of the jammed bleachers, "The sweating crowd." And what is their reaction to her performance? They "speak tongues and prophecies," that is, they shout in strange lingo (we think of the old *sis-boom-ba* type cheer) and they cry out prophecies (even though it is only half-time, they know they'll "Beat Elder! Beat Elder! Beat Elder!") Their priestess, the cheerleader whom they desire, has, through the combination of her physical beauty and her role as intercessor between the crowd and the gods of victory, whipped the fans into an ecstasy—into something resembling the rapt chanting of the pious at the height of worship. The spirits of Pentecost and the Old Testament prophets (as well as the powerful fires of physical passion) have been kindled by her presence.

We see, then, as a result of Miller's mastery of metaphors that are evocative of the strange connection between sexuality and religion, between earthly desire and supernatural force, an overlapping of apparently unrelated things that resolves, in the course of the poem, into a kind of double-sight: at once witnessing the cheerleader and her audience, we are at the same time witnessing what is, in our culture, a quasi-religous event, staged in temples of sport all over the land, attended by millions on Sunday after Sunday. Implicit in the poem, of course, is a criticism. But that's another story. Focusing on the poem's metaphors, we see in "Cheerleader" the shockingly powerful fusion of apparently unrelated realms of human experience. It is a fusion into a whole that makes the reader attend, as if for the first time, as if with new eyes, to what he or she has many times looked at, but perhaps never before actually seen.

If we offer the Creator utter freedom at the beginning of the creative process (and we do, we do), then we have to afford the Critic equal time and equal latitude. In my essay, I really cranked the Critic up and let loose, trying to take an almost microscopic look, so to speak, at one of the aspects of Jim Wayne's poems. We will never come to an understanding or appreciation of how the mind works at work unless we take stock of its products now and then, discovering the many moves a good poem makes and reminding ourselves that ours aspire to such movement as well. Not that we can think our way into writing a good poem; much happens underground, and it is best not too watch too closely, lest we murder the mystery. As in all, it's balance—or not.

And then there is the matter of the more public life of the poem—its existence and influence on its audience. After studying "Cheerleader," I invited students to write to the author if they wanted to, just to reinforce the notion that there really are poets behind these things we more often than not discover between the pages of a book, and so perhaps subconsciously divorce from the actual breathing flesh-and-blood that made them. I must have said something along the lines of "Take the poem seriously, and write a letter to its author about that seriousness; challenge, if you will, something in the poem. Speak out, see what happens." Jaylene Boland, another of the many pairs of sisters I've worked with (her sister is Rory, an equally delightful and lively young woman I run into now and again, always with much talk and reminiscing), took some things in "Cheerleader" to heart, and here is her letter:

Dear Mr. Miller,

I am presently a junior at Purcell Marian High School. Mr. Hague is my American Literature teacher and introduced my class to your poetry. The first poem we studied was "Cheerleader." Mr. Hague asked me my opinion of the poem and thought it would be good to let you know my reaction.

I'll have to admit I was quite offended by your work the first time I read it. In class, we started taking the poem apart, studying each stanza and metaphor. I became angry as I wondered if everyone felt the same way about cheerleaders. You see, I am a cheerleader for Purcell Marian.

I never really noticed or thought how the crowd reacts when I'm cheering. I know that people do judge you on your appearance and your actions but it never really bothered me. I just thought it was my responsibility to keep my school spirit up and represent the school well. But the last time I cheered, I had your poem in the back of my head. I saw cheering in a different and disturbing way. I kept asking myself questions. I was paranoid about how I looked and what I was doing. Does the crowd see me as a sex symbol? Are they watching every move I make? What are they saying as they whisper and point? I couldn't believe how self conscious I was. It was really affecting my cheering.

When I came home that night, I read the poem again. I wrote down points which I noticed at the game and what was stated in your poem. I noticed and realized through my observations the poem spoke the truth about sporting events being like a religious celebration. I couldn't believe how much my eyes were opened because of your poem.

Your work has taught me a little more about myself and cheering. "Cheerleader" is not one of my favorite poems but I guess learning isn't always supposed to be enjoyable. Sometimes it takes a little pain to realize the truth.

I truly think you are a great and talented poet. Thank you for opening my eyes.

Sincerely,

Jaylene Boland

Many things in Jaylene's letter are true about the lives of the poem. The poem does indeed bring us news that is unsettling at times. (Remember "The Poem Rends The Veil.") The poem does indeed invite us to see with newer, sharper eyes what we think we have already beheld and understood—as Shakespeare said of art, it "holds a mirror up to Nature." The poem does indeed remind us of the true nature of learning, requiring us to turn its lessons on ourselves, and as a result, to live a deeper, more examined life. I am sorry—as Jim Wayne would have been sorry, I'm sure—for Jaylene's discomfort. But in the long run, it was a small enough price to pay for a lesson about life—and about poetry—that may never have been learned so convincingly any other way.

* * *

Here's the "write a poem that is a checklist or a set of directions" poem I wrote in the Creator workshop. Much different from Jason's, it reminds me once again of the unpredictable moves poetry can make, even when two may begin in much the same place. I think the poem also owes something to the Ugly/Pretty exercise, and is another attempt to put into action Shelley's and Coleridge's belief that poetry can reconcile and even unify opposites.

Appreciation Instructions: Turkey Vulture

Kill something and let it lie on the ground,
in the open—the mown ellipse
in the freeway cloverleaf,
the ninth fairway,
the field behind the cathedral.

Add summer sun for two or three
days, good weather, calm breezes,
sky the color of a saviour's coat.

Over your shoulder watch for shadows
circling like the pressing of conscience.

Then, suddenly incarnate before you, its meat-red
head, its naked neck, the stink
of its clattering sails!

Watch its beak tear flesh,
stench rising in clouds as dark
as from burning cities.

Remember that this bird is mother, sister,
kin of others for whom it has
an instinctive gentle attachment.

Remember: thrusting its head
into foulness, consuming the womb
of the deer, the maggoty heart
of the woodchuck,
it offers a gift,
a kind of community service.

The Company Poetry Keeps

1

The company poetry keeps
makes widgets, raises snipes,
breeds unicorns.
All its profits go to lighting fires
and defacing ugly buildings.

Its managers sleep on the job.
Every afternoon, the cleaning
crews vacuum up their dreams,

so the night shift,
sifting the bags for loose change,
will have something astonishing
to discover.

2

Poetry hangs on dark
corners with Rastafarians,
tarantulas, and those who
have flunked algebra.
It drinks with
frightened deer
from small
moonlit pools.
It sits patiently
beside the dying,
sending messages
through their comas.

Poetry stretches out
beside all lovers
in their beds
and threads
itself into their
arms and legs, and
smooths their hair, and
licks their sweat,
and oversees their
breathing;

all the while it murmurs,
"Every touch should thrill."

3
Poetry prefers solitude,
silence, empty vast spaces.

Alaska: poetry
loves Alaska,
its ranges, glaciers,
its treeless tundra
cold even in
high summer,

and especially the long
nights of December,
cabin-fevered,
during which
nude maidens of ice
linger smiling
at its windows.

4
On the other hand
(and poetry has more hands than Shiva),
poetry is attracted
to rich or dangerous clumpings:
sleeping bats, armies, champagne grapes,
avalanches, globular clusters,
hornet's nests.

Like the autist, Temple Grandin,
poetry loves to feel
itself pressed on all sides,
the whole weight of things upon it
like ancient coal measures,
till its dense dark
brilliants into diamonds.

The Company Poetry Keeps

This is one of the youngest of the lives of the poem, having been written within a few months of the finishing of this book. It's playing around, of course, with the pun of its title, and remembers Emerson's observation, which I have quoted earlier, about how a man may be known by, among other things, the company he keeps. So too the poem.

But I think what I am most pleased about is getting Temple Grandin and autism into the poem, and in a celebratory way. As I have mentioned earlier, my school is deeply committed to the inclusion of students with special problems that exclude them from many other schools; as a result, we all—students, staff, and teachers—have learned about Down's Syndrome, and Attention Deficit Disorder, and cerebral palsy, and autism, because each has become a part of the lives of the school we attend and work in. Many might remember "Rain Man," the 1988 movie with Tom Cruise and Dustin Hoffman. It was filmed in part less than three blocks from my school. I remember driving by the tiny Owl's Nest Park near one of the film's locations on a swanky street overlooking the river; students would talk the next day about seeing Dustin Hoffman, hands in pockets, crossing Madison Road or Tom Cruise sitting under a bright canopy, eating lunch in the shade.

The character played by Dustin Hoffman is autistic. There are various degrees of severity of autism; the Rain Man's limits his functioning in a complex world. But there are other persons suffering from autism whose lives are relatively normal—though always with odd, even bizarre, twists. Such is Temple Grandin's. A university professor and successful lecturer, she nevertheless has had built for her a machine which, come bedtime, she climbs into. It then presses her tightly, like some kind of mechanical cocoon, and off she drifts into slumber.

Even better than bringing this knowledge alive into the poem is that it suggested a metaphor to me: the Coal Measures among which I grew up, and which surrounded me, literally when I climbed through caves over the hill from my house, the layers of coal and shale and sandstone above me pressing upon me their geological weight, as well as the historical consequences of coal mines and coke plants and steel mills and railroads and towboats that shaped the very life I grew into as a boy on Ohio's Appalachian edge.

And into it entered the Rastafarian Laish, Laisha Dumas's mentor/muse, and Kosmos, up there in Alaska during those long cold winters, and Amanda Lambdin, a student in one of my creative writing classes and in my American Lit. class too, who was excited to her core by Emerson's brief paean to nature and sense and body: "Every touch should thrill." Amanda is also the author of one of the great lines in all the years of my poetry workshop: as a result of us talking about letting go, allowing the poem to take its own direction, she wrote a brief one in which the line "How delicious it is to be far from found" occurs—a moment of genius if there ever was. Lives and lives and lives: a sedimentary accretion of details and connections and influences and locations and depositions of words, things, and people: lives and lives and lives.

Poem Entering The House After A Winter Walk

It smells tonight of snow, that mineral
mixed with brilliance.
It smells of distance, solitude, and dark.
Careful not to disturb me,
it sits down in a corner,
wet boots steaming in the glare.
For a long time I watch it,
silence curled on the hearth
before us.

But as always, I drift drowsily away.
I have forgotten its presence.
Snow seethes softly over the roof.
I listen to the fire's patient epic
hissing on the irons:
blood, dust, armies, sweat, decay.

Across the room the poem clears its throat,
begins.

Poem Entering The House After A Winter Walk

The ending of this poem genuinely surprised me. It was a gift of some sort. As I have observed many times previously, the poem often turns in a way you hadn't expected; it takes its own life and makes things happen you didn't dream of.

Incidentally, insofar as "The Company Poetry Keeps" is a youngster, this poem may well be the *Ur*-poem of *Lives of the Poem,* the most ancient ancestor, in that it came along several years before the collection even suggested itself. Published in *Athenaeum*, the literary magazine of Xavier University, my alma mater, it appeared in 1981. Neither it nor I knew at the time that it was a member of a family that hadn't yet been conceived, of a college that hadn't yet been founded.

The lives of the poem are not subject to the same laws as the rest of nature.

Catching Tigers In Red Weather

Think of these nearly-final words as an outlandishly long epigraph: it's only appropriate that the actual last words of the *Lives of The Poem* arrive in a poem. This one, though as always mothered by The Creator, smells strongly of The Critic. It arose at the end of the *Catching Tigers In Red Weather* workshop, and I am sure is the result in part of the suppression of the Critic that had governed that experience. He is an intent, single-minded and tenacious fellow, and will have his way and be heard despite our strongest resistance.

And it's a good thing. Without the Critic, reasonably and thoroughly trained, we have no chance of making a way through the lives of the poem. We might strike a chance success here and there, the poem exploding from us as Athena exploded fully formed from the forehead of her father Zeus. Most frequently though, such an unconsidered, unfinished poem will wither, unable to bear up under the scrutiny of the reader with high expectations. And it is such a reader we are writing for. We are not writing for ourselves alone; we are writing in response to, and in order to contribute to, the Lives of the Poem, an enterprise that predates history and that goes back, I would guess, to the very beginnings of language. We cannot take such an obligation lightly. We must prepare ourselves, as the bride prepares herself, as the groom himself, as the priest, about to enter into the sacred ritual, prepares.

End of sermon, almost.Though many of the claims this last poem makes, many of the imperatives it offers, sound a little bit crazy, and certainly run counter to a culture of logical and linear thinking, it, too, owes as much to the cold eye of the Critic as it does to the hot heart of the Creator. So be it. The poem will have the final word.

*   *   *

All of us in the *Catching Tigers In Red Weather* workshop—except for Scott Goebel, who as I have said earlier lived there and who had set up the reading—were driving together up to Hamilton, Ohio, to the Fitton Arts Center. Our friend George Ella Lyon from Lexington, Kentucky was to read, and we decided that the trip and her reading and a tavern interlude afterwards would be the workshop for that week. The talk was lively as we drove up, and at one point a quick lane-change out there in the nowhere-land of interstate suburbia snuck up on me; I swerved, gunned it, cut over—and Jason calmly stated from the back seat of the van, "We almost all died there, didn't we?" I laughed. The next week, Jason brought this to the workshop:

The Poetry Accident In A 1976 Pontiac Bonneville

The paramedics saw no irony
in Haap's heart being crushed
by the Bonneville's
steering column.
He always loved that car.

Doctors dug Hague's right index finger
out of Joe's skull like an idea
but no one thought
to write it down.

When the DuMont sisters' bodies
were found thrown from the wreckage,
corpses crumpled like bad rough drafts,
the doctors said revival was hopeless.
Lives don't have the luxury to revise.
Only Pauletta survived,
comatose,
spending long days and nights
breathing in,
breathing out.

Jason not only gets the passengers into the poem, but even quotations of participant work: the last two lines are exact duplicates of the conclusion of a Pauletta Hansel poem, read earlier in the workshop, a serious one, which, beamed over with its molecules all mixed up into this one, gave us some good laughs. And the interesting point is that, in the Lives of the Poem at least, lives *do* have the luxury to revise.

George Ella's reading was wonderful, and we all went out to have a drink at a local pub, and the talk was good and wide-ranging, and even more poems arose from that. George Ella told about a dream she'd had of Jim Wayne Miller, and I said I'd write a poem about her dream, and I did, and it got published in *Appalachian Journal*, from which Jerry Wayne Williamson had recently retired as editor, and George Ella's little book on writing poems, *Where I'm From*, which I had bought a copy of at the reading, wound up on the shelf in my creative writing class, and students and I all wrote "Where I'm From" poems modeled on George Ella's, and mine was published in an anthology of work by teachers which Kathy Wade (a close friend of Pauletta's) and I helped bring into being for twenty-five teachers in the grade schools feeding into my high school, and Pauletta's book of poems *Divining,* which I

300

edited and wrote an introduction for, got published and for it she was honored as Ohio's Poet of the year for 2002, and Kosmos's latest collection was coming together and then was accepted by Iris Press by our mutual friend Bob Cumming, and back in Alaska Kosmos was falling in love, and the DuMonts continued in the bookselling and editing businesses, and Marta's daughter Chelsea went off to Warren Wilson College (Terri Ford's alma mater) to write poems and to keep a garden. Brian Volck was a Finalist for the *Sow's Ear* Poetry Prize and the lives of the poem kept interweaving and braiding themselves into one another like the hair of those two students long ago in homeroom, although even more multiply and more complexly. So the chapbook we all contributed to and published at the end of the workshop itself ended (as does this first installment of *Lives of the Poem* ends) with this advice, summation, admonishment, and valediction:

Catching Tigers In Red Weather

1

The entire effort
is to help them
arise from their
coffins
of thought

put their
lives back
on

and dance

2

When they can't
think of
anything

then poetry
can
begin

3

If thinking

and
poetry
were the
same
thing

they'd have
the same

name

4

Lure or
push them
into the
strangest
corners
and abandon
them there
with a
pencil

5

Every poem
is not only

an undiscovered
country

but also
one they
themselves
having created,
must now
get
lost in,
wander-
ing

6

The Horror:

Up the stream
without
a
paddle

The Ecstasy:

Up the stream
without
a
paddle

7

If the critic
arrives
early,

poison
his coffee

8

Always welcome the
creator

make a large

seat for
her
smooth a place
in your
bed

9

Poems have
their own
rules

sometimes
impossible
to discover

10

Every poem
is
a mirror

that both
tells the
truth
and lies

11

Put on
the night
gowns
then
take
them
off:

know
the
enemy

12

What place
dream
in the
poem?
sometimes
none

Sometimes
the
very
center,
pulsing
like a red
heart
in our
fists

13

Pity
the cliché

set
it aside

like a
child
too young
for the
traffic

14

Peel the
skin from
the cliché

and let
it stand
in the
poem

redly
shouting

15

Kindness,
yes.

But never
at the expense
of
the
poem.

16

After a
time
we must
know
the poem
was never
ours.

17

After a
time
we must
listen
to the poem
as an
equal.

18

After a
time
the poem
will
make
demands.

303

19

Learn
silence
so we
can hear.

20

Sometimes
poems will
want
to make
noise

not sense

21

Sometimes poems
will want
to make
whoopee

right on
the floor
before
us.

22

"We must
be expressed."

23

Restraint
dams
the
river.

24

If the
dam
breaks
what then?

25

The poem
as flood-wrack,
aimless
drift,

expert
canoeist.

26

Poetry
and gardening
require
the same
skills.

27

The seed
does not
know the
planter.

28

"Everything
begins
with the
sun."

29

Small is beautiful,
sometimes.

Big is beautiful,
sometimes.

Keep
them
dancing.

30

Some side
streets
become
freeways.

31

Let the
poems
that
resist
all attempts
at resuscitation
die.

32

Keep the bodies.

33

The sailor
may be
drunk

but he's
got his boots
on.

34

Swimming
with
their eyes closed
is hard, dangerous,
and
irreplaceable.

35

All treasure
is at
our feet.

36

Whatever
students believe,
doubt
it.

37

When they
come over
to our
side too
quickly,
chide
them.

38

In the
poem,
there's
no one
to help
us
but the
poem.

39

Pronounce such
impossibilities
as
"Every line of
a poem
should be
a poem."

40

Read them
"Disillusionment
of Ten O'Clock"
frequently.

Every time
they have
a question,
repeat the poem.

Even when
they grow angry,

repeat the poem.

41

If they say,
as they will,
contentious,
frightened,
lazy,

"So I'm
supposed
to get
drunk?"

Even if they are
young, even

if they
are
innocent,

we
must answer,
after carefully
explaining
what we
mean,
"Yes."

42

Between the
rock
and the
hard place

the
poem
lurks

43

"The houses
are haunted

by white
nightgowns."

44

Every day
a dozen
metaphors

ten strange lines

45

The cougar in the
pantry

46

Space blossoming
like a rose

47

The blood
exclamatory

About the Author

Richard Hague, Xavier University BS '69, MA '71, is a Master Teacher and Teacher of the Year at Purcell Marian High school in Cincinnati, where the Writing Program he designed and administered won the 1994 National First Place in the English-Speaking Union's Award For Excellence in the Teaching of English. He is author of eleven collections of poetry, including *Ripening* (The Ohio State University Press, 1984), *Possible Debris* (Cleveland State University Poetry Center, 1988), *Garden* (Word Press, 2002) and *The Time It Takes Light* (Word Press, 2004.) His collection *Milltown Natural: Essays and Stories From A Life In Ohio*, was a National Book Award nominee; it included work from a manuscript that was named Finalist in the AWP's Creative Nonfiction Award. His poems, essays, stories, columns, and commentaries have appeared in print and online widely, including *Appalachian Journal, Ohio Magazine, Personal Journaling, Religion & Ethics Newsweekly, Poetry, Creative Nonfiction* and *Teachers & Writers*, in which his Bechtel Prize Finalist essay was featured in September 2004. He has won two President's Awards from *Ohio Journal*, the Sow's Ear Poetry Prize, the Black Swamp Poetry Prize, was twice a Finalist for the Pablo Neruda Prize, and has won three Individual Artists Fellowships from the Ohio Arts Council in two genres. He has twice been nominated for a Pushcart Prize. He was a Katherine Bakeless Scholar at Bread Loaf, the recipient of a 1990 NEH Summer Seminar at Oxford University, held A 2000 Teacher In The Arts Fellowship from The Council For Basic Education and the NEA, and returned to the 2004 staff of the Appalachian Writers Workshop in Hindman, Kentucky, where he taught the Poetry Workshop with Frank X. Walker. His *Alive In Hard Country* was awarded Poetry Book of the Year in 2004 by the Appalachian Writers Association, and his story "Fivethree Filson and the Looking Business" won the 2004 James Still Short Fiction Award, judged by novelist Lee Smith.

Born and raised in Steubenville, Ohio, in the upper Ohio River's Steel Valley, Richard Hague lives in Cincinnati with his wife Pam Korte, a potter and Assistant Professor of Ceramics at Mt. St. Joseph College, and their sons Patrick and Brendan.

9 781893 239265